# PRAISE FOR *GOING GOOGLE*

*"Google's presence in our nation's schools is a big one and is only going to increase. Jared Covili has put together an excellent guide—useful for those who are tech savvy and those who are not—for how teachers and students can use these tools for teaching and learning."*

—Larry Ferlazzo, Advice Columnist, *Education Week* Teacher

*"Jared Covili does an excellent job diving into the intricacies of Google so everyone can get the most out of the suite of apps. If you are not 'Going Google,' you might as well just 'Ask Jeeves' for support."*

—Nick Provenzano, Author of *Classroom in the Cloud* and The Nerdy Teacher Blog

*"There are few companies that have had a greater effect on education than Google. Google provides educators and learners many collaborative tools for curation, communication, and creation. These can be daunting to educators struggling to maintain relevance in an ever-evolving environment of teaching and learning. Jared Covili has created a work that provides simple instructions with authentic examples, lesson plans, and teacher-expert perspectives for each Google tool to help the reader navigate what could otherwise be an overwhelming sea of information. This is the ultimate Google Tool companion piece for Educator Relevance."*

—Tom Whitby, Creator of EdChat and Author of *The Relevant Educator*

*"I am not a techie. I am an educator who loves what technology can do to enhance learning for students, but I sometimes feel a bit overwhelmed by the constant creation of new apps, the modifications of existing software, and the abundance of specialized information about how to use the constantly evolving resources available to teachers. I tend to feel one step behind in moving forward in the 21st century. However, help has arrived! Jared Covili's well-written, clearly illustrated, logically laid out book,* Going Google: Powerful Tools for 21st Century Learning, *is a ~~~ ~~~~ of needed answers to questions I didn't even realize I had. Not only does he fully descri~~~ ~ va~~~ty of free Google tools offered for classrooms, he gives important details, shares valuable tips, and explains how they can be incorporated into the curriculum. First and foremost an educator, Covili focuses on usefulness and curriculum integration with each Google tool, and he offers several classroom projects as examples. His book sparked a new excitement in me to start making better use of these 21st Century tools. If I were an administrator, I would buy a copy for every one of my teachers."*

—Debbie Silver, EdD, Author of *Fall Down 7 Times, Get Up 8, Drumming to the Beat of Different Marchers,* and *Deliberate Optimism*

*Thanks to Tara, Kennedy, Alex, and Dylan.*

*Google may provide answers to my questions, but you give meaning to my life.*

# Going Google

## Powerful Tools for 21st Century Learning

### Second Edition

Jared J. Covili

Foreword by Peter DeWitt

CORWIN

A SAGE Publishing Company

FOR INFORMATION:

Corwin

A SAGE Company

2455 Teller Road

Thousand Oaks, California 91320

www.corwin.com

SAGE Ltd.

1 Oliver's Yard

55 City Road

London, EC1Y 1SP

United Kingdom

SAGE Pvt. Ltd.

B 1/I 1 Mohan Cooperative Industrial Area

Mathura Road, New Delhi 110 044

India

SAGE Publications Asia-Pacific Pte. Ltd.

3 Church Street

#10–04 Samsung Hub

Singapore 049483

Printed in the United States of America

Library of Congress Cataloging-in-Publication Data

Names: Covili, Jared, author; foreword by Peter DeWitt.

Title: Going Google : powerful tools for 21st century learning / Jared Covili.

Description: Second edition. | Thousand Oaks, California : Corwin, [2017] | Includes bibliographical references and index.

Identifiers: LCCN 2016027422 | ISBN 9781506325286 (pbk. : alk. paper)

Subjects: LCSH: Internet in education. | Google.

Classification: LCC LB1044.87 .C685 2017 | DDC 371.33/44678—dc23 LC record available at https://lccn.loc.gov/2016027422

Executive Editor: Arnis Burvikovs

Senior Associate Editor: Desirée A. Bartlett

Senior Editorial Assistant: Andrew Olson

Copy Editor: Pam Schroeder

Typesetter: Hurix Systems Pvt. Ltd.

Proofreader: Dennis W. Webb

Indexer: Sheila Bodell

Cover Designer: Scott Van Atta

Marketing Manager: Anna Mesick

This book is printed on acid-free paper.

18 19 20 10 9 8 7 6 5 4

# Contents

# Foreword

Before you can go Google, you have to understand why Jared Covili is the exact person needed to get you there. A few years ago I sat at a table in a crowded room at the Corwin Author Retreat in California waiting for Jared Covili's Google breakout session to begin. Sitting around me were accomplished workshop presenters, consultants, and authors, some who flawlessly use technology and others who struggle using a flip phone.

Jared began the workshop by having us sign into a game, so he could ensure 100 percent engagement among the group. As he asked the first question, you could sense that some people sitting in the room were uncomfortable about how to work the game, while others had no issue at all. Jared slowly talked to the group as they signed on one by one, and he got us to laugh at the same time he moved us to deeper thinking. Sometimes I didn't even realize I was stretching my own thinking because I felt supported as I tried some new tools.

At that moment, Jared became one of the best workshop facilitators I have ever seen. He was able to engage those who were newbies and challenge those who had a great deal of expertise. And he did it all with a very calm and approachable demeanor. The hour flew by, and every single one of us walked out with new knowledge that we could use within the very next day, and that to me is a sign of great professional development. Something teachers, leaders, and even author–consultants are surely lacking these days.

Many times we attend conference sessions or are "voluntold" to attend professional development because someone needs to be a turnkey trainer for some new mandate that the school has to abide by. We don't get to go to professional development where we learn something we didn't even know we needed, and that is why Jared is so talented at what he does. The truth is, teachers and leaders talk to students about learning new material and tools, but they themselves don't like to learn in front of their colleagues because they're afraid of looking as if they don't know enough. Jared has the ability to get participants to drop their guard and dive in.

It's hard to do with a tool like Google, because it's a tool most of us think we know already; we have been using Gmail for a few years or we have created a Google Doc or two. However, that only scratches the surface of what Google offers us no matter what role we play in the education profession. Understanding Google is like peeling back an onion. Each layer brings us to deeper learning, and many of us haven't peeled off enough layers yet. And that is where Jared Covili enters into our learning.

*Going Google* is a book that will help peel back many layers or our learning. Truth be told—I was one of those people before I read this book. I am not a technophile. I have my smartphone and laptop, but I thought I knew more than I did. I realized I use very few apps. Over the last couple of years I have begun flipping my professional development by creating Google Docs that are filled with all of the resources I talk about in workshops and keynotes. I flip them ahead of time, so participants can look through the resources before the event and be better prepared. That is typically where my use of Google, besides email and hangouts, ends.

While reading this book I learned more about Google Voice and Google Drive. I learned from Jared's section called Google Guru. Jared offers practical steps and screenshots to make it easier for those of us who need visuals to move forward with new learning. At the same time as he makes this book a practical read, he also relates it to ISTE standards and other standards that our students need to know to be prepared for their future—not just 21st century skills or other buzzwords but what they need to actually be prepared for their own futures. *Going Google* is a book that matches Jared's excellent workshop style. You will go deeper with your own learning, at your own pace, following the words of someone who has a great deal of knowledge on the topic, with a very approachable style. Now get reading, and go Google!

*Peter DeWitt, EdD*

*Author–Consultant*

*Finding Common Ground blog* (Education Week)

# Preface

A few years ago, I wanted to write a book that helped teachers and students learn about tools that could help them interpret information, collaborate with colleagues, and create content. The answer came back in a word—Google.

In the past 20 years, Google has expanded its role from simply being the leader in online searching to transforming the way in which we communicate with one another. In an era when teachers are being asked to provide more information with little to no financial resources, using Google's free resources may be the best solution to help "every student succeed." And yet, many teachers have a limited idea of the various tools included in the Google library. This book will explore the wide array of Google tools from a K–12 educator's perspective, not simply focusing on how to use the tools but also answering the larger questions: Why use these tools, and how can my students accomplish 21st century learning goals if we utilize Google tools?

This book is broken down into three major areas. Each of these areas reflects a core objective from the Skills for 21st Century Learners. They are as follows: Communicating and Collaborating, Creativity and Innovation, and Critical Thinking and Problem Solving. As we explore these different pedagogical elements, you'll find that various Google tools are used to illustrate how teachers can reach these objectives.

As we discuss the various tenets of 21st century learning skills, I hope you'll find this book addresses three essential areas for K–12 teachers:

1. Which Google tools are essential for achieving 21st century learning skills?
2. How can these tools improve learning and help teachers in their everyday classroom activity?
3. What are some practical lesson plan activities teachers can use with different Google tools as part of their student-centered projects?

To help in digesting key points and features, for each of the main Google tools, you'll find the book has a highlight—Five Things to Know About—at the beginning of the chapter. Also, classroom activities and projects are separated with their own unique headings. This will make the step-by-step instructions easier to find and follow. Another, helpful feature—From a Google Guru—provides you with lesson ideas and practical experience from a variety of educators from around the world. At the end of most of the chapters, you'll find two other highlights for teachers—More Ideas for Going Google and Tips for the Google Classroom. These are quick ideas meant to further your use of the tools and provide an additional framework for classroom application. You will also find a useful glossary at the end of the book. *Glossary terms* in the text are denoted by boldface italics.

Buttons or menu items to select on your computer screen, such as **Save** or **Translate**, are denoted by boldface type.

Another important feature found throughout *Going Google* is the use of screen captures. These images are designed to help illustrate concepts and provide guidance for accomplishing activities. The screen captures are time sensitive, so their content won't be relevant forever, but they provide a valuable resource to help you and your students visualize different Google tools in action.

As this is the second edition of *Going Google,* you'll find that there are several new chapters that reflect the updates to the Google library of tools. Gone are tools such as iGoogle and Picasa, whereas new options including Google Photos and Google Classroom have entered the mix. Screen captures will illustrate the latest updates to the Google tools you and your students use on a daily basis. One new feature for the revision of the book is to tap into the great ideas and experience from classroom teachers and other educators. You'll find their comments for each tool near the end of the chapters. Lesson plan ideas have been selected from a variety of subject areas and are geared for a cross-section of students, representing different backgrounds, ability levels, and understandings. This second edition of *Going Google* will provide educators with the resources they need to succeed as it has the most relevant, curriculum-focused content mixed with the latest tutorials and updates and the combined experiences of educators who are truly Google gurus.

*Going Google: Powerful Tools for 21st Century Learning* should be seen as a handy reference to use with all the other tools in your digital teacher tool belt. I hope you'll learn some new things about the Google you thought you knew. Thanks for joining me in the journey again.

# Acknowledgments

Special thanks to the following:

Peter DeWitt
Tom Whitby
Larry Ferlazzo
Nick Provenzano
Debbie Silver

## PUBLISHER'S ACKNOWLEDGMENTS

Corwin gratefully acknowledges the following reviewers:

Sherry Annee
High School Science Teacher
Brebeuf Jesuit Preparatory School
Indianapolis, Indiana

Avis Canty Duck
Title I Technology Facilitator and Special Education Teacher
Greenville County School District
Greenville, South Carolina

A. L. Hough-Everage
Professor of Education
Brandman University
Victorville, California

Rose Cherie Reissman
Literacy Educator, Director of NYC Ditmas Writing Institute
New York City Department of Education, District 20
New York, New York

Karen Tichy
Associate Superintendent for Instruction and Special Education
Archdiocese of St. Louis
St. Louis, Missouri

Margie Zamora
Project Facilitator, Digital Learning Coach
Clark County School District
Las Vegas, Nevada

# About the Author

 **Jared J. Covili** is a professional development trainer at the Utah Education Network (UEN) in Salt Lake City. Jared specializes in teaching strategies for classroom integration of technology such as social media tools, geospatial learning, and digital devices. Jared received his bachelor's degree in English and his master's degree in instructional design and educational technology from the University of Utah. His background includes four years as a secondary language arts teacher. Besides his work at UEN, Jared is involved with the Utah Coalition for Educational Technology (UCET) and served as president of the organization from 2011 to 2012. Jared also works as an adjunct faculty member in the College of Education at the University of Utah, where he teaches technology integration classes to undergraduate students. In addition to *Going Google,* Jared is also the author of *Classroom in the Cloud: Innovative Strategies for Higher Level Learning* from Corwin.

# Introduction

Years ago I read a bumper sticker posted on a colleague's cubicle that stated "I've Gone Google." *What?* How can someone "go Google"? Sure, we all use Google's search engine on a daily basis, but beyond finding information for work and home, can someone truly "go Google"? I started asking myself, what is the impact that "going Google" can have for teachers and students in the classroom?

What was once a start-up company run out of the garage by a couple of Stanford grad students has become one of the biggest companies in the world. Google spent its first few years developing the number one search engine on the web. For many, that's the only thing they know about Google—it's a search engine. But Google is so much more.

Google has spent the past 20 years developing an entire suite of tools that have revolutionized the way in which we use the Internet. These tools have made the world a smaller place by giving users a chance to work virtually from anywhere, with anyone, at any time they choose. Google has taken advantage of its size and ability to create a large scope for making these tools available to teachers and students—for free.

> Google's mission is to organize the world's information and make it universally accessible and useful. With regard to education, our goal is to leverage Google's strengths and infrastructure to increase access to high-quality open educational content and technology, more specifically, in science, engineering, technology and math. (Google, n.d.a)

So, what does it mean to "go Google" in your classroom? In a nutshell, it means taking advantage of the educational applications, or apps, created and shared by Google as part of your curriculum. Whether it's as basic as conducting a search for a research paper or as complicated as using Google Earth to develop an interactive virtual tour, "going Google" implies that teachers and students utilize Google tools to help them achieve 21st century skills.

## THE WORLD HAS CHANGED

Over the past decade, the world has changed for our students. The students of today have been exposed to more media than any previous generation. Just look at the numbers for households with children ages 12 to 18:

- American teens use an average of 9 hours of media daily, not including for school or homework.
- Teens spend an average of 4 hours and 38 minutes on their smartphones every day.
- Fifty percent of seventh to 12th-graders media multitask while doing homework, for example, IM, TV, Web surfing, and so on (Common Sense Media, 2015).

The problem is that our classrooms haven't changed. Look inside classrooms across the United States, and you'll find a similar arrangement to those of the past century. Students are lined up neatly in rows with the desks facing a board with text written on it. Sure, the board may be a whiteboard instead of a chalkboard, but the method of delivering materials to students is far behind the way in which students absorb material from their portable devices and computers.

Jim Shelton (2011), assistant deputy secretary for innovation and improvement in the U.S. Department of Education, describes the situation in American classrooms:

> For too many of our students around the country, "boring" has become the adjective of choice to describe their experiences. Students have been locked down by the concept of seat time and locked out of the technological revolution that has transformed nearly every sector of American society, except for education.

## TWENTY-FIRST CENTURY SKILLS AND THE MODERN CLASSROOM

As we've moved from a paper-and-pencil past toward a 21st century classroom, we know that the classroom needs to progress. Marc Prensky (2010), founder of Games2Learn, looked at the changes our education system needs to undergo. He says, "The reason a lot of people are stuck, I think, is because they confuse the old ways, the best ways of doing something once, with the best ways of doing those things forever."

We know that our education system needs to improve, but what skills are necessary to empower our students for the jobs of tomorrow? Let's look over the list of skills emphasized for 21st century classrooms, and you'll find that technology's influence is evidenced throughout.

### Communication and Collaboration

Our classrooms should strive to reflect an environment in which students are comfortable sharing their ideas with one another and with external partners as well. The modern work environment demands that employees be able to communicate their thoughts. Simply working on worksheets or taking bubble-sheet tests isn't going to be a huge benefit for students looking to participate in the 21st century.

> Students of today enter an increasingly globalized world in which technology plays a vital role. They must be good communicators, as well as great collaborators. The new work environment requires responsibility and self-management, as well as interpersonal and project-management skills that demand teamwork and leadership. (Pearlman, n.d.)

Collaborative projects were once seen as somewhat of a novelty but now are essential for working in the Internet age. Technology has made work location relatively meaningless—students can work in collaborative groups from anywhere. Yet so many of our classes incorporate assignments in which students work independently, confined to desks, and rarely involving their classmates. A 21st century classroom looks to engage learners in collaborative groups, where learning takes place in and out of school.

### Creativity and Innovation

Most American classrooms can be described as rigid, traditional, even boring—this is not the environment where creativity and innovation typically flourish. Whether it's due to the amount of material that needs to be covered to prepare for a standardized test or the traditional nature of teaching in the current classroom model, bringing in new ideas and allowing students to explore their own creativity is a tremendous challenge facing many classrooms.

Former North Carolina Governor Jim Hunt (2010) shared the following concerning the need for creative thinking in our schools:

> Creative thinking fuels innovation, it leads to new goods and services, creates jobs and delivers substantial economic rewards. However, without adequately cultivating creativity in our schools at the state and local level, states will not be able to compete with other states and countries who already do.

We need to use technology-related activities to facilitate creativity and promote innovation with our students. Kids are excited to show what they know by creating projects that demonstrate their skills. For a 21st century classroom to be effective, our assignments need to give students more than random facts for an upcoming exam; they need to provide students with the opportunity to design projects that inspire and motivate them.

## Critical Thinking and Problem Solving

For several years, there has been an assumption on the part of parents and teachers that our children aren't learning as much as they used to. Our national test scores have gone down over the past few tears, and there is a growing sense that it is due to the overabundance of available technology.

> Fourth-graders and eighth-graders across the United States lost ground on national mathematics tests this year, the first declines in scores since the federal government began administering the exams in 1990.

> Reading performance also was sobering: Eighth-grade scores dropped, while fourth-grade performance was stagnant compared with 2013. (Brown, 2015)

Is technology really to blame for the decrease in test scores? Here is the challenge for the modern teacher—we need to capitalize on our students' interest in and ability to use different technologies, but we don't want to isolate the technologies to the point that computers do the thinking for our students. As Jason Levy (quoted in Dretzin, 2010), principal of I.S. 339 in New York, stated, "Kids are going to need to be fluent in technology. They're going to need to be excellent at communication. They're going to need to be problem solvers. That's just the way the world is now."

One thing we can agree on: New technologies are going to continue to impact the classroom. A teacher of 21st century learners is going to need to use these technologies to enhance their critical thinking and problem-solving skills, not replace them.

## HOW TO USE THIS BOOK

*Going Google* isn't like your typical *Technology for Idiots* textbook. Learning how to use the different tools in the Google library is part of the goal, but you should also come to understand how to use the tools as part of an effective teaching strategy. That being said, *Going Google* wasn't designed to be followed from cover to cover, either. Rather, you should be able to scan quickly to any given section of the book to learn more about a tool and its classroom application.

The book's goals include allowing readers to do the following:

- Preview five major points to consider about each tool or group of tools at the beginning of the chapter or section.
- Discover ideas for implementing a Google tool in your instruction.
- Explore how the tools help students to meet national standards. Chapters begin with a reference to one of the International Society for Technology in Education standards (ISTE) for either teachers (ISTE T) or students (ISTE S). You will also find references to the Framework for 21st Century Learning in various chapters, developed by the Partnership for 21st Century Skills.
- Observe timely screen shots to help you visualize what you're learning.
- Learn from other amazing educators as they share their ideas at the end of each chapter.
- Find tips for "going Google" at the end of most chapters.

Because some of the terms used in *Going Google* may be considered technology jargon or "geek speak," I've included a glossary at the end of the book to help you understand unfamiliar words or concepts (glossary terms are denoted by boldface italics.). I've tried my best to explain terms like HTML and RSS, but some of these acronyms are tough to illustrate quickly. The glossary should help clear up any misconceptions or confusing terms.

It's important to note that the tool tutorials in this book can't stay current forever. Google prides itself on innovation, and the tools in its library are always changing in their look and feel. Just while writing this edition of the book, Google pulled the plug on Picasa and made changes to several features in Google Drive. I want you to learn the essential features found within each of the tools. You'll always be able to add collaborators in Google Drive whether the **Share** button is found in the top right corner of the edit window or not. No book can account for the stylistic changes Google will make, but I hope this book will help you learn the tools' important features and how they can be incorporated into your curriculum.

## POWERFUL TOOLS FOR 21ST CENTURY CLASSROOMS

The premise of this book is simple: Educators want to use the best tools to engage their students and prepare them for their futures. Google has created a comprehensive library of tools that can help teachers accomplish the goal of developing 21st century learners. After reading this book, there are a few things I hope you'll want to do.

- Explore the skills that students will need, moving forward in the 21st century.
- Learn about the different Google tools, and discover how you can leverage the various programs in your classroom.
- Identify several classroom projects you can incorporate into your curriculum.

If you've only used Google as a search engine, this book should provide you with an overview of a variety of tools you can use with your students. If you've been using Google tools for a long time, I hope you'll see some new ways in which you can incorporate the programs you love into your classroom curriculum. Who knows? Maybe by the end of our time together, you'll have "gone Google" as well.

# PART I

# Communicating and Collaborating

Over the past decades, the demands of the modern workforce have shifted. No longer is the factory model of production a viable solution for educating our students. Collaborating with colleagues has become the norm in the business world, and yet our classrooms are still stuck in a 19th-century framework of desks lined up in neat little rows. For the past 150 years, students have been expected to work on projects independent of one another, even though they are sitting right next to each other. The question has to be asked: Why? With so many advances in technology and a deeper understanding of learning theory, why are we still doing things the same way they were done so long ago? *Tradition.* Google tools offer one method of breaking down the constraints of the traditional classroom by providing students with the ability to work on projects at any time, with anyone, in any place. This is an example of the kind of change our classrooms need. Teachers know it, students know it, and our leaders know it.

To remain globally competitive and develop engaged citizens, our schools should weave 21st century competencies and expertise throughout the learning experience. These include the development of critical thinking, complex problem solving, collaboration, and adding multimedia communication into the teaching of traditional academic subjects (U.S. Department of Education, 2015).

Collaboration involves much more than simply working together on a project with others. Collaborative activities ask students and teachers to engage with one another, learn from one another, and rely on one another as an integral part of their education. As Richard Ellwood, technology coordinator and digital arts teacher at Columbia Secondary School, says:

> Collaborative projects really make for an excellent education experience not only because students bounce ideas off each other and improve each other's writing skills, but also because the process itself teaches them how to work well with others—a valuable skill for everyone. (Google, n.d.c)

## CREATING A COLLABORATIVE CLASSROOM USING GOOGLE

We've seen how the classroom needs to be updated. For our students to stay competitive on a global scale, we need to help them develop the necessary skills. In the Framework for 21st Century Learning (Partnership for 21st Century Learning, 2015), collaboration requires students to do the following:

- Demonstrate the ability to work effectively and respectfully with diverse teams.
- Exercise flexibility and willingness to be helpful in making necessary compromises to accomplish a common goal.
- Assume shared responsibility for collaborative work, and value the individual contributions made by each team member.

Google contributes to this framework by offering an online environment for creation and sharing so that students don't have to work on projects alone anymore. The idea of having a group of students standing around while one of them inputs content into PowerPoint presentation is a thing of the past. Using Google Drive, a group of students can contribute ideas to that same group presentation, but now all of them are working on the project at the same time. By having the students working simultaneously on the same project, it gives all of them the responsibility for the work, with each student having an integral role in the project's completion. Using Google tools for collaborative projects is helping teachers prepare students for the jobs of the 21st century.

Now, getting started with new tools and a shift in your educational philosophy isn't always easy. Many students are used to working on projects by themselves, and teachers are comfortable with assignments being an individual rather than a collective effort. Many teachers are still uncomfortable with the learning curve that technology and web-based tools requires of them. Instructors understand the need to share and work together pedagogically, but often they are still hung up on the technology tools themselves.

Google tools provide one important solution to these technological stumbling blocks. Once teachers start using these tools, they will find them simple to implement and see how effective they are for communicating and collaborating with students. Kids don't have issues adopting new technologies; their only concern is whether or not something works. If a suite of programs like Google tools makes their educational lives easier, they're on board.

## USING GOOGLE IN THE CLOUD

So, what are the classrooms of tomorrow going to look like? Will students be organized into tidy rows, each working on handouts individually? Or will we see a structure where tables are found throughout the rooms? The future of our classrooms appears to be one-to-one computing, where each student has access to his or her own computing device. Whether that's on an iPad mini or a Chromebook isn't the issue; we are going to need to use tools that will function well on a mobile computing device. Google tools offer an effective solution for these smaller computers because files are saved "in the cloud."

***Cloud computing*** means that files are saved through websites rather than being stored on a local computer's hard drive. Mobile computers don't have the storage space to house a lot of files or programs, so the need to use the cloud is essential. Google Drive, Calendar, Groups, Sites, and Gmail are all housed on the Internet by Google, so files created in these programs will not fill up space on the devices themselves. Making use of cloud computing is a great way to prepare students today for the tools of tomorrow.

What are the advantages of one-to-one computing? "1:1 and BYOD are game changers, giving students access to digital tools throughout the day, across all subject areas. This paradigm shift challenges teachers to rethink and redesign learning activities to capitalize on their school's investment in technology" International Society of Technology in Education (ISTE) (Soard, 2014).

When we look at districts across the country working to implement a one-to-one computer initiative for their schools, it becomes even more important to have programs that allow students to work and save files in the cloud of the Internet. Students need to have an easy way to access their projects no matter where they are. We can't expect our students to try and keep track of files on multiple computers or various forms of storage. Most of my students couldn't even remember to bring a pencil to class every day. How can I expect them to remember a flash drive?

As you'll see in the upcoming chapters, one of the biggest advantages of Google tools is the ability to access information from anywhere or any device as long as you have Internet access. Adopting a suite of programs like Google tools in the classroom will help prepare your students to work in the modern world. It's a simple investment that will yield both short- and long-term gains.

In this section, we're going to look at some specific tools that promote collaboration, communication, and critical thinking: Google Drive, Google Calendar, Gmail, Sites, Blogger, Hangouts, Google Voice, and Google Classroom. We'll explore how each of these tools can help our students with critical-thinking skills and provide teachers with additional avenues for increasing their productivity. As we look at collaboration and communication as crucial 21st century skills, we need to get students beyond the skill-and-drill education of the past and move our instruction into the global information age in which they thrive outside of the classroom.

## CHAPTER 1

# Google Drive

## FIVE Things to Know About Google Drive

1. Google Drive consists of Docs, Sheets, Slides, Forms, and Drawing.

2. You and your students can create documents from scratch or upload existing files.

3. Google Drive provides you with unlimited free storage for your files in Google Apps for Education (GAFE) accounts or 15 GB of storage in a traditional Google account.

4. You can combine Google Drive with Google Classroom in an easy system for managing student projects.

5. You can add on to the tools in Google Drive with third-party apps and extensions.

Google Drive has a simple premise, but its impact is revolutionary. The basic idea is this: Rather than creating files on one's local computer and sharing them with others via attachments through email, documents are created online, and the files are made available by email invitation. Basically, Google Drive provides an online home for files where people can share their documents by sharing access through a secure link to others for collaboration.

What does that mean for you and your students? There's only one copy of each document. It lives on the Internet, and students can access it anytime, from anywhere. Before, projects were constantly being moved around and relabeled. Old versions and the latest version of a file were getting mixed up, and there wasn't a clear location for saving the file. Everyone had his or her own solution for this problem, from jump drives, to emailing files, to printing

> ### ISTE S Standard 7 Objective c
>
> *Students contribute constructively to project teams, assuming various roles and responsibilities to work effectively toward a common goal. (ISTE, 2016)*

hard copies. Even with all those possibilities, the challenge remained: how can I keep track of the different versions of my files, and how can others work on the project concurrently?

Using Google Drive, there is just one home for your projects. This is a safe and secure way to store them, and you control the files. Old versions and new versions are stored together. Collaborators can be added as needed. It's up to you.

These tools give students unlimited access to work on their projects. They can work collaboratively with their classmates on group projects, without saving and sending different versions. What does that mean for your classroom workflow? Daily projects like self-starting writing prompts or journals can take place online. Your whole class can brainstorm ideas before class even begins. Projects become more collaborative online, taking less time as part of the actual instruction. Having projects take place as part of homework can actually provide the teacher with more instructional time. Who doesn't want more time?

## GETTING STARTED

Thus far, we've shared some different ideas surrounding the need to collaborate and communicate in today's schools. Now you're ready to begin your journey in Google Drive.

So, how do you get started? You can find Google Drive in two ways:

Figure 1.1 Google Drive Menu Options

1. Go to drive.google.com, and enter your Google account username and password.

2. While you're at google.com, click on the **Google 9 key** menu icon. It's located in the top right corner of the screen. You'll find **Drive** in the *drop-down menu*.

You've made it. Welcome to Google Drive!

### A Few Basics About Google Drive

- All documents, spreadsheets, presentations, and other files are housed in the Library.

- The Library is organized chronologically, with new or recently edited documents displaying at the top of the list. You have different options to sort your files, but the default is last modified.

- All files display in the Library unless they are added to folders.

- Folders display along the left side of the Library.

- Create folders by clicking on the **New** button and choosing **Folder** (see Figure 1.1).

## Uploading an Existing Document

- Create an online version of an existing file by selecting the **New** button along the top left of the Library. You'll have two choices: **Upload file** or **Upload folder** (this option only works in Google Chrome).
- You'll be directed to a dialog window prompting you to browse to your existing file.
- You can upload documents up to 50 *MB,* spreadsheets up to 2 million cells, and presentations up to 100 MB in size.
- Or you can simply drag and drop a file or folder into Google Drive.

*Tip—Convert your files into Google Docs. To maximize all the features in Google Drive, you'll want to convert your Microsoft Office files into their Google equivalent. To do this click on the settings icon in the top right corner of Google Drive. Select Setting from the drop down menu. Check the box that says Convert uploaded files to the Google Docs editor format. All of your files will convert automatically from this point on.

## Creating Files in Google Drive

- Create a new file by selecting the **New** button.
- You can create several types of files including documents, spreadsheets, presentations, forms, and drawings.
- These options will all be found in a drop-down menu. Choose the right option for your project, and you're on your way.

As we look at the basic tools available to you in Google Drive, you'll find they are very similar to those in Microsoft Word and other word processing programs. All the basic features are present including alignment options, formatting tools, editing controls, and more.

While working on a project, you'll find there's no need to save your work. Google Drive automatically saves your project every time you make a change in your file.

If you would like to work on your project in an offline environment or share it with someone using Microsoft Office, click on the **File** menu, and you'll discover a **Download as** option to create an offline version of your work.

Most of the getting-started features we've discussed to this point should be fairly familiar to you as they have similar tools in most standard Microsoft Office programs. Now, let's take a look at some of the features that make Google Drive special. Google Drive makes it possible to do the following:

### *Sharing*

- You can control sharing options with others providing them with access to edit, view, or comment on a specific document.
- Folders can also be shared, and the documents inside will have the same permissions as the folder.

### Accessing

- Google Drive is available from any computer or mobile device as long as you have access to the Internet. You can even create offline versions of your files for access when you're "off-the-grid."

- In addition to the latest draft of a document, Google Drive saves all the previous versions of the project as well.

### Storing

- You can store up to 15 GB of files for free in a personal Google account. If you have a GAFE account, you have unlimited storage.

- Files can include items from Microsoft Office, PDF files, images, movies, and more.

### Communicating

- Google Drive provides users with control over who sees and contributes to a project. You can keep it private or share it with the world.

Let's take a closer look at these features and the skills involved.

## SHARING

Google Drive allows students and teachers to create or upload documents and share them with others, which gives you, as the teacher, several options and strategies. What about a class brainstorming session that happens live with all 30 students contributing their ideas? We do this in class all the time, with kids shouting out their answers. But what happens to the shy student who's a bit more reserved? Brainstorming in a shared document means that everyone's voice gets heard.

Group research projects are a natural fit for Google Drive. It doesn't matter whether it's a document or a presentation—you can have groups of students collaborate on their projects. Students can work on creating the content, and revision can take place throughout the project. Imagine having your students working together through the writing process. They are the ones learning how to evaluate one another's writing. Google Drive provides the tools to make collaborative projects happen (see Figure 1.2).

To invite another person to a Google Drive file, you'll want to click on the **Share** button in the upper right-hand corner of any Doc, Sheet, or Slide. Here, you'll be prompted to add collaborators from your contact list, or simply type in a friend's email address and decide what sort of access you wish to provide him or her. He or she can either work on the document as a collaborator, with full editing rights, or the friend can only be allowed to view or comment on the file.

As the teacher, you'll want to have your students invite you to their files as a collaborator, thus giving you the rights to make comments and view changes made to the project in Google Drive. Once a file has been shared with you—you'll find that file in the **Shared with me** folder in your Google Drive Library.

As the teacher, another huge benefit of being a collaborator on student projects is the ability to review the revision history of the document. Located under the File menu, **See revision history**

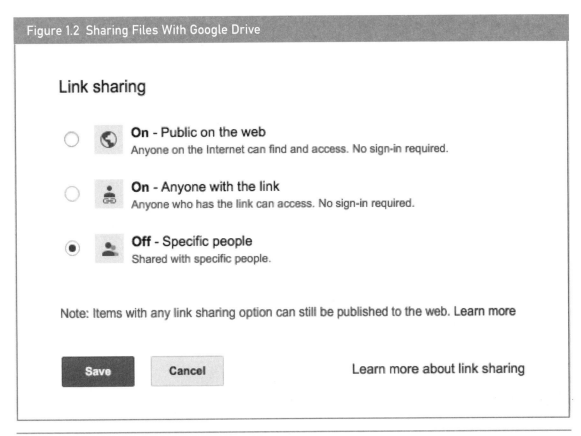

allows the instructor to see how the file has changed over time (see Figure 1.3). For group projects, it also details the contributions of each member of the team. You'll be able to tell, at a glance, what parts of the project were made by each individual in the group. What an asset for managing a group!

Olof Andersson, a middle school teacher from the Kvarnbergss-kolan School in Sweden, shared his thoughts about working through the process with his students using Google Drive.

> Many of my students use Google Drive when they are working in teams. The students invite me to join them and have a look at and give comments on their work. It helps me to be able to participate in the process, not just see the final product. (Google, 2011a)

## Using Templates in Google Drive

If there are two things teachers know how to do well, it's borrowing and sharing. We are willing to share lessons and handouts we've made with our colleagues, and we don't mind using their resources either. Most of us are so busy trying to get through with all the demands of teaching that when a good resource presents itself, we're all over it.

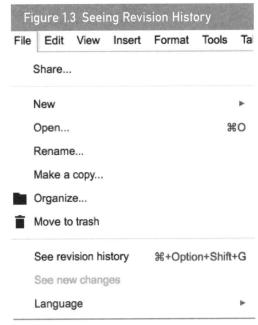

Figure 1.3  Seeing Revision History

Google Drive has a library containing educational Docs, Sheets, and Slides. The Template Gallery is full of useful resources for teachers and students. Instructors can find everything from grade book programs to attendance summaries for classroom management. There are lesson plan *templates* to assist you in creating future activities. Students can find many types of productivity aids including note-taking templates, science reports, and term paper structures. Think of it as an entire portfolio of free resources shared by teachers and students with their peers.

To access the Template Gallery, go to https://drive.google.com/templates. Another option is to create a shortcut to the Template Gallery in Google Drive. Click on **New>More>Connect More Apps** in Google Drive. To find Templates you'll need to conduct a search for Templates in Google Drive. Finally, select the **Connect** button, and you'll have your shortcut. If you create a document you'd like to share with the gallery, choose the **Submit a Template** link from the Template Gallery, and it will become available to other users. The Template Gallery is a wonderful place to find and share some of our best ideas.

*Tip—When sharing your existing files with colleagues, use the **Can View** option in the sharing settings. If you want to collaborate with others, choose **Can Edit**, but otherwise you're simply looking to give a copy of a handout or presentation to someone. Once they have the file, suggest they use the **File menu** to **Create a Copy** of the file for their own editing. You'll give them access to file but without having to worry about them making unwanted changes to your original.

## ACCESSING

Students are no longer bound to a location when working on a project. If you have Internet access, you can work on a Google Drive file. What a great solution for students working on a project from school and at home. They can simply pick up right where they left off because Google Drive has saved a copy of their project, just as they left it! This may not seem like that big a deal to some of your students, but wait until they experience the dreaded "computer crash." As an example, take the experience Julie Meloni (2009) had with one of her students.

> A student ran into class one day and said, "My computer died in the middle of my essay."
> I calmly opened my laptop, logged into my account, and showed the student the essay—
> saved constantly by Google until her computer crashed.

As a teacher, your access to students and their work increases dramatically as well. Gone are the days of searching through an endless number of drafts. Once students share their projects with you, you can look through the single copy of the document and find all the changes with one click. What's more, you can manage all of the work in a paperless environment! Student projects can easily be organized into online folders, so managing documents is a snap.

### Never Buy Software Again!

Google Drive also makes moot the debate as to which format to have student use to save their documents. It doesn't matter which software they have on their home computer. Because Google Drive is an online set of tools, you and your students don't even need to have Microsoft Office. As long as they have access to the Internet, they have access to their files on Google Drive.

Because Google Drive is a free tool, this can be part of a school- or districtwide technology plan. Imagine the savings to our financially challenged schools when they stop buying software and use that money elsewhere. As one teacher commented, "I guess I really don't need to have Microsoft Word anymore. As long as I have the Internet, I can use Google Drive."

## STORING

Google Drive might just remedy the eternal student declaration, "The dog ate my homework." No longer will students lose their projects between home and school. Now, all their files will be in one location, easy to access and share. Google provides users with 15 **GB**, or gigabytes, of free online storage, meaning you can probably store every document, spreadsheet, and presentation you own for free!

In addition to being able to store Docs, Sheets, and Slides, Google Drive also allows users to store other files like PDFs, images, videos, and so forth. This gives you additional options, but remember, the more multimedia files you include, the quicker your storage space gets filled. If you need to increase your storage, Google provides a cheap solution. For $2 a month, you can expand your personal storage from 15 GB to 100 GB. But don't forget, GAFE accounts have unlimited storage.

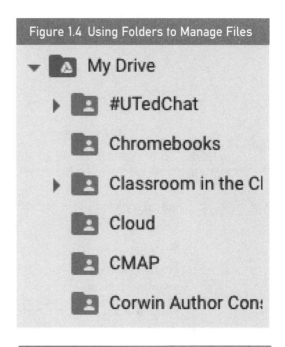

Figure 1.4 Using Folders to Manage Files

Previously, I mentioned that you can create folders in Google Drive as storage for your files. This is another nice aspect of the program—it can become your personal filing cabinet online (see Figure 1.4). While this may seem unnecessary as you begin using Google Drive, over time you'll continue to amass more and more files until it can become very overwhelming. Remember, a little file management in the beginning can save you huge headaches in the long run. Folders are an easy way to store your documents and find them later!

## COMMUNICATING

Google Drive provides you with several ways to communicate with parents and students. We've already explored how you can share Docs, Sheets, and Slides with individuals, but you can also make files public and share them with everyone else. What a great way to publicize your classroom newsletter or share your disclosure document!

Although getting your message out is important, it may be even more vital to get the students' and parents' opinions. Remember, students and their parents are your main clients. If you aren't in touch with their desires and needs, you may be setting yourself up for unnecessary challenges. One of my favorite components in Google Drive is the Forms feature, which can be used to get authentic feedback from the people who matter most. As with the other tools in Google Drive, it's easy to share a form—you can either email it to people or share a public link.

The power isn't so much in the form itself but in your ability to take the information gained and plan your teaching strategy accordingly. Most kids want their opinions to be heard, but few feel comfortable sharing verbally with the teacher. The Forms function allows individuals to give their

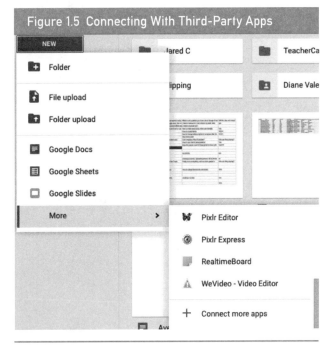

Figure 1.5 Connecting With Third-Party Apps

© 2016 Google Inc. used with permission. Google and the Google logo are registered trademarks of Google Inc.

input and provides the teacher with an easy way to access the feedback.

## Expanding Google Drive

Another great option for using Google Drive in the cloud is to extend the tools with a variety of third-party applications. These tools can be found and added through the **New>More>-Connect More Apps** (see Figure 1.5). Once you open the menu you've just unlocked a treasure trove of resources and tools from the cloud.

The great thing about these apps is that many of the tools are free. Another advantage is that you can use your Google Drive logon to provide you with access and storage for the tools. Some apps that are essential for the cloud classroom include:

- Pixlr Editor: This is a fantastic tool for editing your photos. It has many similar features to the popular photo editing tools that users have been using for years.

- WeVideo: This tool allows users to upload and edit their videos in the cloud. It creates finished projects that can be stored in Google Drive, shared online, or saved to devices.

- MoveNote: This is a tool for making video-narrated presentations. The cool thing about MoveNote is that it allows you to use your Google Slides presentations and add on a video narration alongside the other content.

- Lucid Chart and Lucid Press: Chart is a tool for creating graphic organizers for your classroom. Press is for desktop publishing and allows your students to create newsletters, brochures, and more.

## THE GOOGLE DRIVE SUITE

To this point we've discussed using the Google Drive programs as part of a collection. Combined, all of the tools share many things in common with regard to sharing content, storing files, and so on. However, each of the unique tools in Google Drive have some amazing features that we should explore a bit. Let's learn about a few key features for each program in Google Drive.

## Google Docs

- Be sure to check out the Tools menu in Google Docs. Here you'll find some of the best advantages to using an online word processor. Some of the best tools are listed here:
  - *Research:* The Research feature allows students to search for new information while still working on documents. Research opens a side panel in Google Docs that allows you to search the web, images, Scholar, and more.

○ *Voice Typing:* This is a new option in Google Docs that allows you the chance to use the microphone in your computer as a dictation device. You literally can speak your sentences, and Google Docs will transcribe them for you. This is amazing to help younger students share their ideas.

○ *Translate Document:* Capitalizing on Google Translate, you can take your documents and create foreign language versions to share with others. This is a great option when creating documents for your English-as-a-second-language (ESL) students.

- Editing, Suggesting, or Viewing: Found in the top right corner of Google Docs (see Figure 1.6), this new feature allows collaborators different rights when working on a shared document. Rather than making corrections on a student project, teachers can select the **Suggesting** option. Your suggestions will appear in the document, but it's up to students to accept or reject changes.

- Add-ons: Google Docs has some terrific add-ons to extend the power of this tool. Simply click on the **Add-ons** menu and look for a few of these options:

  ○ EasyBib—You can quickly create bibliographies for research projects using this tool. Add books, websites, and journals in no time. Format the citations in a variety of different ways including MLA, APA, and Chicago Style. When you've added all your sources, EasyBib will create a works cited page in your document.

  ○ Kaizena—Using this add-on will enable voice comments in a Google Doc. This is a great way to personalize your feedback on student documents. When students checks your comments, they'll simply click on a **Play** button and hear your feedback.

  ○ MindMeister—This tool will let you take content and turn it into a graphic organizer. Imagine making your agenda a mind map, so you can visualize the important elements of your upcoming module or lesson.

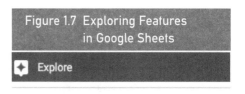

Figure 1.6 Editing Options in Google Docs

**Editing**
Edit document directly

**Suggesting**
Edits become suggestions

**Viewing**
Read or print final document

© 2016 Google Inc. used with permission. Google and the Google logo are registered trademarks of Google Inc.

Figure 1.7 Exploring Features in Google Sheets

Explore

## Google Sheets

- Explore the numbers in Sheets, located in the lower right corner of your Google Sheets, which can provide a summarized snapshot of different elements of your data. With one click, you'll be able to visualize and compare your numbers (see Figure 1.7).

- Import web data. Using formulas within your Google Sheets, you can bring in data from tables or charts on the web. This will allow the data to be updated in real time as the data updates on the web. This can be a great to have students explore information that updates frequently—such as the weather or stocks.

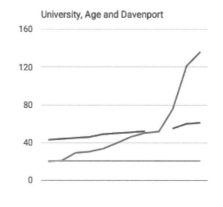

University, Age and Davenport

© 2016 Google Inc. used with permission. Google and the Google logo are registered trademarks of Google Inc.

- As with Google Docs, Google Sheets also contain some amazing add-ons that you can install in your program. Here are a few favorites:

  ○ Flubaroo: Used in combination with Google Forms, Flubaroo is a great tool for quickly assessing responses from your forms. With Flubaroo you can turn your Google Form into an online quiz. This is an easy way to evaluate what your students are learning.

  ○ Yet another Mail Merge: One of the biggest complaints from Microsoft users is the lack of a mail merge tool. Well, in add-ons you'll find several different tools to help you merge data from your Google Sheet into a Google Doc. In seconds you'll be able to send mass emails using your Google data.

  ○ gMath for Sheets: Math teachers rejoice! gMath is a fantastic tool in both Sheets or Docs that allows you to use your favorite math formulas as part of your file. In the past, it was always difficult to type mathematic formulas in Google Sheets, but with gMath you can solve equations, create graphs, type formulas, and more.

## Google Slides

- Publish to the web: Google Slides allows you to publish your presentations to the web, so they can be shared with larger audiences. This feature is also available in Google Docs and Google Sheets, but Google Slides capitalizes on this sharing feature.

- Edit images: You have several different options for editing your images as part of a presentation. Simply select a photo on your current slide, and you'll find that you have access to a variety of image editing tools. Using the crop tool, you have the ability to mask your image to a variety of shapes. You'll also find different color, light, and transparency choices.

- Use the PowerPoint factor. You can upload your existing PowerPoints into Google Slides. This will save you a ton of extra time. Now, there are several PowerPoint templates that don't exist in Google Slides, but you'll have access to dozens of effective templates. Also, you can download your Google Slides presentation into a PowerPoint presentation.

- Add Q&A to your presentation. While in the Present mode, you can turn on Presenter View, which allows your audience to ask questions using a custom **URL**. The URL will appear at the top of your slides (see Figure 1.8). Once questions are submitted, others in the audience will see all the questions from the custom URL and can vote (thumbs-up or down) on questions. The presenter will be able to see all questions and will also have the ability to filter the questions based on the number of votes from the audience. This is a great way to involve your audience in the presentation!

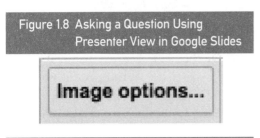

Figure 1.8 Asking a Question Using Presenter View in Google Slides

© 2016 Google Inc. used with permission. Google and the Google logo are registered trademarks of Google Inc.

## Google Forms

- Customize your forms. You can create your own custom headers in Google Forms. Use your school logo, or pick from the provided templates based on content or event type.

The tool looks like a painter's pallet, and you can access the custom header icon in the top right corner of the screen.

- Add images, video, and more. In addition to adding questions, Google Forms provides for incorporating other types of content.

  - Video: You can embed YouTube videos into your Google Forms. This can be used to provide background information in your form.

  - Images: Using digital images in your Google Form gives you different options. You can use images as part of questions in a quiz or as another way to share information.

  - Sections: This option provides you with the ability to break forms up into separate parts. This is helpful for having answers direct users into different sections. For example, if someone answers yes to a question, they are directed to a different section of the form than someone answering no.

- Add-ons: There aren't as many add-ons in Forms as we find in Sheets and Docs. Here are a couple to explore:

  - Form Limiter: Use this add-on to automatically shut your Google Form off. This is great when you want to set it and forget it. You can also limit the total number of responses in a form if you choose.

  - Form Notifications: This add-on allows you to receive an email when someone completes your Google Form. This is useful if you have a form open for a long period of time. You'll simply get notifications if someone completes the form.

## Google Drawings

- Improve your layout. In Google Drawings be sure to explore the Grid and Guide options as ways to get exact in adding objects to a drawing. You can also use Auto Distribution to create the right spaces in your drawing.

- Insert drawings into other tools. Images created in Google Drawings can be added into Google Docs, Google Slides, and more. Once the drawing is inserted, with one click you can go into an edit mode to make last-minute corrections.

- Save drawings as JPGs. You can save your Google Drawings in many different image formats. This gives you the option to use the pictures in a variety of different ways.

> **ISTE S Standard 7 Objective c**
>
> *Students contribute constructively to project teams, assuming various roles and responsibilities to work effectively toward a common goal. (ISTE, 2016)*

## Project Idea: Student Writing Group

As a former language arts teacher, I think Google Drive is an incredibly effective solution for student writing groups. Here's why. As our students work through various drafts of a research project, many of us have the students engage in some type of peer review. This helps the writer get feedback on what's working and what isn't going as well. Peer review also helps the reviewers; they see some of the mistakes they're making in their own writing as they evaluate another paper.

## Setting Up a Peer-Reviewed Paper

Have the author create the document using the **Create New** button and selecting **Google Docs.** The author of the document needs to "share" the project with the rest of the peer reviewers. Once the author uses the **Share** button, he or she will be prompted for the email addresses of the peer reviewers (see Figure 1.9).

One management strategy I like involves using the Comment feature. Found in the **Insert** menu, **Comment** provides peer reviewers with an easy spot to make suggestions without deleting any of the original work. If you have more than one peer reviewer, have the students pick a specific font color to use when they make their own comments.

Once the author reviews the comments made by peers, he or she can make future revisions. Using the **Revision History**, the student can compare various versions of the paper and see the progress he or she has made.

To help students work through the revision process together, I would suggest not asking to be added as a collaborator until the students are a good distance into the project. Too often, once the instructor becomes part of the process, the other reviewers tend to defer to the teacher. Refrain from joining the project to begin with, and let the students work through the process.

Using the revision history is a good management strategy for you as the instructor. Once you are added to the document, you can quickly assess the work of each student, not just the author. Because the revision history keeps track of each change on a document, you can see what contributions each reviewer has made. This illustrates to the students that each of their comments is observed and that everyone contributes to the success of a project.

As the time comes for the final draft to be submitted, the nice part for teachers is they already have access to the document. Now it's time to move the file from the Library into a final versions folder. You can create a folder that gets placed along the left side of the Google Drive Library. Folders can be set up for different subjects, class periods, or however you want.

With the advent of Google Classroom, you'll find that setting up these collaborative projects has gotten even easier. Even better, once you've gotten the completed writing assignment, you can quickly grade the paper and provide students with the necessary feedback.

Working in student writing groups uses several different elements of sharing, revising, and evaluating. Google Drive provides the structure and the support to help students work through any peer-reviewed project.

**Figure 1.9  Inserting Comments in Google Docs**

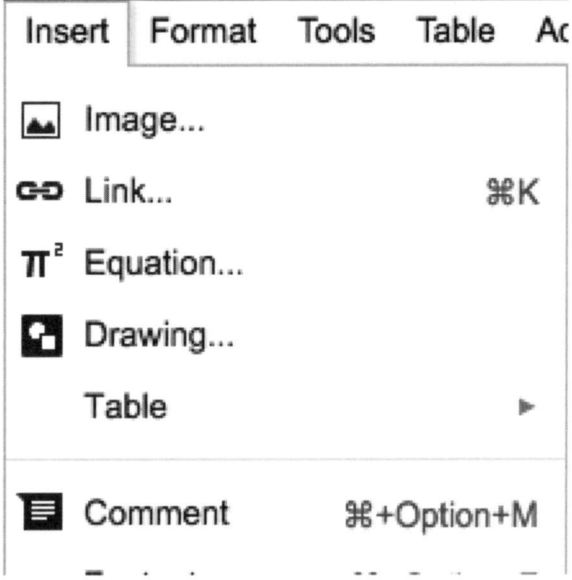

Insert | Format | Tools | Table | Ac

- Image...
- Link...                           ⌘K
- π² Equation...
- Drawing...
- Table                             ▶
- Comment                    ⌘+Option+M

© 2016 Google Inc. used with permission. Google and the Google logo are registered trademarks of Google Inc.

**ISTE T Standard 3 Objective b**

*Teachers collaborate with students, peers, parents, and community members using digital tools and resources to support student success and innovation. (ISTE, 2008)*

One of the first things a teacher needs from his or her students at the beginning of the school year is contact information for parents or guardians. We want to know whom we can contact, where, when, and how. Sure, the school can provide us with a lot of this information, but much of it is out of date or just incorrect, and it requires us going through the administration to access the data. Creating a Google Form is an easy solution to this beginning-of-school-year problem. Here's how to get started (see Figure 1.10).

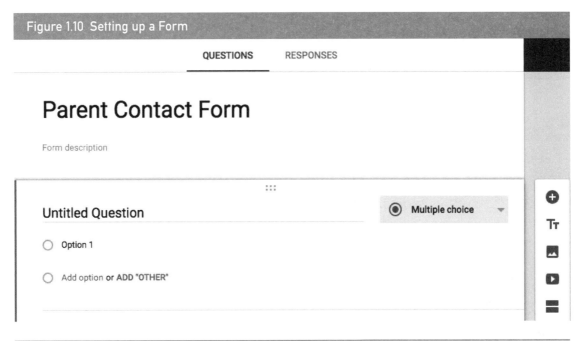

Figure 1.10 Setting up a Form

## Creating the Form

- Select **New** from the button along the top left side of the Google Drive Library and under the **More** header, you'll drop down to **Forms.**

- As soon as you start a form, you'll find it has a basic structure: name the form, provide instructions, and ask questions.

- For our sample project, you'll need to name your form something like "Parent Contact Form."

- Following the title, in the **Form description** field, be sure to provide a basic overview of what information you'd like from parents and how you plan to use that information in the future.

- Next we'll start creating the basic **Questions** we need for our form). Note: The default type of question in a Google Form is text (see Figure 1.10). Simply put, you want your respondent to enter his or her answers manually.

So, we need to create basic text questions that will provide us with important contact information about our students' parents. Examples of text questions may include parent name, student

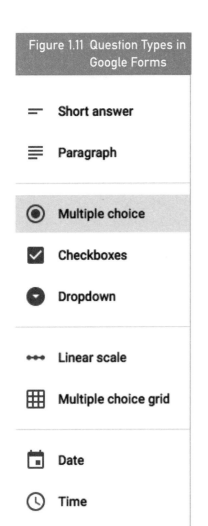

**Figure 1.11 Question Types in Google Forms**

— Short answer

≡ Paragraph

◉ Multiple choice

☑ Checkboxes

⏷ Dropdown

••• Linear scale

⊞ Multiple choice grid

📅 Date

🕐 Time

© 2016 Google Inc. used with permission. Google and the Google logo are registered trademarks of Google Inc.

name, or parent contact number. To enter in this data, you'll simply type in the **Question Title** for what you'd like to know. For example, if I'd like to know the parent's name, I'll enter that in the Question Title.

There are a few additional aspects to each question in a form. Google provides a space for clarifying information. You'll see a space to choose your question type (see Figure 1.11). I mentioned that the default style of question is text, but there are several types of questions at your disposal. Currently the list includes Short Answer, Paragraph, Multiple Choice, Checkboxes, Dropdown, Linear scale, and Multiple choice grid. Each one of these options can be useful for gathering specific types of data.

The final option in creating a question is whether or not to require the answer. This means a form cannot be submitted without a reply to that question (see "Required" button below). For our example, items like student name, parent name, and phone number or email are essential to the success of our project. These items would definitely be required before someone could hit submit.

**Required** ⬤

### Adding Additional Questions

When you first create a form, you'll find that two sample text-style questions automatically populate the fields. If you want to add additional questions, look in the top left corner of the form, and you'll find the + button. This is a drop-down menu that allows you to select from the options mentioned previously (i.e., Checkboxes, Linear scale, etc.).

### Editing a Question

Once you've established a field of data, changing it doesn't require starting over. Instead, you just need to do the following:

- To edit the text or style of question simply click on the field you wish to change, and you'll be able to make any corrections you'd like. Changes are saved automatically, so there isn't a button to save changes.

- On the right side of each question, you'll find two editing buttons—an overlapping box icon to copy a question, or a trash can icon to delete the question.

- The overlapping box is useful if you have a series of similarly formatted questions. Simply duplicate the question, and make the minor adjustments you need without retyping the entire field. A great example of this would be a multiple-choice quiz. Perhaps two or three of the questions have the same options for answers. Rather than retype the five or six answer choices, simply copy and paste the entire entry and adjust the question, leaving the answers intact. This can save quite a bit of time.

- We all have a pretty good idea that clicking on the trash can will delete the selected question.

## Sharing the Form With Parents

So, you've put the final touches on your form, and you're ready to get parents to respond. Now what? You have a couple of different choices.

1. You could use the **Send** button and enter in all the parents' email addresses, so you can send the form directly to them. One problem here is that you need the email addresses, which is why you made the form in the first place. Here's a better choice.

2. Along the top right of your form is an eye icon. This is to preview the public URL. The URL is a site's address on the web. This one is a long, ugly address, but we've got a nice solution to work around that issue. There's a great website from Google found at http://goo.gl, which allows you to transform a nasty very long URL like https://spreadsheets0.google.com/viewform?formkey=dDZKdzlZOXpBYWh FQlcxOFlDRk16QWc6MQ into an easy-to-use URL: http://goo.gl/T3DE5y. Which URL would you rather type?

Now that you've created a usable address for parents to find the form, your next job is to distribute it. How do you get this form into the hands of the parents?

- Perhaps you could include the address to your form in your disclosure document, distributed on Back to School Night or during the first week of class.

- Another good option is to add the web link to your classroom website (if you don't have a website yet, we'll get to that shortly).

Once the parents start filling out the form, the final question is, where do the answers go? Here's the beauty of Google Drive. There are two options for looking at the responses.

Figure 1.13 Options in Form Menu

- First, you'll find the form has two tabs in the top center of the screen. To this point, we've been working in the **Questions** tab. Alongside is the **Responses** tab. Here you'll have a snapshot of all the responses to your questions.

- Here is a second option for viewing your results. When you created the form, Google Drive started a Google Sheet for the answers. The easiest way to access the sheet in on the **Responses** tab in Google Forms. Simply click on the **Sheets** icon, and you'll be prompted to enable the spreadsheet (see Figure 1.12).

If you want to edit the form or use any of its data, click on the **Form** option in the menus, and you'll have a variety of choices (see Figure 1.13). You can end submissions, summarize the data, edit the form, and more. It's a great system and an easy way to organize the information you need to start the year off right.

**ISTE T Standard 2 Objective d**

*Teachers provide students with multiple and varied formative and summative assessments aligned with content and technology standards and use resulting data to inform learning and teaching.*
(ISTE, 2008)

Assessment is such a major part of your classroom. Using Google Drive, you can create a form that will help you uncover student understanding and compile the data in an easy-to-use spreadsheet.

As we've learned about Google Forms, creating an online quiz is as simple as developing a series of questions you want to ask your students. Remember, there are several different types of questions, so you can write the questions to look at many kinds of data. Whether you want to use multiple choice or a paragraph response, it's up to you.

*The key for assessment is being able to use the answers to quickly identify student comprehension or identify teaching areas that need improvement.* Once the quiz is completed, all student responses are submitted into a spreadsheet that allows you to compile the data in many useful ways.

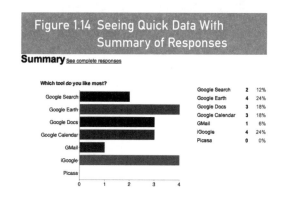

**Figure 1.14 Seeing Quick Data With Summary of Responses**

© 2016 Google Inc. used with permission. Google and the Google logo are registered trademarks of Google Inc.

One of the best ways to analyze the data is with the **Responses** tab in your Google Form. Remember, with this option, you can view a chart representing the various responses. For a quick formative assessment, this is a lifesaver. Within seconds of the quiz ending, a teacher can see how the class performed as a whole. It's an easy way to view what your students are thinking and determine where you need to spend your instructional time. In Figure 1.14, you'll see how easy it is to find out what students are thinking and learning.

Another useful option for scoring your quiz is the add-on called Flubaroo. I know it's a funny name, but it works great. Flubaroo is found in the **Add-on** menu in Google Sheets, under the **Get Add-ons** option. Just type the word "Flubaroo" in the search box, and you'll find it. Once you install the add-on, you'll find that Flubaroo has an option in your **Add-on** menu within your Google Sheet. Click on this menu option to get started.

Setup is easy as Flubaroo runs a little wizard to help you install the script. As you run the wizard, you'll find that Flubaroo wants to use one of the submissions as the answer key, so you'll either have to take the quiz yourself or use one of the students (provided they get all of the answers correct).

With the answer key established, Flubaroo will quickly score all of the quizzes and provide you with a detailed summary of each student's score. Here's a hint: Be sure to include a question on the quiz that requires an email address. You can then use the email address to send students their scores. This is an option in the Flubaroo menu.

## FROM A GOOGLE GURU

I do a lot of Google trainings with teachers, and we love Google. Our state is even a Google Apps state, so we can turn Google on for every district with a state email address.

We use Drive in a number of ways. First, Google has now enabled Apps to have unlimited storage in Drive. So we talk to teachers about uploading all of their school documents—no matter what format—into Drive so that they can access them from any device they are on. This means that if they have computer problems on their school device, they don't have to worry about losing things they have saved on the hard drive. They are very excited that they don't have to carry their documents around on a flash drive either.

I have teachers and students download Drive to their computers so they can access their documents and files even when they are offline. This has proven to be extremely useful when the Internet has been down in schools. Kids were still able to access their work and continue with their projects. Some students and teachers don't have Internet access at home (South Dakota is a pretty rural state), and they are able to work from their devices even without it. Using the downloaded Drive also makes it easier to pull the files from your computer over to the Drive. You can do a drag and drop and bring multiple files and folders into Drive without having to upload one at a time.

Google Drive allows you to share not only documents but folders as well. Many of my teachers will set up folders for each of their students and share them. That allows students to share documents with each other without having to use the share feature on each document, which is particularly easier with younger students. We also use this feature with the schools we work with. We are working on a grant with 10 schools, and we will have to both share information to help them move forward and to collect data to report back. We set up folders that we share with them as in Figure 1.15.

Figure 1.15 Teacher Folders in Google Drive

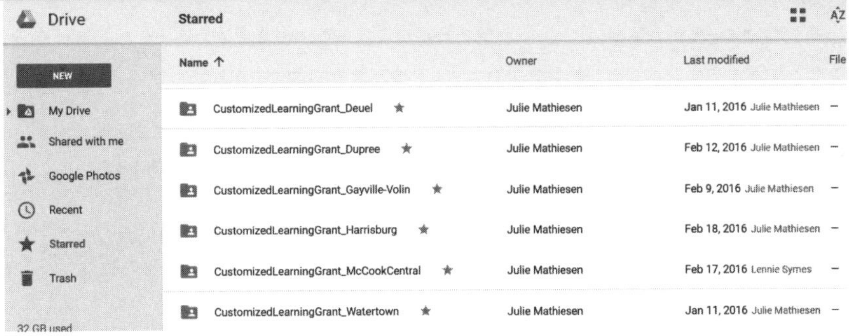

© 2016 Google Inc. used with permission. Google and the Google logo are registered trademarks of Google Inc.

We all can add and edit documents in the folder as in Figure 1.16.

Figure 1.16 Filtering Folders Using the Starred Option

© 2016 Google Inc. used with permission. Google and the Google logo are registered trademarks of Google Inc.

This is just such an efficient way to share a volume of documents. We will be working with these schools for three years, so we will have everything organized in one place.

Another tool I use all the time is the Starred feature. For the documents or folders that I am currently using often, I click on the star. Then I only have to click on the **Starred** on the left navigation bar, and I will focus on just those files. This has saved me much time. You can also use the **Recent** in much the same way, but Starred ensures that I can find specific files immediately, whether I have opened them recently or not.

One of the newer features is Google Photos. I have an Android phone, and I set all my photos to back up in Google Photos. (I don't want to be the one that drops her phone in the pool and loses everything!) I also have my iPad backing up here as well. (I love that it works cross-platform.) I can access all my photos from any device I am on, including my computer.

I would also like to point out that documents that are in other formats can both be stored in Drive and converted to Google documents. For example, I can take a Word file that is stored in my Drive and select it, as in Figure 1.17.

### Figure 1.17  Storing Microsoft Word Files in Google Drive

| | Name ↑ | Owner | Last modified | File size |
|---|---|---|---|---|
| NEW | | | | |
| My Drive | W  BCJH Curriculum Unit checklist.docx | me | Aug 25, 2015 me | 16 KB |
| Shared with me | PDF  Best-Practices-in-Personalized-Learning-Environments.pdf | me | Mar 11, 2015 me | 744 KB |
| Google Photos | W  Breakouts.docx | me | Jul 28, 2015 me | 31 KB |
| Recent | Brian Pete | me | Dec 10, 2012 me | — |
| Starred | Brookings Example | me | Jun 18, 2015 | |

By right-clicking on it, I have the option to **Open with:** and **Google Docs** (see Figure 1.18).

### Figure 1.18  Converting Word Files Into Google Docs

Once I select Google Docs, it opens another document, and I have the same document, which is now a Google Doc. But it also leaves the original Word document in my Drive, so I have a version in each platform.

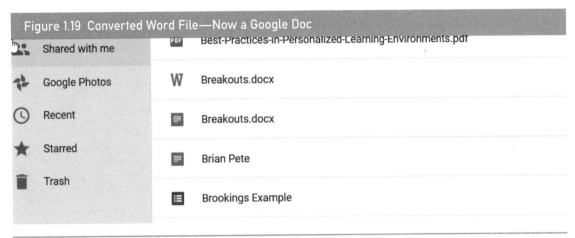

Figure 1.19 Converted Word File—Now a Google Doc

| | |
|---|---|
| Shared with me | PDF Best-Practices-In-Personalized-Learning-Environments.pdf |
| Google Photos | W Breakouts.docx |
| Recent | Breakouts.docx |
| Starred | Brian Pete |
| Trash | Brookings Example |

Clearly, I use Google Drive every day. I have more than one account—one for work and a personal one. It has made organization easy when I travel and when I use multiple devices. The schools I work with find it to be easy to work with and just as useful.

## BIOGRAPHY

Sherry Crofut

TIE (Technology and Innovation in Education),
Rapid City, SD, US

Learning Specialist

Twitter: @SDSherry

Website/blog: tie.net

### More Ideas for Going Google

- Develop an online writing portfolio for students.
- Create choose-your-own-adventure presentations for students.
- Brainstorm a class activity or learning topic using an open spreadsheet.
- Develop a classroom newsletter.
- Create an online checkout list for classroom books.

## TIPS FOR THE GOOGLE CLASSROOM

- Tying in Google Classroom is a great way to maximize using Google Drive. Instead of having students create Drive files and share them with the teacher, Google Classroom will automatically create student files when teachers create class assignments. Classroom organizes all the files and makes it easy to find student assignments.

- Embed your Google Slides presentations into your online courses. This is a terrific option to help you keep your content current without having to constantly update your presentations in your learning management system (LMS). Once a slide presentation is embedded, changes are automatically updated in your online course.

- Check out the two new features in Google Drive—Presenter View in Google Slides and Quizzes in Google Forms. Both tools will help you assess your students' understanding.

## CHAPTER 2

# Google Calendar

## FIVE Things to Know About Google Calendar

1. Calendars can be shared with different permissions for multiple people.

2. Calendars can be public or private.

3. You can attach files to calendar events.

4. Calendars can be embedded in your website.

5. Parents and students can subscribe to your classroom calendar.

As we look at our hectic lives, many of us would be lost without some type of planner, calendar, or notebook. We jot down events and plans into our three-ring binders, knowing that we rely upon these books to keep us on time and focused. Whether it's for our personal or professional lives, a calendar is our essential system for maintaining our schedules.

One of the most important communication tools a teacher has to share with parents is the classroom calendar. Over the years, there have been several different methods used by teachers for sharing important dates and events. For years, teachers have created a classroom newsletter with a one-page calendar included that covers the next 30 days. This has been a useful system for presenting information, but it is soon out of date and is easy to misplace. As we moved into the digital age, a teacher's webpage became a perfect place to share an electronic version of the schedule. This was and is a great way to share information, but many websites are difficult to update, and the calendar can be easily neglected as a result.

Google has developed a calendar tool that is easy to use. It doesn't require any knowledge of web design, and there are no special programs to purchase. The calendar is dynamic, and it can be updated instantly to share information with parents and students. It can be easily shared, so parents and students don't have to hunt around the web to find the events that are important to your class. Let's learn more about Google Calendar.

## GETTING STARTED WITH GOOGLE CALENDAR

To create a Google Calendar, you need to use your Google account. Once you have your account, you'll find Google Calendar in one of two ways:

1. Go to www.google.com/calendar, and enter your Google account username and password.

2. Or, while you're on google.com, click on the **Google** icon in the top left corner of the screen. Within the drop-down list you'll find **Calendar** among the options that pop up.

By default, Google will want you to create a personal account with your first and last name as the calendar's name. This is automatic and something you'll want to let occur. Still, a personal calendar isn't something you'll want to share with others, so let's go through the process of creating your classroom calendar.

## CREATING A CLASSROOM CALENDAR

Your classroom calendar is going to be a public calendar you can share with parents and students. You should plan on including only events that everyone can see and that relate to assignments and activities associated with school. To create a new calendar, follow these steps.

1. Click on the ***drop-down menu*** next to the **My Calendars** menu along the left side of the screen.

2. Choose **Create New Calendar**. You'll find yourself on the **Calendar Details** page.

3. Basic settings for your new calendar include **Calendar Name**, **Description,** and **Location** (see Figure 2.1). These elements should provide enough information to enable parents and students to find your calendar, but you still want to keep all the information strictly related to your classroom.

    a. Calendar Name: The name of your calendar will appear in any Google searches for your events and information. This means if someone types "Mr. Covili's Classroom Calendar" into the calendar search box, he or she will be able to find my specific calendar.

    b. Description: A brief description will help you ensure that your calendar finds its target audience. This doesn't need to be more than a line or two, but it provides that extra information to help parents.

    c. Location: As with the description, including a location helps parents to make sure they have the correct Mr. Smith. Including the name of your school is a good way to make this happen.

4. Once you've filled in all of the Calendar Details, you have the option to make your calendar **Public**. Your school calendar will need to be public to help parents and students

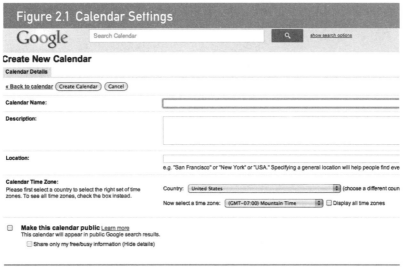

**Figure 2.1 Calendar Settings**

© 2016 Google Inc. used with permission. Google and the Google logo are registered trademarks of Google Inc.

find it. If this calendar is private, the only way for parents to access it is through direct contact with you. Although that may be "safer" and keep the information more private, it really hinders interested parties from finding your school calendar. We want this calendar to be accessible to more parents, and making it public is a good way to help this happen.

5. The last step is to save all of your information for the new calendar. To do this, click on the **Create Calendar** button along the top or bottom of the screen. That's it; you've just created your new classroom calendar!

## ADDING EVENTS AND MANAGING YOUR CLASSROOM CALENDAR

Now that you've created your calendar, it's time to start adding content to share with parents and students. Google Calendar makes this as simple as clicking and typing. Here are the basic steps:

1. Click on the calendar on the appropriate date and time for your selected event. This will create a new 1-hour event (see Figure 2.2).

2. When you first create the event, the only requested information is the **What**, or the event's title.

3. Because you have both a personal and classroom calendar, you'll want to use the drop-down menu to select the appropriate calendar.

4. To add information to an event on your calendar, click on the existing event. Select the option to **Edit event details**.

5. On this screen, you can add or edit several pieces of information including the name of the event, the date and time, the length, a description, the location, privacy settings, and any specific guests.

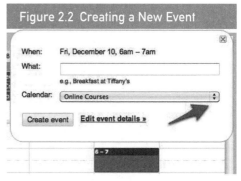

**Figure 2.2 Creating a New Event**

© 2016 Google Inc. used with permission. Google and the Google logo are registered trademarks of Google Inc.

6. Once you complete the event, be sure to click **Save** along the left side of the screen. You can now go **Back to calendar**.

Your updated event is now displayed on the calendar.

## Event Basics

- Creating All-Day Events: Click in the area without a specific time at the top of each day.

- Creating Repeat events: Use the radio button in the **Edit Event** settings to have an event repeat. You can choose from options such as repeating **Daily, Weekly, Monthly**, or **Yearly**.

- Changing the day or time of an event: Simply click on the event you wish to change, and drag it to the correct day or time. If you click on the bottom of an event, you can drag out the time (i.e., you can lengthen an event beyond 1 hour).

## ATTACHING FILES TO AN EVENT

A valuable feature in Google Classroom is the ability to attach files to individual events. This gives teachers the ability to provide valuable information to parents and students. Imagine that a specific calendar event is titled **"TEST."** This provides very little information for anyone looking at

**Figure 2.3  Adding Attachments to Google Calendar**

© 2016 Google Inc. used with permission. Google and the Google logo are registered trademarks of Google Inc.

calendar events. What parents and students are looking for when they go to the calendar is information. What if you could attach the study guide for tomorrow's test to your calendar? Suddenly the calendar is an information station rather than simply a list of due dates.

To attach a document to a calendar entry, use these steps:

- Click on an existing calendar entry to edit the event.
- About halfway down the event, you'll find an option to **Add Attachment** (see Figure 2.3).

You have a few main options for attaching a file—you can select something from **Google Drive,** or you have the option to **Upload a file** from your machine.

Once you save the update on the calendar event, anyone who accesses the calendar will now have the ability to view and download your attachment. This is a fantastic way to share important files with parents and students.

## WHY USE GOOGLE CALENDAR?

Many of us already have a calendar system we use and love, so why would we want to switch to Google Calendar? A big reason to create your classroom calendar in Google Calendar has to do with communicating. A paper classroom planner is personal and can't be shared with others. The same thing holds true for calendars on Outlook or Groupwise. These are great tools for individual use, but they don't help parents and students find out about classroom events. Your Google Calendar can be shared with anyone you want, making it a terrific system for spreading the word about the great things going on in your classroom.

Because your calendar is online and public, another big advantage to parents and students lies in the diverse methods in which they can access the information. Each Google Calendar can have a public *URL,* giving users the chance to bookmark a link to the teacher's calendar. This works, but there's an even better option for most parents and students.

With the average online classroom calendar, the only place to access the information is from the teacher's website. The problem is that most of us don't check a classroom website on a daily basis. Information gets missed and is often overlooked. Rather than going out for information, Google Calendar brings the information to you. Here's how it works.

## SUBSCRIBING TO A CLASSROOM CALENDAR

Once a calendar is made public, it has a unique URL. Anyone with that address can access the calendar online. In the past, this is the address most of us would have bookmarked, never to be seen again among the virtual pile of "favorite" websites. With Google Calendar, instead of bookmarking, you "subscribe" to any public calendar. This means the events from that calendar show up on your own Google Calendar. Here are two ways to subscribe to a Google Calendar.

One way for parents to subscribe to your calendar is to type your email address in the search box under the **Other calendars** heading (see Figure 2.4). This means you'll want to provide parents with your Google account email. Most likely, this is your Gmail account address.

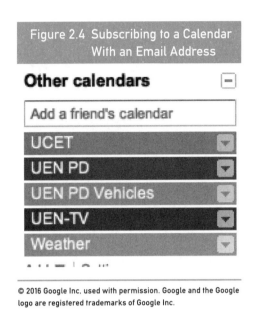

**Figure 2.4 Subscribing to a Calendar With an Email Address**

© 2016 Google Inc. used with permission. Google and the Google logo are registered trademarks of Google Inc.

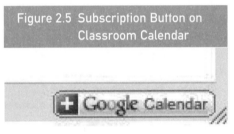

**Figure 2.5 Subscription Button on Classroom Calendar**

© 2016 Google Inc. used with permission. Google and the Google logo are registered trademarks of Google Inc.

Once parents add your public calendar to their list, it will display in the **Other calendars** section of their Google Calendar account. Even though your classroom calendar is public, the default sharing setting is "view only," meaning they cannot change anything on it.

Another option for adding your classroom calendar involves visiting the calendar online and subscribing directly. Here's how this works. When parents and students visit the URL of your calendar, they will find a **Subscribe** button in the lower right corner of the calendar. Hitting this button will add your classroom calendar to the subscriber's Google Calendar account under the **Other calendars** section (see Figure 2.5).

As with the other method for subscribing, using the + **Google Calendar** button provides the person with view status of your classroom calendar. They do not have privileges to edit or add events to the calendar.

One big advantage to having parents subscribe to your Google Calendar is that it provides them with access to your calendar using their mobile devices. Once someone subscribes to a calendar, it becomes part of his or her available calendars under their Google account. This means they can turn your classroom calendar on using their Calendar app on an iPhone or Android device. Parents will love the convenience of having access to your classroom events from their smartphones!

## GOOGLE CALENDAR AND THE CLOUD

We've already discussed how the cloud provides better access to our information online. Because Google Calendar lives in the cloud, we can have access to our calendar from any computer or device with Internet access. This makes it easy to update events from school or from home. It also means that our calendar can be accessed on several different devices, both desktop and mobile.

Here, Google (2011d) describes the advantage of having your data in the cloud:

> Data is stored in the cloud—not on one particular computer—so [users] can connect with all of their information and get work done from any Internet connection. Google's infrastructure gives users seamless access to their information at work, at home, on the road and from their mobile devices. With traditional technology, important information can be trapped in software only available on a limited set of devices, preventing [users] from being their most productive.

Having access to your calendar in the cloud not only provides you with more options to update and share events; it also means that parents and students can access your events from their smartphones and tablets. Anytime you can share data to someone's cell phone, your chance of the person seeing the information increases.

# SHARING YOUR GOOGLE CALENDAR

Google Calendar is a wonderful tool to use for communicating with others, but what about using it to collaborate? Google Calendar is useful for departmental calendars, the school website, or club calendars. One nice thing is that because it exists as part of the cloud, multiple individuals can add and manage events on the same calendar. Here are the steps to share your Google Calendar with collaborators (see Figure 2.6):

**Figure 2.6 Accessing the Sharing Settings**

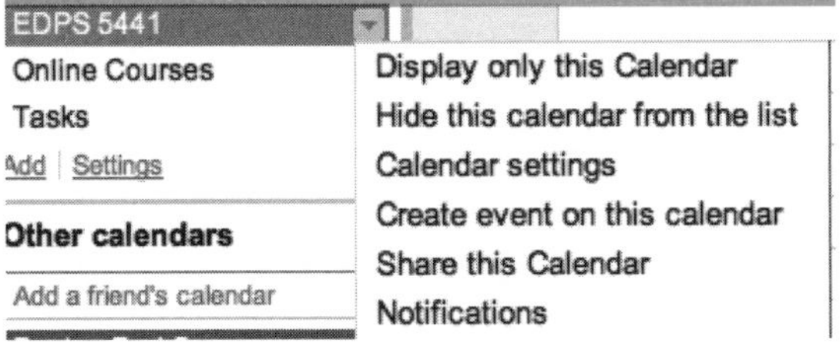

EDPS 5441

Online Courses
Tasks
Add | Settings

**Other calendars**

Add a friend's calendar

Display only this Calendar
Hide this calendar from the list
Calendar settings
Create event on this calendar
Share this Calendar
Notifications

© 2016 Google Inc. used with permission. Google and the Google logo are registered trademarks of Google Inc.

1. Go to your list of **My Calendars** (in the menu along the left side of your calendar display).

2. Click on the drop-down menu for your calendar.

3. Select the option to **Share this Calendar**.

4. Under the option to **Share** with specific people, you'll find a window to type in someone's email address. To add a collaborator to your calendar, you'll need the person's email address.

**Figure 2.7 Sharing Setting Options**

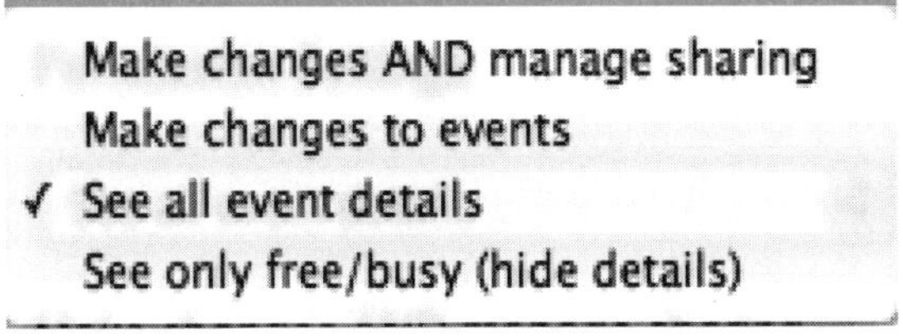

Make changes AND manage sharing
Make changes to events
✓ See all event details
See only free/busy (hide details)

© 2016 Google Inc. used with permission. Google and the Google logo are registered trademarks of Google Inc.

5. Once you've entered the email address, the next step is to select the **Permission** settings for that person. You've got four choices to pick from (see Figure 2.7):

   a. Make changes and manage sharing: This enables the person to add or edit events, but it also gives him or her the right to share the calendar with others.

   b. Make changes to events: This gives the ability to add and edit events.

   c. See all event details: This provides user access to view events on the calendar.

   d. See only free/busy (hide details): Viewer can see only blocked-out times for events with no other details.

## Project Idea: Adding Your Calendar to Your Website

Many of you have a classroom website that you've spent hours creating. In the past, one of the hardest things to update on your site was the calendar page. No more. Rather than recreate your Google Calendar for your website, you can simply embed it. The best part is that once your calendar is embedded in your school website, any new events you create are automatically found on both versions of the calendar. Let's set this up.

1. Find your classroom calendar in the **My Calendars** menu (along the left side of your calendar display).

2. Click on the drop-down menu along the right side of the calendar.

ISTE T Standard 3 Objective c

*Teachers exhibit knowledge, skills, and work processes representative of an innovative professional in a global and digital society. Teachers communicate relevant information and ideas effectively to students, parents, and peers using a variety of digital-age media and formats.*
(ISTE, 2008)

3. Select **Calendar Settings** from the menu.

4. You'll find yourself on the Calendar Details page for your classroom calendar. Look toward the bottom of the page for the heading **Embed this Calendar**.

Embedding a calendar requires copying some HTML *embed code* and pasting it onto a page on your classroom website (see Figure 2.8). Before you copy the code, however, you have the option to customize the code to make it work on your site. Let's look at a couple of useful choices (see Figure 2.9).

Perhaps the most important element you'll want to customize on your calendar is the size. Depending on the *pixel* dimensions of your classroom website, you may need to adjust the width and height of your calendar before you embed it.

Size also plays a part in the default view you choose for your calendar. Most teachers use the month view because it's the default choice. The problem is that the calendar view doesn't give you much information because the individual days are fairly limited in size. Try choosing **Agenda** view, and see how it displays more details about a specific event.

Another key option for your calendar is selecting the correct calendars. You'll find that if you have several different calendars, you can pick and choose which calendar you wish to display on your site. Why is this important? If you're a secondary school teacher, you may have created a calendar for each class you teach. Rather than display events for different preps, you can choose to only include the event for a specific calendar.

Once you finish customizing the code, be sure to use the **Update HTML** option to save the changes.

Now that you've customized your calendar, you'll want to copy all HTML code in the window (see Figure 2.10).

Once you arrive at your website, you'll need to paste the code on the appropriate page for your site. If you're using Dreamweaver, be sure to paste your selected code into the Code View of your page. If you're using Blogger, Weebly, WordPress, or most online web creation tools, look for a *gadget* that accepts HTML code. (A gadget is an element of a blog or website that can be customized. It will be discussed more fully later in the text.)

Paste your code, and you're done!

**Figure 2.8 Embedding Code for Calendar**

**Embed This Calendar**
Embed this calendar in your website or blog by pasting this code into your web page. To embed multiple calendars, click on the Customize Link

Paste this code into your website.
Customize the color, size, and other options

```
<iframe src="http://www.google.com/calendar/embed?src=1om1pjb7m36et5pa6q4dl0eco0%40group.calendar.google.com&ctz=America/Denver" style="border: 0" width="800" height="600" frameborder="0" scrolling="no"></iframe>
```

**Figure 2.9 Customizing Your Calendar for Embedding**

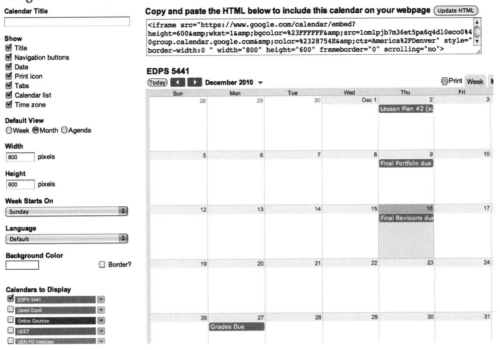

As you've seen in this section, Google Calendar is easy to set up and share with others. It's a great way to provide information about the events of your classroom and an effective collaborative tool to use with colleagues. The hardest part of using this system is staying up-to-date and being organized on your end. All you have to do is know your schedule; Google Calendar makes everything else happen.

**Figure 2.10 Copying the HTML Code for Your Calendar**

## FROM A GOOGLE GURU

From top-level administrators to our district's teachers and students, optimized calendars are the antecedent to and consequence of productive academic, professional, and social lives. Solid calendaring practices can help our students in a variety of ways: from establishing proximal and distal goals to improving how they respond to organizational change. However, although Google Calendar provides an incredible platform for this type of personal improvement, it is one of the most challenging applications to promote in our classrooms and, therefore, is often neglected or lost among the other "more prominent" Google tools.

Knowing the important role a calendar can play in our students' day-to-day lives, my team of instructional specialists attempts to increase student calendar usage by introducing students to Google Calendar's multitude of features as part of their introduction to Google Apps and teaching them how to leverage this powerful tool to self-regulate their learning. At the most basic level, we focus on helping students learn to schedule critical due dates, customize notification rules, and use the various views to personalize their user experience. We have found that students, even with a basic skill set, have been able to use Google Calendar to greatly reduce uncertainty, which in turn has helped reduce stress.

Once we see our students begin to broaden their repertoire within the Google Calendar app, we aim to help them use it to connect to their classmates to further promote shared learning experiences. In this regard, we have seen students invite classmates to study sessions, copy teacher-created events to their calendars, and attach collaborative agendas to events for shared access. At this level of use, our students move beyond using Google Calendar to simply organize their schedules and start putting it to work as platform from which they launch their academic and social ventures.

Regarding our ongoing work with Google Calendar, my team's proudest moments come when we observe students instinctively turn to their calendars as problem-solving mechanisms for a host of daily challenges. To observe students employing multiple shared calendars to meet a variety of objectives, using integrated task lists to stay on top of ongoing projects and embedding shared calendars on their personal or team Google Sites give us a sense of accomplishment, for we then know that we have fulfilled a critical role in preparing them for future success.

I feel compelled to acknowledge that developing effective calendaring habits takes perseverance and patience. Yet, if we truly believe in building our student's capacity to tackle the inherent complexities of both college and career, then we must promote effective calendar use and help our students unlock Google Calendar's features as a means to organizing their complex lives.

## BIOGRAPHY

Adam McMickell

Ogden School District, Ogden, UT, US

District Assessment and Instructional Technology Coordinator

Twitter: @mcmickell

+AdamMcMickellEdu

Website/blog: www.osd3t.org

### More Ideas for Going Google

**Possible Google Calendars for School**

- Use Google Calendar to create the calendar for all school events. You can enter everything from sporting events to the lunch menu on a given day.

- Create a sign-up calendar for shared school spaces like the computer lab or library. This can be an easy way to let teachers know if these "prime" spaces are available on a given day.

- Use Google Calendar to show your available or busy times during parent-teacher conferences. Using Appointment Slots, you can actually have parents schedule their appointment with you.

- Create a department calendar to share materials with your fellow teachers (i.e., iPads, Chromebook cart, projector, etc.).

## TIPS FOR THE GOOGLE CLASSROOM

- Parents and students don't need to have a Gmail account to view a Google Calendar. However, if individuals want to subscribe to a Google Calendar, Google will prompt them to create an account.

- Once events are created in the calendar, they are permanently saved. This means you can go back to events and update from year to year if you continue to follow the same basic classroom schedule. This can be a huge time-saver once the events are created.

- As you create events, add more details in the description field. It's much easier for parents and students to understand "Today's test covers Chapter 11 in your textbook" than simply "Big Test Today."

- Sync your Google Calendar with other services like Outlook or the calendar app on your Mac or iPhone, so you can have all your events in one location.

## CHAPTER 3

# Gmail

## FIVE Things to Know About Gmail

1. Gmail provides you with 15 **GB** of storage for your personal account. GAFE accounts have unlimited storage.

2. Gmail groups messages into threaded conversations, making it easier to follow a discussion.

3. Gmail incorporates Google **Hangouts** to improve personal communication using video conferencing or instant messaging.

4. Gmail uses Google search technology and has an effective spam filter.

5. Gmail has many different settings and tools that can simplify your transition from other mail programs.

For most of us, email is one of the best ways to stay in touch with everyone. Think about the way most of us start our workdays. As soon as the computer is up, most of us open our email to see what messages are waiting. Email is the primary communication tool between parents and teachers. Even if students may say "email is for old people" (Anderson, 2006), it is still the most common way for teachers to communicate with students. Why?

Email is a great way for teachers to communicate with parents and students in a documented format. If you have concerns with grades or performance, email is an effective method of sharing those issues. It creates a "paper trail" and can be a useful way to ensure that information is "on the record."

Email also allows us to communicate with several people at once. You can send messages to select groups of students or to your entire class. It provides a quick way to get your message out to everyone who needs it. Gmail provides teachers with a practical way to communicate—there's a reason it was the first tool created by Google!

## GETTING STARTED WITH GMAIL

Earlier in the book, we talked about the need to create a Gmail account when you first start using Google tools. *Please note: If you created a Google account using an email account other than Gmail, your login will change the instant you create a Gmail address.* I know this seems a bit proprietary, but I think it makes things simpler in the long run. For all your Google tools, the login will be your Gmail address. In case you still need to create your Gmail account, let's look at how this is done (see Figure 3.1).

1. Access Gmail at mail.google.com. You can also find a link to Gmail along the top left side of the Google homepage.

2. Here you'll be prompted to log in with your account and password. Because you don't have this information, you'll find a large button beneath the login window inviting you to **Create an account**.

3. The most important part of creating your Gmail account is twofold: picking a username and a password. The username has to be something unique, and with several million Gmail accounts in use, this can be pretty tricky.

Also, because you're going to be using this account as part of your classroom, you'll want to ensure you pick something that's not a distraction. I'd suggest creating a username that implies you're a teacher—that is, coviliclassroom or mrcovili. You might have to be a bit more creative than that, but you get the idea.

Selecting a password is something we're all getting used to in the Internet age. Google will help you in choosing a password that is the most secure.

As you type in the letters and numbers, Google will indicate how secure the password is with a security strength meter. Remember to keep track of your username and password—but try not to write it down on a sticky note and put it on your computer!

### Figure 3.1 Creating a Gmail Account

Create your Google Account

## GMAIL BASICS

As with other email programs, the basic functionality you're looking for is to send and receive messages. You want to be able to organize your messages into categories. You want the ability to attach files both large and small. These are the things you expect an email client to do; Gmail does all these things and more.

Here are a few of Gmail's available tools:

- Composing mail—To create a new message, click on the **Compose** button along the top left of the Gmail screen.

- Attaching a file—Gmail allows you to attach files up to 20 *MB* in size. This is considerably larger than your average email client. If a student wants to send you an assignment, 20 MB allows him or her the space to send various types of files. You can even send relatively small videos and photos!

- Organizing email—Gmail organizes your emails a bit differently than most traditional email clients. Here are some of the major differences:

  - Threaded conversations: Rather than emails simply being placed in your inbox chronologically, Gmail keeps conversations (replies to an email thread) together. You don't have to search through your inbox to figure out how someone's comments or questions relate in an old message. It takes a few tries at this to get used to this new way of organizing messages, but most find this feature really helps them to keep up with an ongoing conversation.

  - Organizing your inbox: This is a fairly new feature in Gmail. Google keeps track of your most important contacts and messages and moves them into the Primary Tab. (It does this by determining which mail comes from LISTSERVs or other commercial entities and which comes from individual senders.) When parents, students, and colleagues email you, the messages will go into the Primary Tab instead of getting mixed in with the rest of your messages. It's a convenient way to keep track of your most important messages.

  - Applying labels: This is a major departure from Outlook and other traditional email clients. Rather than organizing messages into specific folders, Gmail has you apply labels to messages. Your labels are color coded, so you can set up different colors for various types of messages. You can set up specific labels for parents, colleagues, and students. If you teach in a secondary school, you may want to set up labels for your individual preps or for each period of the day. Once labels are applied to messages, you can sort for the specific labels, or messages can be moved out of the inbox and into the labeled folder.

- Searching messages—Gmail utilizes Google's superior search technology to help you find emails. How often do you know that there is a certain message in your inbox but you can't find it among the rest of your mail? Using the search box in Gmail, you can look for names, addresses, key words, and more to help you find those "lost" messages.

## ADVANTAGES OF USING GMAIL

So let's say you're comfortable using Outlook. Why would you want to use Gmail? I can't say that you should completely abandon whichever email service your school is currently using. (I'd rather argue that your school or district should make the switch for everyone, but we'll talk about that later.) For now, here are some of the pros of using Gmail as your main email client.

### Storage

We all want more room when it comes to saving our messages and their attachments. Gmail has up to 15 GB of storage available, meaning you'll probably never get the dreaded "Mailbox has exceeded its allotted storage amount" message again. Add this to the 20 MB attachment size limit, and you can see why Gmail has all the storage you could want.

For students, extra storage can help eliminate the issues of losing files due to lack of allocated space. It also gives them an additional backup for any projects they're working on while at school.

## Spam Filter

No one wants to get advertisement emails or spam in their inbox. Most of us spend a lot of time trying to create filters to eliminate unwanted solicitations and junk mail. At the same time, we can't run the risk of important emails accidentally getting the spam label and never making it to our inboxes.

> None of my real emails have slipped into the spam folder and I remember only one spam reaching my inbox in the period I've been using Gmail. Spam is the bane of the Internet and it is refreshing to see Gmail put up such a good fight against it.
>
> —Eric, who wrote into our support team. (Jackson, 2007)

As teachers, we don't want to spend countless hours poring over junk mail and deleting from our inboxes. We don't want students to encounter "adult" content in email or phishing scams either. With Gmail's advanced filtering services, this is no longer a concern.

## Google Hangouts in Gmail

This is a big advantage to using Gmail over a traditional email client. Gmail has the ability to enable two or more users to live chat with one another. Imagine, rather than running down the hall to ask a colleague a question, you can simply type the query and get an immediate response. The old method involved sending a message that went into someone's inbox to be retrieved some time down the line. Hangouts put you in touch with a contact right when you need the person. Located along the left side of the Gmail page, you'll find it's easy to use and a great way to communicate.

Google Hangouts in Gmail is a good tool for students to use while working on group projects. In Google Hangouts, multiple students can communicate with one another at the same time. As we've mentioned, collaboration shouldn't be limited to a particular location, and having access to live chat is an effective way to have students share ideas with one another.

# SETTING UP GOOGLE HANGOUTS IN GMAIL

To set up the Google Hangouts function, take the following steps (see Figure 3.2):

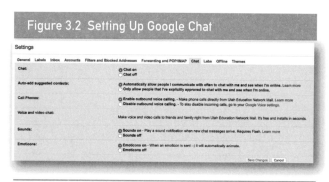

Figure 3.2 Setting Up Google Chat

© 2016 Google Inc. used with permission. Google and the Google logo are registered trademarks of Google Inc.

1. You'll want to add your colleagues to your list of contacts. That way, when they are available for chat (i.e., when they are at their computers using Gmail or Google Hangouts and you see they have a green light next to their names), you can jump right into a live conversation.

2. To add a contact, you'll need your colleague's Gmail address. With the address in hand, go into the chat search box, and enter the address.

3. You'll be prompted to send the person either an email or an invite to chat. Once a chat invite has been sent and accepted, that contact will now be part of your chat list in the future.

## Project Idea: Using Google Hangout With a Guest Presenter

One of the coolest classroom innovations is the ability to video chat right in Gmail (Simple K12, 2010). Although there are other programs that can facilitate this happening (e.g., Skype), probably the biggest advantage with Gmail is that because it is so widely used, it's easy to access video chat without having to create a new account. When you're trying to get a guest lecturer for your classroom, the easier you can make things, the better. Imagine bringing an author, athlete, politician, or entertainer into the walls of your classroom to talk with your students. Our "schools will go from 'buildings' to 'nerve centers,' with walls that are porous and transparent, connecting teachers, students and the community to the wealth of knowledge that exists in the world" (21st Century Schools, 2010).

> **NETS S Standard 7 Objective b**
>
> *Students use collaborative technologies to work with others, including peers, experts, or community members, to examine issues and problems from multiple viewpoints. (ISTE, 2016)*

Setting up the chat is easy, but let's be sure to cover how this is done (see Figure 3.3).

- The first items you'll need to make a video chat work are a microphone and a webcam. Depending on the computer you're using, these may already be part of the internal tools (i.e., if you have a Mac computer, you're set!). If you don't have a mic and a webcam, they're fairly inexpensive to purchase and well worth the money.

- The most important step to enabling video chat within Gmail is acquiring a simple plug-in from Google.
  - To download the plug-in, click on the ***drop-down menu*** in the Hangouts area along the left side of the Gmail screen.
  - You'll find a menu for **Chat Settings**. Look in the area for **Voice** and **Video Chat**. You'll find a link that will help you access the plug-in.
  - Alternatively, you could use the following link to download the tool: http://google-voice-and-video.en.softonic.com/.

- Once the plug-in is installed on the computer, you'll find that you now have a green video camera icon next to your name in the Hangouts window. This means you can now launch audio and video chats in addition to normal text chats.

- Any of your contacts that have enabled video chat on their computers will have the video camera icon next to their names as well.

- Now that the plug-in is up and running, the only remaining settings for video chat involve enabling a camera, mic, and speakers. Once they're all hooked up to the computer, you're ready to go!

Figure 3.3  Setting Up Video Chat in Gmail

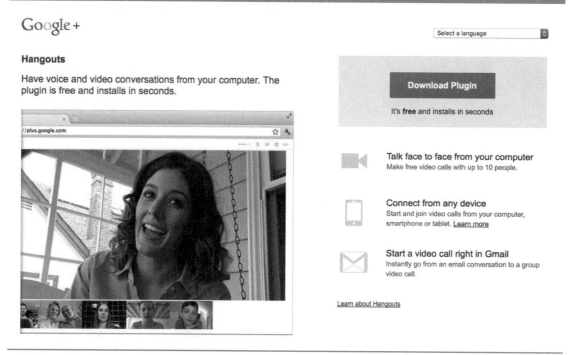

© 2016 Google Inc. used with permission. Google and the Google logo are registered trademarks of Google Inc.

Here are a couple of pieces of advice when it comes to microphones:

1. Buy a microphone that has a USB connection. The mini-plug type may be cheaper, but they don't work on every machine, and it's easy to overlook the connection as the problem.

2. If you're broadcasting the audio from your guest speaker to the entire classroom, you'll want a mic that isn't part of a headset combo. It's easy to find a stand-alone microphone, and they generally work well.

## FROM A GOOGLE GURU

Google's addition to email many years ago was monumental to many people. I remember my really nerdy cousin giving me an invite really early on. Today, it may seem rather mundane to use a web-based email client. The reasons can be many; for one, what if I have more than one email account? How can I check them all? Switching windows? That doesn't seem that productive. For another, the use of filters is a powerful way to get through that way-too-full inbox. In education, many of our district use GAFE, which means that as teachers we have an additional email address to check and maintain. Also, our students have accounts, which may or may not be additional for them. With all this email pulling on us, it seems that all we do is read, reply, and manage email. Gmail may not at first blush seem like the best tool to use; it is rather complicated, but with a little digging, and using some online tutorials, you can customize it to do exactly what you need done to make email much easier to manage.

I would like to give you five reasons for using Gmail in your classroom.

1. Gmail is a client that can gather your email from other sources. You can add your personal account, your school account, or have your other Gmail accounts come to one Gmail inbox.
   - Start in the upper right hand corner with the **Gear menu>Settings**.
   - Go to **Labs>Multiple Inboxes>Select Enable**.
   - Go to **Accounts>Check mail from other accounts**.
   - Add your accounts, up to five. You will need to know your passwords and account usernames, but it is worth the effort.

2. You are able to use the tabs at the top of the Gmail page to sort through your email and get to the messages most pressing.
   - Start in the upper right-hand corner with the **Gear menu>Configure Inbox**.
   - Select tabs to enable.

These tabs are Gmail's way of sorting your email. The Primary is basically person-to-person conversation, Social would be conversations from social networks, Promotions is generally from people trying to sell you things, and so on.

3. Messages in Gmail that have dates and times in them will link to your calendar if you add them as events. This saves time and energy getting you directly to the tasks you need, and because many of our appointments are set up via email conversations, this should save you tons of time.

Some messages highlight the date in blue, but even if they don't, just click on the **More** menu above your message and select **Create Event**. This will take you to a calendar event, with the event name being that of the email subject. Just adjust the time and date.

4. With Gmail you can use add-ons. One that you should look at is Boomerang:
   - Boomerang allows you to set a time to resend the message to you, so you can deal with it later. It also will send your reply to an email at 6 a.m., even though you answered at 11 p.m. the night before.
   - Find more at http://www.diygenius.com/15-free-gmail-plugins-that-will-improve-your-email-workflow/.

5. The last reason is ubiquity. Any computer you sign into becomes your email computer. Everything stays the same—the same tags (folders), same tabs, same filters, same everything! There is no setup needed when you switch computers.

If I were back in the classroom today, the first thing I would do is gather the email of each student's parent. This is easily done with a form, giving me the ability to send a personalized message to each parent via a mail merge.

## BIOGRAPHY

Robert Gordon

Canyons School District, Sandy, UT, US

Secondary Team Lead, Educational Technology Department

Twitter: @trainerob

### More Ideas for Going Google

- Students can have fun doing the morning announcements using video chat in Gmail. They can use the program to conduct interviews with other students or various members of the community.

- Parent-teacher conferences may be changed forever in the future. Can you imagine having a one-on-one with a parent from your computer screen? You can quickly look up information and share it with parents without leaving your classroom. Conducting meetings like this could be very valuable for reaching those living in rural areas.

## TIPS FOR THE GOOGLE CLASSROOM

- If you're already using a different email client at school, try using Gmail for a while as a personal email account. It will give you the chance to test some of the features we've discussed while providing you with options to retain both accounts.

- Tired of having multiple email accounts to check daily? Gmail can receive emails from other clients. Here are some instructions from Google for how to make this happen: http://gmailblog.blogspot.com/2009/05/import-your-mail-and-contacts-from.html. It takes a few minutes to set up the Gmail system, but once it is in place, you can check all your email from one location.

- Even students who don't have a Gmail account can still access email and use Google's spam filters with a new feature called Gmailify. Students can use other email addresses in the Gmail mobile app and then have access to many of the unique filters and protections from Google.

CHAPTER 4

# Google Sites

## FIVE Things to Know About Google Sites

1. You can create multiple sites, but there is a size limit of 1 *GB* for your account.

2. The new design interface for GAFE accounts will consist of drag-and-drop elements you can add to your site.

3. You can use a variety of files on your site, including images, docs, videos, and more.

4. Sites can be public or private.

5. Student projects can include an ePortfolio or a WebQuest.

## TWENTY-FIRST CENTURY LEARNING

*Use communication for a range of purposes (e.g., to inform, instruct, motivate and persuade).*

—Partnership for 21st Century Skills (2004)

Creating a classroom website is an important way to communicate and share with your key stakeholders: parents and students. Using Google Sites, not only can you create your own classroom site, but students can also create a web presence to share some of their ideas and projects.

In this chapter, we'll look at how you can create your classroom website using Google Sites. We'll also discover how you can help students build an online portfolio of their work. Finally, we'll explore a classroom project called a WebQuest that has students conduct research in an online activity that encourages higher-level thinking.

> ### ISTE T Standard 3 Objective b
>
> *Collaborate with students, peers, parents, and community members using digital tools and resources to support student success and innovation.*
> *(ISTE, 2008)*

By the end of this I think you'll understand why Kyle Pace calls Google Sites the "digital hub for your classroom. You can combine video, documents, forms, calendars, and other resources all in one place for student and parent access" (Pace, 2016).

## Project Idea: Building a Classroom Website Using a Template

For this Google Sites project we're going to use the Classic Sites version of the tool. This will allow us to create a classroom website using a school-formatted *template* from Google. Here are the steps to take:

1. Go to sites.google.com.
2. Be sure to select **Classic Sites** in the bottom left corner of the screen (if available).
3. Select **Create**.
4. Choose the **Schools & Education** category from the left menu and select the **Classroom Template**.*
5. Provide your site name. It must be a unique name.
6. You may be required to type in the word verification security code.
7. Click **Create Site**.

You've now got a default template on your Google site. Now let's customize the site for your information.

The site you've created is specifically formatted for a teacher. As you've probably noticed, though, it is already populated with generic classroom content. You'll need to go through and customize the pages with your announcements, assignments, a calendar, and more. As you edit the different pages in the site, be sure to think about what pages you'd like to keep and which ones you'd like to change or remove. For example, you may not want to have an extra credit page on your site, but you will want to keep the calendar page.

*If you teach in an elementary school—you might want to consider using the **Simple and Easy Teacher Site** template. You can search for it in the template gallery.

## ADDING, EDITING, AND DELETING PAGES

The classroom template comes with certain links and pages already intact, but there may be a page or two you'd like to create for your classroom website. Perhaps you'd like a page to display your grading policy, or you'd like to have a page of student work for display.

In addition, you will certainly want to edit the pages with Latin instead of English text. The calendar page will also need to be edited, so you can include your classroom calendar instead of generic filler.

Finally, there are bound to be pages that don't fit with your classroom structure. These pages will need to be deleted from the site.

## Adding New Pages

1. Click on the **Create Page** button. It's located in the top right corner of the screen.

2. Select the appropriate template for your new page. There are four types of page templates for you to choose from: Web Page, Recent Announcements, File Cabinet, or List.

   a. Web Page: This is the basic style of page. You can insert any type of content you'd like on this page.

   b. Recent Announcements: This is the blog-style page in Google Sites. Content is added in posts and appears chronologically on the page.

   c. File Cabinet: This page is used for file storage in Google Sites. You can add a variety of file types including PDFs, images, Word files, and so on.

   d. List: If you want to create a list of items, this is your page. Perhaps you want a weekly spelling list or a page for vocabulary.

3. Name your new page.

4. Choose whether to have your new page on the top level of your site or if it will be a subordinate page.

5. Click **Create Page**.

## Editing Your Pages

- Click on the **Edit Page** button. It's a pencil-shaped icon located in the top right corner of the screen. ✏

- As you first get started, you'll want to click on the **Tip** at the top of each page. This will give you a step-by-step list, helping you adjust the current page.

- Different sections of the page are editable: You can delete the sections and create your own content or change the current content.

- To change the name of a page, click on the current name and edit the text. Doing this will change the link name along the left side of the screen.

- To remove an existing content element from the page, click on the object (see Figure 4.1). The properties bar will display along the bottom of the element. Click **Remove** (the **X** button) from the properties, and it will delete the content.

- To add new content to the site, click on the **Insert** menu. Located in the top left corner of the screen, you'll find various options for content elements you can add to your site.

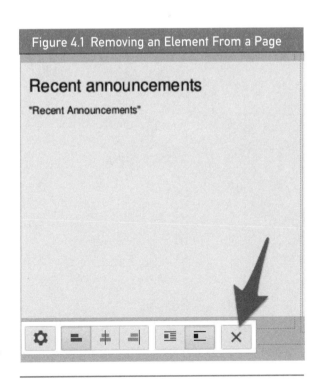

Figure 4.1 Removing an Element From a Page

**Recent announcements**

"Recent Announcements"

## Deleting a Page

- Click on the **More Actions** button. It's located along the top right side of the screen.

- Choose **Delete Page**. Even though the page is no longer present, there will still be a link in the sidebar navigation. We'll need to delete that at some point.

## ADDING CONTENT TO YOUR SITE

Using the Insert menu, there are several different elements you can add to your Google site (see Figure 4.2). It's important to consider some of the key information parents and students will want from your classroom site. Parents and students want to know due dates for assignments in a calendar. They want information about projects from online documents. Let's look at adding some of the elements found under the Insert menu.

## Adding the Calendar

A calendar is an essential element that should be part of every classroom website. Parents and students are extremely interested in understanding when assignments are due and when classroom activities will occur. Because the calendar is a Google tool, it integrates seamlessly into Google Sites.

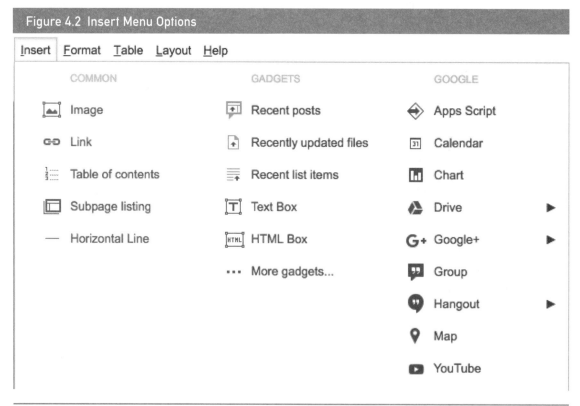

**Figure 4.2 Insert Menu Options**

© 2016 Google Inc. used with permission. Google and the Google logo are registered trademarks of Google Inc.

To add a Google Calendar, follow these steps:

1. Select **Calendar** from the **Insert** menu. You'll see the list of your Google Calendars.
2. Pick the calendar you'd like to add, and the **Settings** window will appear.
3. Choose from the different options (size, color, etc.), and your calendar will show up on your page.

Once the calendar is on your website, any additions or edits you make in Google Calendar will appear in Google Sites.

## Adding Images

1. Select **Image** from the **Insert** menu.
2. You can choose to upload an image from your computer, or you can select an image from the Internet. If you choose to add an image from its *URL*, be sure you aren't violating copyright. Choose only images from the Creative Commons or another site that provides users with permission to use the images.

The photo will display on your page. You can then adjust the size of the image.

## Adding Video

Video can serve a few different purposes for your classroom website. You can share videos from classroom activities with parents and students. These can include student presentations in class, club activities, field trips, and more.

Video can be used as an instructional tool. Whether it's making your own videos to help students with concepts and assignments or finding videos online to help students understand your curriculum, video can dramatically enhance your students' ability to grasp concepts.

Another effective method of sharing video on your website is as a student showcase. When students create videos for their projects in class, Google Sites allows them to easily promote those videos.

It's important to note that the only video tool that is included in Google Sites is YouTube. If you want to display a video on your site, you'll want to upload it to YouTube first.

1. Select **YouTube** from the **Insert** menu.
2. Choose among using YouTube, Google Video, or Google Docs Videos to display your movie.
3. To insert a YouTube video, you'll need to know its URL. Go YouTube, and search for your video. You'll find the URL beneath the video using the **Share** button. Copy this URL.
4. Paste the URL in the **Open** field in the dialog window.
5. Choose from other video options, including adding a border or a title.

One of the best ways to utilize Google Docs as part of your website is to embed forms on your Google site. The form is easy to find, and the results are sent to you immediately.

## ADDING DOCS, SHEETS, SLIDES, AND FORMS

As part of your instruction, you utilize a variety of files to help students with the curriculum. You make handouts, teach using multimedia presentations, compile data to make analysis, and gather information from students. We've already looked at Google Drive as a way to make these different types of files. Now Google Sites can be used to display the files on your website.

### Adding Docs

To add a document to your site, do the following:

1. Select **Drive>Documents** from the **Insert** menu.

2. A pop-up window containing your Google Docs will appear. They will be ordered by most recent to oldest (you can change the order using the sort tools in the top-right corner of the screen).

3. If you can't find your desired file, try using the **Search** box along the top of the screen.

4. Add your file by choosing it and clicking on the **Select** button.

5. A properties window will open giving you a few options for displaying the document. Using **100%** for the width gives you a large enough window to view the document.

### Adding Forms

To add a form to your site, do the following (see Figure 4.3):

1. Select **Drive>Form** from the **Insert** menu.

2. A list of your Google Forms will appear in the window. Choose the file you'd like to display on your Google site. The spreadsheet will have one additional display option as you can choose between a published spreadsheet and an editable spreadsheet.

3. Once you pick the desired file, you'll have several display options to choose from, including title of the form, a border for the file, and the display size of the file in *pixels*.

4. Align your file on the Google site using the **Options** bar. After setting up the way your file looks on the page, the **Properties** bar helps you determine how other elements on the page will interact with the file.

5. Click **Save** to preview your file. Use the **Edit page** button, and select the object to change.

## Adding Presentations

To add a presentation, do the following (see Figure 4.4):

1. Select **Drive>Presentations** from the **Insert** menu.

2. A list of your presentations will display in the window. Choose your selected presentation.

3. As with the other Google Docs tools, you'll be able to create borders or use titles with your presentation. Unique to presentations is the ability to auto start the presentation or to have the slideshow loop once completed. Also, size matters for your presentation. You'll have several different size options available.

Adding Google Slides is a great way to share content from your class with parents and students. Those students who were absent from class can follow along with materials from home. Students looking to review a concept learned earlier can recap information at their own pace.

### Figure 4.3  Adding a Form

Insert Google Spreadsheet Form

Get to Know [Form]     Change

**Display:**

☑ Include border around Google Spreadsheet Form

☑ Include title: Get to Know [Form]

Height: 600 pixels

Width: ___ pixels (leave empty for 100% width)

SAVE     Cancel

Source: © 2016 Google Inc. used with permission. Google and the Google logo are registered trademarks of Google Inc.

### Figure 4.4  Adding a Presentation

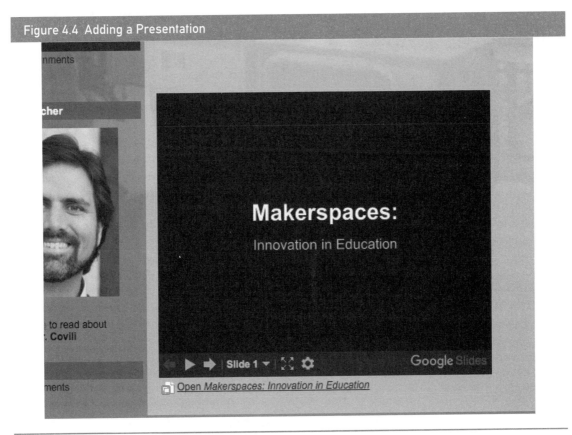

# NAVIGATION FOR YOUR SITE

As you customize your classroom website from the premade template, you'll find there are several links to pages going down the left side of the screen. Whereas there are some great ideas for possible pages for your classroom site, you should adapt the links to the pages you want on your site.

A classroom website should be easy to navigate and straightforward regarding content. Parents want quick access to the most important information, which includes due dates, project requirements, contact information, and classroom resources. The template we used to set up a classroom website has several of these pages. The template includes three separate submenus of links to pages.

The first set of links includes the home page for the site, Homework Assignments, Extra Credit, and Contact Me. Remember, earlier we saw how you can delete unwanted pages. The problem was that the link still remained in the sidebar. You can remove any of these links to deleted pages (see Figure 4.5).

## To Remove a Link in the Sidebar

1. Click on the **Options** menu. Choose **Edit Site Layout**.
2. Select **Edit Sidebar**. This is located at the bottom of the sidebar.
3. You're now on the **Site Layout** page. Click on the **Edit** button below the first **Navigation** area.

Figure 4.5 Deleting an Existing Link in a Sidebar

4. A page will display showing the links in this section of the sidebar. Select the page you'd like to remove, and click on the **X** button in the lower right corner of the menu.

You have successfully removed that link from the sidebar.

## To Add a Link in the Sidebar

By creating a new page in your website, you'll be prompted to include a link to the page in your sidebar navigation.

1. Choose the **Put Page at the top level** option when creating the page, and the link will be automatically added.
2. You can add a link to an external site using the **Add URL** link.

## To Edit a Link in the Sidebar

You can't change an existing link in the sidebar. You'll need to just delete the unwanted link and create a new one.

## Adding or Editing Content in the Sidebar

Not only can you have a navigation menu going down the sidebar of your page, but you can also add or edit other types of content in this area (see Figure 4.6). Because we're using the Classroom Template, let's explore how to edit the existing sidebar content.

Click **Edit Sidebar**. You'll find several different elements in the sidebar that you can edit. Each field is named based upon its content style. Click **Edit** in the left corner of the element you wish to change. The element will open, and you can edit the content inside.

For example, let's change the image and link in the Meet Your Teacher text element.

1. Click on the top text field. This will launch the edit mode for this field. You can change the text by typing your own content.

2. To change the image, click on the existing image and use the **Remove** link.

3. To insert your own image, click on the **Insert** menu and select **Image.**

4. Either upload an image, or use an image from the Internet as your profile picture.

5. The link that goes to the About Me page doesn't need to be changed. You'll just need to open that page and update the information with your own bio and images.

6. Click **Done** when finished.

Adding new content to the sidebar can provide your users with the information they're interested in. Here's how to create a new field in the sidebar:

1. Click **Add a sidebar item**.

2. A window will open giving you a variety of new page elements to choose from. You can add a link through the **Navigation** element, text and images using the **Text** element, or site information using either the **Activity** or the **Site** elements.

3. Add your desired elements. They will appear in the list along the sidebar.

4. Click the **Save Changes** button when you're done.

Figure 4.6  Editing Elements in the Sidebar

Don't forget, this template has different tutorials to help you make certain customizations. The **Template tips** are found in the lower left corner of your site. These types of tips are found throughout this template, and they can really help you work with the various pages. Check them out!

## CUSTOMIZING THE LOOK AND FEEL OF YOUR SITE

One of the best things about Google Sites is the ability to adapt the way the site looks to your individual taste. Because we've used a template, much of the design was previously customized. Still, there are several changes we can make to customize the site. Let's change the site's general appearance

1. Click on the **Options** button to get started.
2. Select the **Manage Site** option.
3. To change the appearance of the site, go to the **Site Appearance** area in the lower left corner of the screen. Here you can choose **Themes, Colors, and Fonts** to edit the look and feel of your site. Under the **Site Layout** option, you can change the Header, Footer, and Sidebar of your website.

### Colors and Fonts

You have the option to change everything about the page, from Background Color, to Link colors, to fonts themselves. You even have a Preview window to see your potential changes.

### Themes

When we started this teacher website, we used the Classroom Template. If you want to use something else, however, there are a variety of themes to choose from in the Sites Gallery. There are two major options for changing the theme of your site.

1. Choose from the basic **Sites Gallery**. There are about 30 different themes that can replace the Classroom Template. Select the theme you'd like and click **Apply**.
2. Browse the **Templates Gallery**. There is a collection of templates for schools and education. Once you find the template you like, you can apply it to your site.

## USING YOUR CLASSROOM WEBSITE

Once you have your Google site together, there are a few things to consider in making your site an effective tool.

### Updating the Content

It is so important to keep the content on your site current. No parent or student will value a site that is woefully out-of-date. Make sure the calendar has current events being displayed. Homework should reflect the projects the students are currently working on. Google Sites makes it easy to replace old content with new, but it requires having a plan to make the necessary changes.

## Providing Relevant Content

The information on your website should help students accomplish assignments and learn more about the materials they are studying in class. Be sure you share any handouts or training materials you used in class. Other important documents for your website may include a syllabus, disclosure statement, grading policy, fieldtrip permission slips, and any additional forms for class. It's also useful to include links to sites where students can get additional information about the content from your curriculum.

## Marketing Your Site

I'm not suggesting you need to place an ad on the web or in the local paper, but you should have an idea of how you'll let parents and students know about your website. First, be sure your site is linked to your school's website. This is the first place parents will look for you online. Next, let parents and students know you keep the site up-to-date and that you'll be using the site to share helpful information with them. Give them the address to your site at Back-to-School Night or at a parent-teacher conference. Add the URL for your site to the disclosure statement or syllabus you give to students during the first week of school.

## Project Idea: Creating a WebQuest

Creating a WebQuest using Google Sites is an excellent way to have students conduct research online using a structured, self-paced method. Often, when students are asked to perform a research activity online, it falls into one of two camps: an Internet-based scavenger hunt or a loosely organized Google search where anything goes. A WebQuest looks to provide students with high-quality web resources that offer content-based information in an organized, online activity.

## What Is a WebQuest?

A WebQuest is an inquiry-oriented lesson format in which most or all the information that learners work with comes from the web. The model was developed by Bernie Dodge at San Diego State University in February 1995, and since its inception, tens of thousands of teachers have embraced WebQuests as a way to make good use of the Internet while engaging their students in the kinds of thinking that the 21st century requires (Dodge, 2007).

A WebQuest consists of five major components that are developed in an online environment. These elements include the Introduction, Task, Process, Evaluation, and Conclusion. All of these parts work together to provide students with a rich online experience. Let's take a closer look at the basic elements of a WebQuest. You'll also find a lot of great WebQuest information at http://teacherworld.com/webquest.html and www.internet4classrooms.com/using_quest.htm.

ISTE T Standard 2

*Teachers design, develop, and evaluate authentic learning experiences and assessment incorporating contemporary tools and resources to maximize content learning in context and to develop the knowledge, skills, and attitudes identified in the ISTE•S. Teachers design or adapt relevant learning experiences that incorporate digital tools and resources to promote student learning and creativity. (ISTE, 2008)*

## Introduction

In a short paragraph, you'll want to do the following:

- Introduce students to the WebQuest.
- Set the stage or provide background for the upcoming activity.
- Motivate students and capture their interest. Think about creating an educational "hook" for your activity.

## Task

Next, write a short paragraph or outline of expected results.

- The task is the end result of student efforts, not the steps involved in getting there.
- This section helps focus the learner and clearly describes the essential questions and student learning objective.
- It is important to engage students in an authentic task, something that has meaning beyond the classroom.

## Process

The process section lays out the entire activity. Be sure to provide enough information that students can work independently.

- Describe how the groups will be assigned and the role of each member.
- List the steps that the students will need to follow to complete the activity.
- List any materials and resources that the students will need for the activity. In particular, you will need to list websites in this section.

## Evaluation

Traditional forms of assessment usually don't fit into the WebQuest model. One popular form of assessment is a rubric for evaluating WebQuests.

- Provide students with the evaluation criteria.
- Make students aware of their responsibilities with the WebQuest.

## Conclusion

Encourage the students to form their own conclusions from what they learned as a result of the WebQuest.

- Provide students with additional information, activities, or links that will enable them to explore information beyond this WebQuest.
- Give students the chance to reflect upon the activities and what they've learned.

## Why Use WebQuests?

Developing a WebQuest is a fairly involved process that will require the teacher to prepare a lot of information and find a variety of online resources. So, why would a teacher want to put the time into developing a WebQuest? Here are some key ideas on the rationale behind this effective teaching tool from Tom March, one of the leading innovators of WebQuests.

*Student Motivation and Authenticity*—When students are motivated, they not only put in more effort, but their minds are more alert and ready to make connections.

*Developing Thinking Skills*—One of the main . . . features of any WebQuest is that students tackle questions that prompt higher-level thinking.

*Cooperative Learning*—[I]n WebQuests, students take on roles within a small student group and this tends to promote motivation.

*Process and Access*—Research has shown that the most important factor related to student learning and technology use is how teachers relate the technology-based activity to other learning activities (Teacher Created Materials, 2002).

## DEVELOPING A WEBQUEST USING GOOGLE SITES

We've seen how a WebQuest can be an effective teaching and learning tool for your classroom. Google Sites is a great way to build and share your WebQuest with students. Here are some of the basic steps for creating your WebQuest and some ideas for using Google Sites in its development.

1. Go to sites.google.com. Be sure to select the **Classic Sites** option (if available).

2. Click **Create**.

3. Choose **Browse the gallery** for more options.

4. Type WebQuest in the search box.

5. A great option is the WebQuest Template from Patricia McGee. Select **Preview Template**.

6. By previewing the WebQuest template, you'll find the site already includes the five main elements you need for your WebQuest. Each of the pages includes details concerning the steps of the WebQuest and provides you with ideas for developing the page. Apply the template with the **Use this Template** button located in the top right of your screen (see Figure 4.7).

7. You'll be prompted to name and establish the settings for the WebQuest. This follows the same procedure you've done before with other Google sites.

8. Your WebQuest structure is now set. You'll need to update the pages with the appropriate content. Remember, each page has suggestions of possible content and formatting ideas. There are also links to existing WebQuests to give you examples.

9. Customize your pages by deleting the current content, and add the content for your subject. Remember you can add images, links, documents, videos, and so forth to help provide activities and resources for your WebQuest.

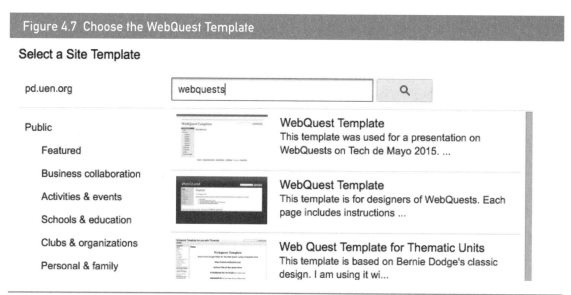

**Figure 4.7 Choose the WebQuest Template**

Select a Site Template

pd.uen.org

webquests

Public

Featured

Business collaboration

Activities & events

Schools & education

Clubs & organizations

Personal & family

**WebQuest Template**
This template was used for a presentation on WebQuests on Tech de Mayo 2015. ...

**WebQuest Template**
This template is for designers of WebQuests. Each page includes instructions ...

**Web Quest Template for Thematic Units**
This template is based on Bernie Dodge's classic design. I am using it wi...

## Project Idea: Creating a Digital Student Portfolio

A student portfolio isn't a new concept. Many of you have been tracking student writing and assignments in folders that have been stored in the classroom. Portfolios are a great way to help students organize their materials as the content is all located in one place.

The problem is that the traditional portfolio has become fairly antiquated. It only allows for a paper-based project and doesn't account for the wide array of digital assignments currently being created. Although it's still a useful way to track student writing, the portfolio has needed an update to meet the needs of 21st century learners.

The electronic portfolio has evolved as an effective method for storing and sharing students' digital projects. A website is a terrific venue for this content as it can be updated and shared with parents, peers, and teachers.

**ISTE S Standard 3 Objective c**

*Students curate information from digital resources using a variety of tools and methods to create collections of artifacts that demonstrate meaningful connections or conclusions. (ISTE, 2016)*

### What Is a Student Portfolio?

A student portfolio is a collection of student works over a period of time. A portfolio generally is seen as a performance-based assessment tool. It is used for evaluation as it demonstrates how and what the student is learning. An electronic portfolio simply means that the portfolio is digitally created and shared.

A portfolio is the story of knowing. Knowing about things.... Knowing oneself ... Knowing an audience ... Portfolios are students' own stories of what they know, why they believe they know it, and why others should be of the same opinion.

Students prove what they know with samples of their work. (Paulson, Paulson, & Meyer, 1991, p. 60)

## What Are the Key Elements of a Student Portfolio?

Portfolios can come in several different media types. The projects can reflect a wide array of standards. But there are a few things that are common among portfolios, regardless of their purpose and format. Student portfolios should include the following elements:

- Learner Objectives: These objectives can come from state and national standards. You should have students clearly identify what skill(s) they are looking to illustrate with an artifact in the portfolio.

- Guidelines for Selecting Materials: Working with the teacher, students should choose projects that reflect their best work. "The portfolio is a laboratory where students construct meaning from their accumulated experience" (Paulson et al., 1991, p. 61).

- Artifacts: These consist of student projects that demonstrate the learning objectives. As part of a Google-enhanced classroom, many of these projects should be stored in Google Docs, Picasa, or other Google tools. Working collaboratively, the teacher and student will determine the appropriate number of artifacts for the portfolio.

- Self-Reflection: One of the most important elements of a student portfolio is reflection. As students choose artifacts for their Google site, they should reflect upon how the project is an accurate depiction of their content knowledge. Reflection can come in the form of a blog post, or it can be shared as a simple text box.

- Teacher Feedback: Assessment from the teacher is a key difference between a student portfolio and a student website. Once the student has identified curriculum standards and demonstrated his or her understanding of those learning objective through artifacts and reflection, the teacher provides important insights into the success of those academic measures. In many ways, teacher feedback validates the effectiveness of the student portfolio.

## Five Key Stages to Creating an Online Portfolio

Stage 1:   Setting Up the Definitions of Your Portfolio

Be sure to identify the purpose of your portfolio, select the standards of your portfolio, and recognize the audience for your portfolio.

Stage 2:   Developing Your Portfolio

Create the Google Site for the portfolio. This should include creating the various pages you intend to use as part of the site.

Collect the educational artifacts for the portfolio. Students should identify which projects they intend to include in their portfolio.

Stage 3:   Student Reflection

Students should write reflective statements about each artifact and why it was included in the portfolio.

Students should set goals for improvement on educational skills.

Stage 4:  Adding the Artifacts

Artifacts should demonstrate the student's understanding and application of the desired standard.

It's good to have students use a variety of projects that reflect different types of media and literacies.

Google Sites is an effective tool for adding artifacts as the site can incorporate files from documents to videos.

Stage 5:  Presenting the Portfolio

Students will share their portfolios with the appropriate audience. This is typically the teacher, but it may include a potential employer or recruiter (EPortfolio Step-by-Step Process, n.d.).

## Building a Student Portfolio Using Google Sites

Using Google's tools makes creating a student portfolio much easier as many of the artifacts you will want included are stored in Google Drive, Google Photos, or other Google products. Because the tools work hand in hand with one another, you can insert these files into your Google site seamlessly.

Rather than using a premade template for the student portfolio for this project, we'll be building our Google site from scratch. Let's get started.

1. Go to sites.google.com.
2. Click **Create New Site**.
3. Select the **Blank Template**.
4. Select a **Theme** for your site. There are several to choose from, and you can always update this later.
5. Under **More Options**, you can add a **Description** of your site. You can also choose whether to make your site **Public on the web** or only to **Specific people**.
6. Provide the name of the site, and enter the appropriate security code.
7. Click **Create Site**.

As this is a blank site, you'll need to create all the pages for your student portfolio. Remember that you'll want to use the different page templates to create the right style of page for the intended content. For example, you'll want your students to use the announcements style of page for their personal reflections.

### Creating the Pages

To get started with our new portfolio site, let's make the pages we'll need to display our content. Pages are all created in the same manner; only the template you use will differ. Here is the basic outline for creating your pages:

1. Click **Create Page**.

2. Choose the template.

3. Name the page.

4. Choose the **Put the page at the top level** option.

5. Click **Create Page**. The page will appear on the screen, and a link to the page should display in the sidebar.

Possible pages for the site include Introduction, Reflection, Artifacts, Learner Objectives, and Teacher Feedback. Let's look at some content options for these pages.

*Introduction:* Students should use the standard web template option when creating this page. This page should contain an overview paragraph that states the general purpose for the portfolio. Other possible elements for this page include the following:

- Image—Use either a picture of the student or some picture that deals with the content of the portfolio (i.e., for a writing portfolio, you could use a picture of a pencil and paper).

- Table of Contents—Share which pages are part of the portfolio and a sentence about each one's content.

- Contact Information—If students plan to use the portfolio as part of a job search, contact information is a must.

*Reflection:* The template for this page is the **Announcements** option. To use this page, your students will be blogging. Rather than writing in text boxes, blogs utilize posts. These posts will be organized chronologically on the page, with newer entries at the top and older content further down the page. Here's how to blog in Google Sites.

1. Click **New Post** to create your first entry.

2. Provide a **Title** for your entry by replacing the **Untitled Post** text in the appropriate box.

3. Use the provided text box to compose your thoughts. There are editing controls along the top of the page. The editing tools give you options from formatting text to adding content to the layout and more.

4. You can use the Reflection page as a way to display portfolio artifacts and reflect upon them on the same page. Use the **Insert** menu to add artifacts using different Google tools as part of your site. Remember, you can insert images, Google Docs, YouTube videos, and more into a post on your blog.

5. When you complete a post, click **Save**.

*Objectives and Learner Standards:* Students can use the web template to create these pages. The basic elements for these pages include national and state standards embodied by the artifacts in the portfolio. A great place to find these standards may include the National Educational Technology Standards (*NETS*), ISTE, or a variety of national and state curriculum standards.

*Artifacts:* One option for the artifacts page is to use the **File Cabinet** template. With this template, you can upload a variety of files for evaluation. The size limit is 12 *MB* per file, so you can include documents, PowerPoints, spreadsheets, images, and more (see Figure 4.8).

Figure 4.8 Artifacts in a Student Portfolio

## Artifact #1

**Description: This is a project for EDPS 5441**

**Reflection: I learned about using Makerspaces to promote student learning.**

**Proficiencies: ISTE T Standard 4 Objective A**

To add files to the artifacts page,

1. Select the **Add File** button.
2. A window will appear, prompting you to browse your computer for the file or to provide the URL for a file.
3. Choose the text to display. If none is provided, the file name will display.
4. Provide a file description. This is a good place to reflect upon the artifact or to share a brief summary of the file.
5. Click the **Upload** button.

*Teacher Feedback:* The final page in the student portfolio is for teacher feedback. To create this page, let's use the Announcements template. For the teacher to provide feedback, he or she needs to first be added to the site as a collaborator.

To add a collaborator to your site, follow these steps:

1. Select the **More** button in the top right corner of the screen.
2. Choose **Site Permissions** from the list of settings. It should be the last item.

3. Enter the email address of the collaborator.

4. Select the level of permission you'd like to give the new collaborator. To make someone an editor, he or she will need to have the option **To Edit** chosen.

5. Hit the **Share** button, thus sending the person an email invitation to collaborate on the site. This gives the teacher the ability to add comments and provide feedback for the portfolio.

Once you've created all the pages for your site, it's time to add all the content to the pages. We've already discussed possible content for the various pages. Google Sites makes it easy to add and edit all of your desired content.

## Sharing the Completed Portfolio

So, the students have created their portfolios, and now it's time to share them with the appropriate audience. There are three permission levels that allow students to share their portfolios (see Figure 4.9):

1. **Public on the web**—The site is searchable and viewable to anyone online.

2. **Anyone with the link**—If you share the link to your site, anyone who uses the link will have access to the site. Both this and the previous option are open to the public as they do not require a sign-in to view the portfolio.

**Figure 4.9 Sharing Settings in Google Sites**

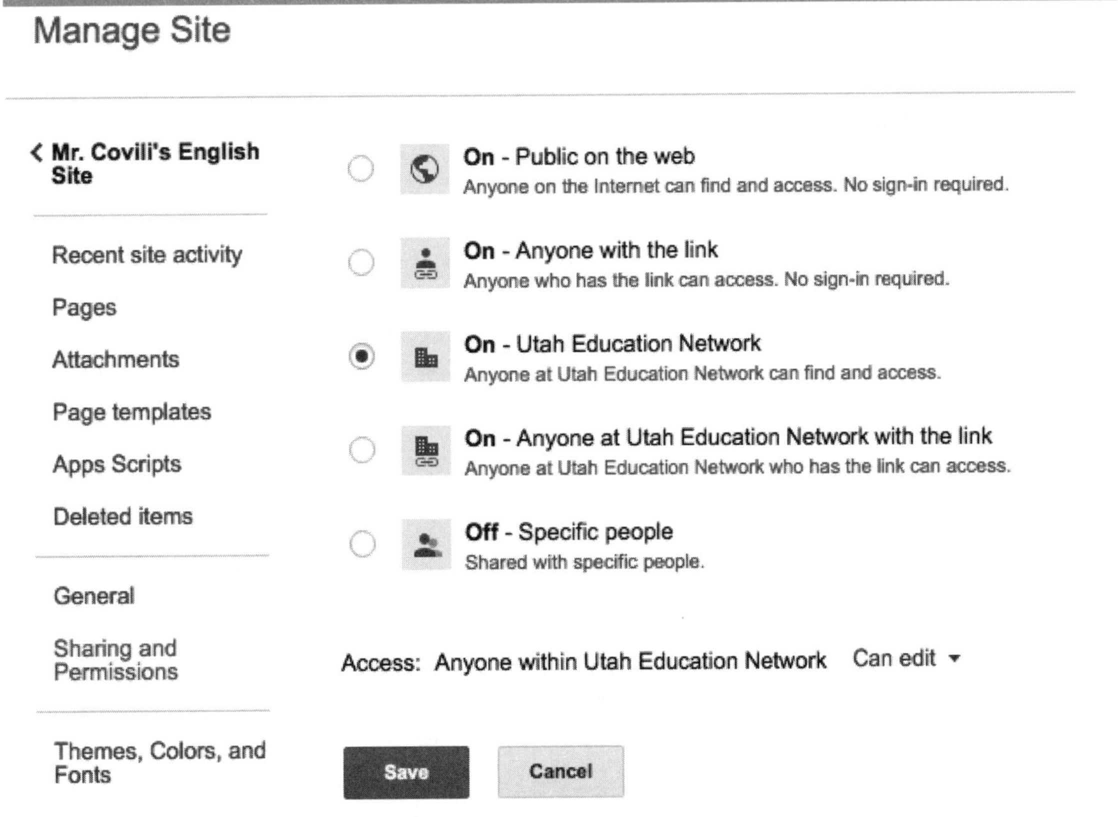

## Manage Site

< **Mr. Covili's English Site**

Recent site activity

Pages

Attachments

Page templates

Apps Scripts

Deleted items

General

Sharing and Permissions

Themes, Colors, and Fonts

○ 🌐 **On - Public on the web**
Anyone on the Internet can find and access. No sign-in required.

○ 👤 **On - Anyone with the link**
Anyone who has the link can access. No sign-in required.

● 🏢 **On - Utah Education Network**
Anyone at Utah Education Network can find and access.

○ 🏢 **On - Anyone at Utah Education Network with the link**
Anyone at Utah Education Network who has the link can access.

○ 👤 **Off - Specific people**
Shared with specific people.

Access: Anyone within Utah Education Network    Can edit ▾

[ Save ]    [ Cancel ]

INSERT    PAGES    THEMES

**Aa**
Text box          Images

</>              ☁
Embed URL         Upload

Google Drive

⬗ From Drive

⬙ Drive Folder

Google Embeds

▶ YouTube

📅 Calendar

📍 Map

Google Docs

📄 Docs

🖼 Slides

➕ Sheets

🗒 Forms

📊 Charts

3. **Private**—Only a site administrator can provide access to this site. Users must sign in to the site, and their email addresses must be preapproved. This is the most secure form of access to the student portfolio, and it is the preferred one for many teachers.

4. If you're in a GAFE district, you'll find that there is also an option to share within **Your Organization**.

One of the best things about sharing an electronic student portfolio is that it can be updated from year to year. Once the structure is in place, content can be added and removed. Reflections can be updated to show student growth. Evaluation can take place over a student's career instead of merely focusing on a particular assignment or grade level.

## New Google Sites in GAFE

Google Sites is getting a makeover as part of GAFE. If you're part of a GAFE district, here are some basic instructions for setting up a new site.

### Creating a Site

To create a new site click on the + button in the lower right corner of the screen. Type a name for your site in the header, and you're off and running.

### Basic Features

There are three basic tabs for your Google Site: Insert, Pages, and Themes.

- *Insert:* In this tab you'll be able to add content like text boxes, images, and links (see Figure 4.10). Simply drag content around on the screen to adjust its location. You can wrap text around images or alter the size of pics with drag commands. You'll also find that you can embed content from many of your favorite Google tools. Insert videos from YouTube, calendars from Google Calendar, or embed your favorite Doc, Sheet, Slides, or Forms right into your site.

- *Pages:* Create new pages for your site using the + Pages button. As you create new pages, a simple navigation menu automatically appears at the top of your site. To rearrange the order of pages, drag and drop the various buttons on the Pages tab.

- *Themes:* Change the look and feel of your site with a single click. From the Themes tab you'll be able to adjust your header, colors, and fonts. Google Sites will automatically adjust the content once you choose your specific theme.

### Sharing and Publishing

As with other versions of Google Sites, your new website will allow for multiple editors. To add contributors to your site, simply click on the **+person** button located along the top of the screen. Add the email address for any collaborators you wish to invite to your site.

- Keep in mind that your site will be private until you change the settings. You'll find an option to change viewing permissions when you're in the sharing settings. You'll have the same sharing options as with the Classic Version of Google Sites.

One big change with the new version of Google Sites is the addition of a Publish button. This button allows you to make your updates public to the world. Conversely, if you want to work on your site without needing to share changes, simply avoid the Publish button, and you're the only one who can see your latest updates.

Google has more plans in store for Google Sites, so it will be interesting to see all the upcoming changes. One thing is certain—the new Google Sites will be simpler and better looking than ever.

## FROM A GOOGLE GURU

I have been a Google Sites user since 2010 when there was a fear of a possible bird flu outbreak and a possible closing of schools in my district. We were told we had to have some sort of web presence, so we could communicate with parents and students as well as have a place to store possible assignments. Due to the fact that my district was a GAFE district, I figured I'd try my hand at a Google Site and have stayed with it ever since, even though that dreaded bird flu never came to pass. It's been fairly simple to create, update, and tie in the many other Google tools available to a GAFE district.

I keep my site fairly plain and unassuming, with the exception of the vanity URL, Larsonlandia. com, I purchased to make it a touch easier to find when typing in the name.

I love that I can bring in my different Google Calendars that I am already using to keep things organized. I also like that I have the option to include a blog-like page, announcements theme, to keep my parents informed more than a quick email. I am also using the file cabinet-themed page to host different assignments and templates, so parents and students can more easily find the important papers that tend to get lost when coming home from the elementary school I teach at.

I also enjoy the fact that I can modify my site in a multitude of ways to really make it my own. Changing the colors, fonts, and even the physical size of the site is so simple to do.

I'm very pleased I decided to go with a Google Site all those years ago because it has helped to keep my parents more informed and better organized. And the fact that it plays so nicely with my other necessity GAFE apps is just such a nice bonus!

## BIOGRAPHY

J. Derek Larson

Classroom Teacher

Washington County School District St. George, UT, US

Twitter: @lars3eb

Class Google Site: www.Larsonlandia.com

Personal Site: www.EdTechBabble.net

### More Ideas for Going Google

#### More Possible Google Sites

- **Create a site for your school club or sports team:** Google Sites can help you share announcements or calendar items about upcoming events for your group. Parents can see photos from recent activities. As the teacher or in the role of coach or advisor, you can provide access to different materials that are important for your students.

- **Create a student *wiki* for a research project:** Because Google Sites has the ability to add collaborators, you can have students work on a wiki in groups. Each of the students can add his or her own content to the site and develop a really interesting research wiki.

## TIPS FOR THE GOOGLE CLASSROOM

- Before students start creating their sites with Google Sites, have them create an outline of the content they would like to add to their projects. It really helps to have an idea of what pages you'll need to create for your site and what material you plan to put on each page.

- Be sure the students add you, as the teacher, as an editor on their sites. Often, students will forget to give you access, thus making the site private. Be sure you can add comments and suggestions to the students' Google sites.

- You have up to 100 MB of space per site. This provides you with ample room for data storage, but you won't be able to load tons of multimedia files to your Google site. Be sure to take advantage of additional Google tools (i.e., Google Drive, Picasa, and YouTube) to house a lot of your larger multimedia files. Remember, you can always insert a copy of the files into your Google site from the other Google resources.

- Another simple idea for students working online in collaborative groups is Google Spaces. Not considered a full website, this is a quickly shared workspace where students can share text, images, and links with one another. Even though the tool is relatively basic, expect to find updates coming soon.

## CHAPTER 5

# Blogger

## FIVE Things to Know About Blogger

1. Creating a blog takes about 5 minutes.

2. Blogs post information chronologically, with newer information at the top.

3. Students can leave comments on blogs as a way to communicate with one another.

4. Blogs can contain multimedia content including images, video, presentations, and more.

5. Teachers can follow colleagues' blogs as part of their personal learning network (**PLN**).

We've all heard about blogs for years, but what is a blog, and what makes it unique?

At its core, a blog provides a space where people can share their thoughts and ideas with one another. Used in the school setting, it is an online journal where students can reflect and collaborate with their classmates. A traditional website generally consists of one-way communication; the teacher shares information about the classroom with parents and students. With a blog, the audience can also contribute by making comments.

> **ISTE S Standard 7 Objective b**
>
> *Students use collaborative technologies to work with others, including peers, experts, or community members, to examine issues and problems from multiple viewpoints. (ISTE, 2016)*

Blogs are also different from traditional websites because they are subscribable. This means that parents and students can receive updates from your blog, and they can read your blog entries through a variety of online tools using an **RSS** feed. This makes your blog more available to your audience.

# WHY SHOULD STUDENTS BLOG IN SCHOOLS?

We often hear of students sharing too much personal information online. Students can put comments on the Internet that have unintended consequences and that can cause them a variety of social problems with peers, family members, and school officials. So, why would we encourage them to blog as part of our curriculum? Here are a few reasons from David Warlick, author of www.twocentsworth.com and a leading voice on educational blogging:

> Number 1: A blog is a Web-publishing concept that enables anyone—first graders, middle school teachers, high school principals, district superintendents—to publish information on the Internet.

> Number 2: Blogs . . . or blogging has become a journalistic tool, a way to publish news, ideas, rants, announcements, and ponderings very quickly, and without technical, editorial, and time constraints. It essentially makes anyone a columnist. In fact, many established columnists now publish their own blogs.

> Number 3: Blogs, because of their ease of use, and because of the context of news and editorial column writing, have become a highly effective way to help students to become better writers. Research has long shown that students write more, write in greater detail, and take greater care with spelling, grammar, and punctuation, when they are writing to an authentic audience over the Internet. (quoted in Jackson, 2007)

As students blog, they open their thoughts up to their classmates as part of the public discourse. This helps students participate in a group forum where ideas are exchanged, opinions are discussed, and comments are provided. One of the key 21st century learning skills involves collaboration:

- "Demonstrate ability to work effectively and respectfully with diverse teams" (Partnership for 21st Century Learning, 2015).

Blogging truly encourages students to respectfully share ideas with their peers. Even though an individual produces each post, the blog is an effective way to get feedback and communicate in a group process.

## Why Should Teachers Blog?

Blogging has become a major tool in the 21st century teacher's bag of tricks. Because it is so easy to set up and maintain a blog, many teachers find it is an effective way to get their message out. Here are a few reasons teachers love to blog:

### Communicate With Parents

A blog is a great way to communicate with parents. Unlike a traditional website, a blog provides a more personal way to share information. Whereas a website is really good at providing the details about a classroom activity, a blog lets the teacher share the *effect* of that event on the students. Using images and video as part of the blog gives parents an intimate look into your classroom and helps build a strong sense of community.

## Communicate With Colleagues

Teachers love to talk about education. Lots of educators blog, so they can have a professional dialogue with their colleagues. As teachers share their ideas and advice on a variety of classroom issues, they can form a network of support for one another. Blogging also provides the teacher with a forum to share his or her ideas related to the classroom. More than just a how to on the act of teaching a lesson, blogging provides many teachers with a place to share their thoughts on the role of education.

## Highlight Student Work

We've seen how many student projects are moving into the digital age. Not only are these assignments more engaging for the kids, but also electronic assignments can easily be showcased on a classroom blog. "Blogs can be used as a platform for highlighting the best work of your students, showcasing their talent to an audience that goes beyond the classroom" (Carvin, 2006).

So, now that we've looked into the *why* of blogging, it's time to explore the *how* of creating your classroom blog. This section will detail how you go about making a blog, adding posts with multimedia content, and establishing the different settings you'll want for your blog.

## CREATING A CLASSROOM BLOG

There are many different blogging tools available online (even with other Google tools like Google Sites), but we will be discussing Blogger because it is used so widely used and is simple to manage. Once you have your Google account, setting up your blog is a breeze through Blogger. Let's get started.

1. Go to www.blogger.com.

2. You'll be prompted to login using your Google account or create an account if you don't already have one.

3. The next step is to **Create a new blog**. There are a few elements to complete on this screen.

    a. Blog Title: This will appear at the top of your blog. It can be anything you'd like, but for a classroom blog, you'll probably want it to sound professional.

    b. Blog Address: This will be your blog's web address, or **URL**. You'll find that every Blogger blog has the same ending—blogspot.com—but you must provide a unique beginning for your address. This can be a little tricky because there are millions of blogs in Blogger's database. You can always **Check the Availability** of your address with the provided link. Again, pick something you're willing to use with parents and students as the address will be something you'll share with others.

    c. Pick a starter *template:* You can always change this later; in fact, after your blog gets created, there will be a lot more choices.

4. You've successfully created your blog with Blogger. Now it's time to add content and customize how your blog looks.

## Writing and Editing Posts on Your Blog

With your blog created, you can begin sharing announcements, homework help, and other thoughts on your classroom with parents, students, and colleagues. Blogs are different from traditional websites in that they consist of individual bits of news and information called *posts*. As you write posts on your blog, older content moves down the page as newer content gets added.

### Writing a Blog Post

1. To write your first entry on your new blog, click on the **Start Blogging** button. If you've created a blog in the past and want to add a new post to it, you'll find a **New Post** button on your Dashboard in Blogger.

2. Blogger will load the New Post page (see Figure 5.1), where you'll find a basic word processor.

3. Start your post by providing a **Title**. The title should relate to the content of your new post. For example, a title might be "Field Trip on Friday" if you're looking to make an announcement of the class's upcoming activity.

4. Type the body of your post in the provided text editor. The editor should look familiar to you as it shares several of the same features as Microsoft Word or Open Office.

5. You can change the style, size, and color of the fonts.

6. Formatting includes options like bold, italics, and underline.

7. Once you've typed your post, click the **Publish Post** button to make your comments live.

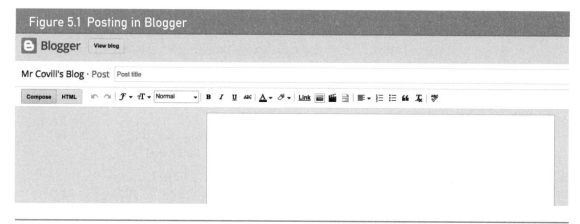

Figure 5.1 Posting in Blogger

© 2016 Google Inc. used with permission. Google and the Google logo are registered trademarks of Google Inc.

### Adding Multimedia to a Post

The ability to add multimedia to your posts is one of the big differences between blogging and traditional journaling. Creating links, adding pictures, or using video gives the blog a modern twist and engages students so much more than written journals. You can insert different multimedia content into your post using the provided controls. Let's see how it's done.

- Inserting a link in your post (see Figure 5.2):

  1. Highlight the word or phrase you wish to turn into a hyperlink.

  2. To create the link, click on the **Link** option.

  3. A window will open to create the link. Type in the **Text** to display. If you previously highlighted an existing word or phrase in your post, it will appear in the Text field.

  4. Next, provide the URL or web address of the link. You can test the link to ensure you entered the correct information.

  5. Click **OK** when done.

- Inserting an image in your post:

  1. Select the **Add Image** icon from the toolbar.

  2. A window will open with your choices for adding an image. You can add the image by **Uploading** (see Figure 5.3) it to your blog, using an existing image from a previous blog post, including a photo from your Picasa Web Album, or copying the URL of a photo already on the Internet. Photos you use on your blog should either be original, or you should have permission to share the images online.

  3. Once you choose your desired image, click the **Add Selected** button to make the image display in your blog post.

  4. To change the properties of an image once it's in a post, click on the image. You'll be able to change the display size, the alignment, add a caption, or complete a bit of basic editing on the link or image.

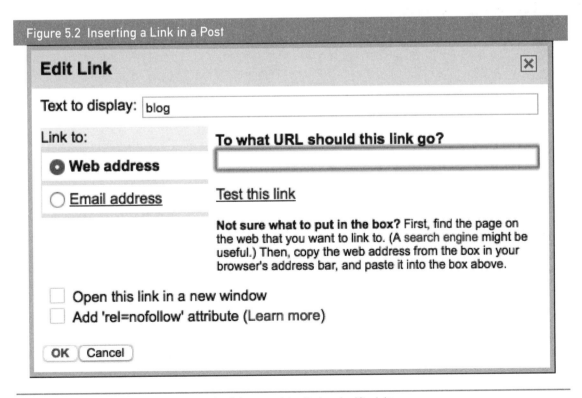

Figure 5.2 Inserting a Link in a Post

**Edit Link** ☒

Text to display: blog

Link to:
- ● **Web address**
- ○ **Email address**

**To what URL should this link go?**

Test this link

**Not sure what to put in the box?** First, find the page on the web that you want to link to. (A search engine might be useful.) Then, copy the web address from the box in your browser's address bar, and paste it into the box above.

☐ Open this link in a new window
☐ Add 'rel=nofollow' attribute (Learn more)

OK  Cancel

- Inserting a video in your post:
    1. Select the **Add Video** icon in the toolbar.
    2. A window will open with three choices for adding video to your blog. First, you can upload your own video to a post. Or, you can add a video from YouTube by copying the video's URL. You can also add any of your own videos from YouTube.

Videos and images uploaded to your blog are stored by Google in the Picasa Web Album as private content, meaning they are not searchable in the Google database. They do count toward your storage limit in the Picasa Web Album—remember that you get 1 *GB* of free storage.

Figure 5.3  Setting the Image's Properties

Small - **Medium** - Large - X-Large - Original size  |  Left - **Center** - Right  |  Add caption  |  Properties  |  Remove ⊠

## Editing a Post and Saving a Draft

Once you've written a post, there may be many occasions when you'll need to reopen the entry to make some revisions. There will be other times when you aren't quite ready to publish a post, so you'll want to save the entry as a draft.

1. On the Dashboard, click the **Posts** button.
2. A list of all your previous posts will appear.
3. Select the desired post, and click **Edit**.

This will put you back in the **Post Editor,** where you can make the necessary adjustments and republish the post. If your post isn't ready to publish, you'll find a **Save** option next to the **Publish**

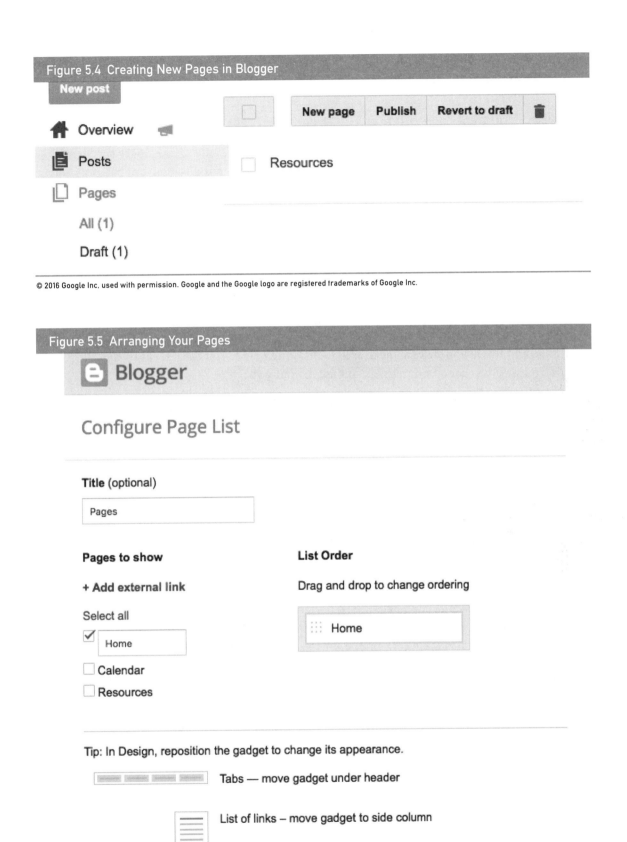

Figure 5.4 Creating New Pages in Blogger

New post

🏠 Overview 📢

📋 Posts

📄 Pages

All (1)

Draft (1)

New page  Publish  Revert to draft  🗑

☐ Resources

Figure 5.5 Arranging Your Pages

🅱 Blogger

## Configure Page List

**Title** (optional)

Pages

**Pages to show**

+ Add external link

Select all

☑ Home

☐ Calendar

☐ Resources

**List Order**

Drag and drop to change ordering

⠿ Home

Tip: In Design, reposition the gadget to change its appearance.

▭▭▭▭  Tabs — move gadget under header

▤  List of links — move gadget to side column

Save  Cancel  Back

button. Even if you don't use the **Save** button, Blogger has an automatic backup on your posts. You should find the system backing up your changes within a few seconds of your typing.

### Creating Pages for Your Blog

In the past few years, Blogger has added the ability to create stand-alone pages for your blog. It's a great way to have all the features we love about blogging but also some of the functionality we like about a traditional website. By creating pages, you can have some information accessible all the time rather than moving down the blog page as new posts are written on the blog. Here's how to make additional pages on your blog and then build the navigation to them (see Figure 5.4):

1. Start on the Dashboard in your blogger.com account.

2. Select **Pages**.

3. Choose the **New Page** button.

4. The editor will appear very much like the Posting editor. You can use all of the same formatting and content options as you use in your post.

5. Add your content, and **Publish** the page to your blog.

6. To choose the layout for the links to your new page, click on the **Show Pages** *drop-down menu*. You can select to add the links to your new pages along the side of your blog or across the top of your blog (see Figure 5.5).

7. Click on the **Save Arrangement** button at the top right corner of the screen.

## ADDITIONAL SETUP FOR YOUR CLASSROOM BLOG

### Using the Dashboard

When you first log in to Blogger, you'll find yourself on a page called the Dashboard (see Figure 5.6). Think of this page as the hub of your blogging world. From the Dashboard, you can create new blogs, edit existing ones, manage your profile, and learn about updates on the service.

The Dashboard helps you manage all the blogs you have rights to. It's a convenient way to add a new post, change permissions, update the design of your blog, or keep track of your blog's stats.

Some of the quick access links for each blog on your Dashboard include New Post, Blogger Options, and View Blog. You'll find these links are an easy way to jump into your blog and work on the content or customize the functionality.

### Blogger Options in the Dashboard

Most of the editing controls are available from the Dashboard. The trick is that they are available from a drop-down menu. When you click on the **Blogger Options** button in the Dashboard, you'll find a host of controls for your blog (see Figure 5.7).

- **Overview:** This is a quick look at blog features. Learn the latest news from Blogger Buzz. Access tips and tricks as well.

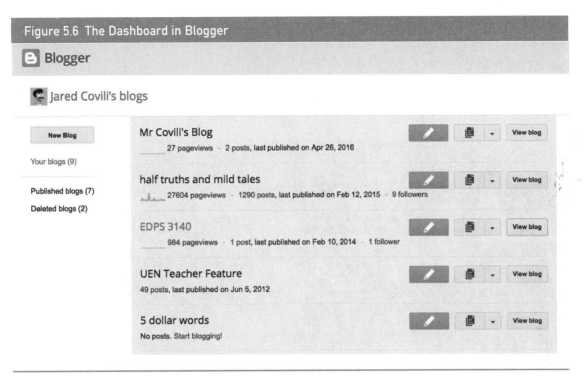

Figure 5.6 The Dashboard in Blogger

**Blogger**

Jared Covili's blogs

New Blog

Your blogs (9)

Published blogs (7)
Deleted blogs (2)

**Mr Covili's Blog**
27 pageviews · 2 posts, last published on Apr 26, 2016
View blog

**half truths and mild tales**
27604 pageviews · 1290 posts, last published on Feb 12, 2015 · 9 followers
View blog

**EDPS 3140**
984 pageviews · 1 post, last published on Feb 10, 2014 · 1 follower
View blog

**UEN Teacher Feature**
49 posts, last published on Jun 5, 2012
View blog

**5 dollar words**
No posts. Start blogging!
View blog

- **Posts:** Create a new post, or edit posts from your archive.

- **Pages:** Here you can create new pages with static content on your blog.

- **Comments:** Find out what viewers are saying about your posts. You can quickly view readers' comments about your blog.

- **Stats:** Users can find stats for the blog. See how many visitors have viewed your blog, and find out which posts are most popular.

- **Earnings:** Find reports of earnings if you've chosen to include ads on your blog. This is not something to be concerned about for your classroom blog.

- **Layout:** Customize your blog by adding *gadgets*, or applications from third party providers, adjusting the column placement on your blog, and more.

- **Template:** Change the look and feel of your blog. Change colors, backgrounds, fonts, and so on.

- **Settings:** You can control all the other elements of your blog here. Change the name or address of your blog, choose permission settings, add more authors, and so on.

## Using the Template Tab

The Template tab allows you to easily change the look and feel of your blog (see Figure 5.8). People love to give their blog a one-of-a-kind

Figure 5.7 Blogger Options Menu

Overview

Posts

Pages

Comments

Google+

Stats

Earnings

Campaigns

Layout

Template

Settings

look. Changing the look of your blog used to require understanding a bit of **_HTML_** or downloading a template from a third-party website. With Blogger in Draft, you have tons of fun options for updating the appearance of your blog.

Figure 5.8 Blogger's Template Designer

## Changing the Background

1. Click on the **Template** link from the **Blogger Options** button.

2. Choose a new template option.

3. When the Template Designer opens, you'll have a wide variety of choices to customize your blog. Pick a different template, change the background image, or pick a new layout. It's up to you. Blogger even gives you a preview window right in the editor, so you can see your changes before applying them to your blog.

4. Click on the **Apply to Blog** button when you're finished.

5. Note that you'll also have the ability to create a mobile version of your blog in the Template Designer. This is great for students who typically view webpages from the browser on their mobile devices.

## Adding a Gadget

Gadgets provide you with the ability to customize your blog in many different ways. One of the best things about blogs is how personal they are for their owners. By using gadgets, you can share important information with your users, but you can also give parents and students a little look into some of the fun sides of your classroom and your own personality.

1. Go to your Dashboard and click on **Layout** from the **Blogger Options** button.

2. The **Page Elements** page will load. Here you'll see your current configuration of elements.

3. Click on the **Add a Gadget** link.

4. A window will open with a list of available gadgets for your blog. There are various categories to look at including **Basics, Featured,** and **Most popular.**

5. There are dozens of gadgets to pick from, but the most popular include the following

   a. Link list—Lets you share links to resources and other popular sites

   b. Blog roll—For sharing links to your network of colleagues and fellow bloggers

   c. Pages—For creating static pages for your blog

   d. Polls—Where you can have students share their opinions—this is a great way to get a quick assessment for your class's views

   e. Picture or Text—For sharing a favorite image or inspirational quote.

6. In the **Link** window, you need to enter the name of the link and the URL or address for the website.

7. Once you've added the gadget, click the **Save** button in the top right corner of the **Page Elements** page.

## Using the Settings Tab

There are several elements and options available to you in the Settings tab. You can control features related to publishing, emailing, commenting, formatting, and more. Rather than explore each of these options, let's focus on the elements that are most important for educators (see Figure 5.9).

Under the Basic settings for the blog, you have several different choices to consider, perhaps the most basic of which is deleting the blog. In addition, you have the option to rename your blog or change the search settings. If privacy is a concern, then you may want to change your search settings so that your blog is not available for public search. For more on privacy issues, see the following section.

## Permissions for a Blog

As I've taught educators about blogging, one of their biggest concerns is about privacy. They worry about who can post to a blog, who can comment on a blog, and who can view a blog. Teachers should know that Blogger gives you control over all three of these issues and makes changing permissions a snap. Here's how to set limits on posting and reading (see Figure 5.10):

1. Go to your Dashboard, and click on the **Blogger Options** button.

2. Choose **Settings** from the menu.

3. In **Settings**, click on **Basic**.

4. Look for the **Permissions** options.

5. To set limits on reading a blog, under the heading **Blog Readers**, you can select from three options: **Anybody, Only these readers,** or **Only blog authors**.

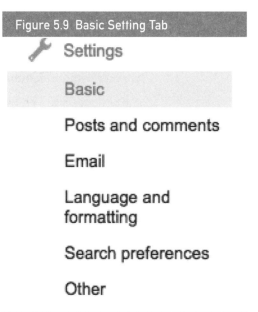

Figure 5.9 Basic Setting Tab

Settings

Basic

Posts and comments

Email

Language and formatting

Search preferences

Other

6. The **Only these readers** option offers the greatest security as you can determine who looks at your blog though an email invitation. For your class, you can determine the level of security for the blog. Remember, if you select the **Only these readers** option, no one will be able to read the blog unless you have previously entered his or her email address on an approved list.

7. To allow multiple students to collaborate on a single blog, use the **Add Authors** button in the **Blog Authors** section. You'll be prompted to add an author by providing his or her email address as verification.

Using these privacy settings is a useful way to have students work with one another but maintain a level of personal privacy that's important to their parents and to the school.

Figure 5.10 You Choose Who Reads and Edits Your Blog

**Permissions**

| Blog Authors | | | |
|---|---|---|---|
| | Jared Covili | covili@gmail.com | Admin |
| | + Add authors | | |
| Blog Readers | Public   Edit | | |

## Comments and Your Blog

Comments are one of the key elements that transform a basic website into a collaborative blog. For your classroom blog, you will want to allow students to make comments on your posts. This will enable a discussion about information and ideas versus an announcement from the teacher. However, although we want to encourage comments, we still need to have some control over who can make comments and how we can monitor the discussion. To manage these settings for your blog, do the following:

1. Go to **Settings**.

2. Click on **Posts** and **Comments**.

3. You need to decide **Who Can Comment** on your blog. There are four choices:

   a. Anyone—This is the least secure option as anonymous readers can leave comments on your blog.

   b. Registered Users—This allows anyone with a Google account or an Open ID account to comment.

   c. Users with Google accounts—This allows just those with a Google account to comment.

   d. Only Members of this Blog—Only those who've been invited using their email addresses are allowed to comment. This is the most secure and a favorite option of many schools.

4. Next, be sure to decide on Comment Moderation. There are different choices for this setting, but choosing to moderate comments means that the thoughts can only appear on the blog if you approve them.

The advantage of comment moderation is that you control what is posted to the blog (see Figure 5.11). You can ensure that nothing inappropriate is said and that all the comments relate to the topic. The downside is that you lose the spontaneity and immediacy that students love about blogs. It's very engaging for students to hit **Post** and then immediately see their comments as part of the blog.

5. There is one last option to enable on your blog—Word Verification. I know many of you don't like it when you have to type those crazy letters that appear in a box when you go to make comments on a blog or site, but it prevents blog comments from being hit by spammers. By enabling Word Verification, you ensure that computers cannot auto-post inappropriate content to your classroom blog.

6. Once you've finished setting the comment options on your blog, select **Save Settings**, and you're done.

Figure 5.11 Comment Moderation Helps You Control the Content

© 2016 Google Inc. used with permission. Google and the Google logo are registered trademarks of Google Inc.

## Mobile Blogging

A great feature for posting is to set up your mobile device for posting. This allows students to post to their blogs using email instead of needing to open the browser. To set up posting using email, use the steps:

1. In your blog select **Settings>Mobile and email**.
2. Choose **Email,** and enter your email address and settings in **Posting using email**.
3. Choose whether to **publish automatically,** or **save as a draft** and publish them later.

To post to your blog using email, follow these steps (see Figure 5.12 on page 84):

1. Create a new email, and use your post title as the subject of the message.
2. The body of the email will be the body of the blog post.
   ○ To mark the end of your post, enter # end.
   ○ To include an image, simply attach the picture to your email.
3. Send the email to your Blogger email address.

## FROM A GOOGLE GURU

My teaching partner, Melissa Hellwig, and I run an extensive, pure 20% Time program. Kids come up with their own learning projects, curricular or non-curricular, and pursue that learning during the course of the year. Part of the project includes blogging. We ask kids to tell the story of their learning, to share the *why* of their project and give the readers insights about the project process. After all, readers are not only interested in the happenings of their 20% Time projects; they are also interested in *why* this learning is meaningful to the students.

Melissa and I keep our own blog and have since we launched 20% Time a few years ago; see harmonizedlearning.blogspot.com. We have built this blog into a hub of student learning and teacher resources. All of our students' blogs are linked from our blog, our students' TED Talks are on our blog, and our weekly podcast is featured on our blog. Because we expect our students to narrate their stories on their blogs, we model blogging by keeping an extensive blog of our own.

When we introduce blogging to our kids, some gravitate to it quickly. They are writers. These kids create clever blog titles, begin drafting their first entries, and spend hours creating just the right design. We use Blogger as our tool, and the kids love it because it is easy enough to learn quickly while also being complex enough that kids can really individualize their blogs. Some of the more techie students even get into the code and tinker in HTML, creating some visually stunning designs. After a while, kids discover the Stats tab where they can see how many page views they have and where those views are coming from. Kids have varying degrees of success with blogging. Some kids are natural storytellers, and some don't think that their stories matter. For these kids, it takes more work to help them discover their voice.

And then there is Steve. A couple of years ago we had a student named Steve. He was hardworking and quiet. Steve would not talk much in class, but we knew that there was an intelligent kid underneath that quiet exterior. For Steve's 20% Time project, he wanted to create a line of environmentally friendly bass baits. Now, neither Melissa nor I knew anything about bass baits, but Steve was sure that he wanted to pursue this learning project. We said, "Go for it!" And he did! Steve created and maintained one of the best blogs we have seen during our years of 20% Time. His blog, snbbassbaits.blogspot.com, is an awesome record of Steve's learning. He tells the story of his project idea and the *why* and goes on to show the successes and failures during the course of his project. He tells his story in words, pictures, and videos. Indeed, Steve's blog is one that we still use as a model for other kids who are having difficulty telling their stories. Steve is now selling his bass baits online at snbbassbaits.com.

## BIOGRAPHY

Don Eckert

Webster Groves School District, MO, US

Teacher

Twitter: @dayankee

Website/blog: curiouslycollaborative.blogspot.com, harmonizedlearning.blogspot.com

### Classroom Ideas for Blogging

- Student writing journals—Have your students create a daily writing journal as a way to work on their writing skills and share their thoughts. The blogs can be private, so they are only available to the student and the teacher. This provides the students with a modern twist on the notebook journal they may already be using. Have students write their blogs using the **Posting Using Email** option, so it's simply a matter of composing an email on any device.

- Student portfolios—We mentioned this project as part of the Google Sites section of this book, but you can also use Blogger for creating a student portfolio. It's a great way to focus on reflection for the different learning goals in the portfolio, but it is a bit more difficult to include artifacts.

## TIPS FOR THE GOOGLE CLASSROOM

- Think about maintaining a blog in which you discuss educational issues. With all the demands that are placed upon teachers, I know this can sound like "one more thing," but sharing your thoughts on education can be a great release for a lot of the stress of teaching. It also provides a way to join in the conversation and share your insights. Start slowly, and don't feel obligated to blog on a daily basis. Share at your own pace.

- I mentioned that blogs are part of many educators' PLN. Some great blogs to consider reading if you're interested in educational issues include the following:

  - Two Cents Worth (http://davidwarlick.com/2cents/)

  - Cool Cat Teacher (http://coolcatteacher.blogspot.com/)

  - Drape's Takes (http://drapestak.es/)

  - dy/dan (http://blog.mrmeyer.com/)

  - The Nerdy Teacher (http://www.thenerdyteacher.com/)

- Public versus private blogging is a big debate in blogging *circles,* but I would argue on the side of public blogging. Part of the magic of blogging is that the conversation is available as part of an open blog. In the classroom, you'll need to establish clear guidelines for student posting, and you'll need to follow your district's legal guidelines for web content, but sharing comments publicly is one of the best things about blogging.

## CHAPTER 6

# Google Hangouts

## FIVE Things to Know About Google Hangouts

1. Google *Hangouts* allow video conferencing for up to 10 people.

2. Hangouts can be scheduled, broadcast, and recorded as part of the Hangouts on Air feature.

3. Beyond video conferencing, Google Hangouts can also incorporate streamed YouTube video, Google Drive, Fun Effects, and Screensharing.

4. Hangouts can be accessed on mobile devices, tablets, desktops, and laptops.

5. Instant messaging in Hangouts can include text, images, animated gifs, and more.

Communication for teachers and students has undergone a dramatic shift in the Internet age. Where classrooms would have previously created relationships through written correspondence like pen pals, now everything has gone to video. The ability to have live video conferencing gives classrooms a convenient way to learn from teachers and students from anywhere in the world. Google Hangouts is your tool to facilitate communicating in the cloud.

Google Hangouts allows you to create an online video conference call between you and up to nine other people. Additionally, you can use Google Hangouts to place phone calls to any number in the domestic United States for free. You can also instant message your Google Contacts using Hangouts. In fact, you'll be able to chat with up to 100 of your friends.

Google Hangouts are available from most devices with an Internet connection. This provides teachers and students incredible flexibility as they can participate in the video chat regardless of which device they have in their hands. In fact, Hangouts can start on a mobile device and switch to a laptop when the user gets in front of a computer.

> ### ISTE T Standard 4 Objective a
>
> *Develop and model cultural understanding and global awareness by engaging with colleagues and students of other cultures using digital age communication and collaboration tools. (ISTE, 2008)*

## GETTING STARTED

To create a video hangout, take the following steps:

1. Go to hangouts.google.com. You'll find a few different options for using Google Hangouts—**Video Call**, **Phone Call**, or **Message** (see Figure 6.1). Select the **Video Call** option, and a new window will open, ready to begin setting up your video call.

2. You'll be prompted to add members of a particular circle from Google +, or you'll find a list of your contacts to add to the Hangout. Your other option is to enter the specific email addresses of those you want added to the video call. Remember, you can have a total of 10 users in your video call. This means you can invite nine others to be part of your video chat.

3. Once you invite others to join the Hangout, you'll have to wait for them to accept your invitation. One quick way to know who's available for an immediate chat is to look for the green camera icon next to your contacts' names. The green icon indicates that a person is currently logged into their Google account and ready to chat.

4. After your invitees join the Hangout, you're all set. You should see a split screen of all participants along the bottom of the room and a larger shared canvas for video chatting with one another.

5. You can adjust the settings to display your video or improve your audio. Those buttons are found along the upper edge of the hangout room.

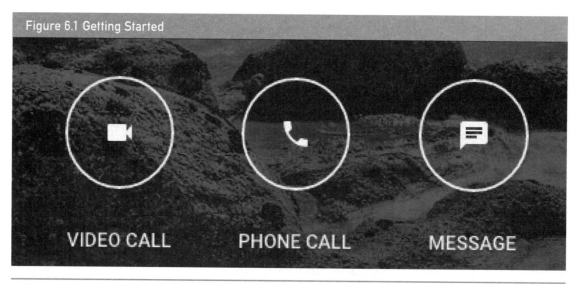

Figure 6.1 Getting Started

VIDEO CALL     PHONE CALL     MESSAGE

© 2016 Google Inc. used with permission. Google and the Google logo are registered trademarks of Google Inc.

## GOOGLE HANGOUTS FEATURES

You can enable your Google Hangouts with many different features to enhance your video chats and bring collaboration to a whole new level (see Figure 6.2).

- Live Chat: In addition to your video feed, use the chat feature to share links, images, and back-channel discussions in the sidebar. This is a great way to moderate a panel discussion with your students.

- Screenshare: Switch from the video camera to display the computer screen and share information with your audience. With Screenshare you can do a live presentation from your computer. Share websites, navigate through classroom assignments, and more.

- Google Drive: Enable Google Drive in your Hangout and share documents with your audience. This will allow the members of your Hangout to collaborate in real time while having a conversation about the document using your microphones.

- Remote Desktop: Allows you to get help from someone in your contacts. They can take over your screen and provide you with the assistance you need. You can also enter Remote Desktop to provide help for others.

- YouTube: Enabling the YouTube feature allows all the members of your Hangout the ability to stream a video and provide commentary using the chat. This is a great way to get your Hangout all watching the same video at the same time.

- Video Effects: OK, so there isn't as much of a classroom use for Video Effects, unless, of course, your classroom needs a little awesomeness! Effects allow you to paste different digital props in the Hangout for speakers to use. Imagine having your guest speaker as a visiting pirate!

**Figure 6.2 Features for the Classroom in Google Hangouts**

## HANGOUTS ON AIR

One of the best features of Google Hangouts is the ability to manage the video conference using Hangouts on Air. Google allows users to schedule a Hangout for a future time and then invite their guests to attend. Hangouts on Air can be broadcast from your YouTube Channel or Google + channel, or you can embed the Hangout onto your own website. Even though there is a limit to the number of people who can actually participate in a Hangout, there isn't any limit to the number of individuals who can watch a broadcast for your Google Hangout.

The other major feature of Hangout on Air is the ability to record the presentations for archiving purposes. Imagine saving the guest lecture or panel discussion, so your students can go back and review the materials later. This is perfect for those students who were absent on the day of the Hangout, either due to illness or other circumstances. Hangout can have a recording time of up to several hours, so you can feel confident in using this tool for archiving a variety of video chats.

A new feature in Hangouts on Air is the Q&A option. This allows users to provide questions in advance of the chat, thus giving the moderator a chance to "preload" some of the best ideas for the upcoming video chat. This can greatly reduce the stress of making sure time in the Hangout is efficiently spent sharing ideas, not querying the audience.

## Creating a Hangout on Air

- Access your Hangout on Air through the menu icon inside of Google Hangouts. Just look for the three bars along the top left of the screen.

- You'll be prompted to add a few elements to make your Hangout available to a desired audience (see Figure 6.3).

  - Name your Hangout—This can be important if you want to invite a larger audience or share your Hangout to a public space.

  - Description of Hangout—Let your audience know the purpose of the Hangout.

  - Determine a Start Time—Hangouts on Air can start immediately, or they can be scheduled for a future day and time.

  - Invite Your Audience—As with any other Google Hangout, you can add your contacts using their Google account. You can also enter email addresses for those not in your contact list. Your invitees will receive an email notifying them of your upcoming Hangout on Air.

### Project Ideas: Using Google Hangouts in the Classroom

- Student Study Group: A Hangout can be a fun way to get your students collaborating in small groups. Hangouts have plenty of options including instant messaging (IM) or video chat, live video streaming from YouTube, and more. Students don't need to meet at the library any more to go over notes and prep for the big project. Now the study group is only a click away using the Hangouts mobile app on their devices!

- Student Film Festival: Taking advantage of the YouTube feature in Google Hangouts, set up a class film festival. You can invite students to be the judges of the different student videos and have everyone watch the festival using Hangouts on Air.

- Mystery Visitor: Taking a page from the hugely popular Mystery Skype program. Invite a mystery guest into your classroom using Google Hangouts, and have your students ask questions to determine how your visitor relates to content they are learning in class. You can bring in guests based upon their careers, experience, backgrounds, and more.

## FROM A GOOGLE GURU

Of all the Google tools I have used in my classroom, I have to say that Google Hangouts has been a real game changer when it comes to communicating with people. Before my school board adopted GAFE, I had used Hangouts to connect with other teachers to collaborate on a variety of projects.

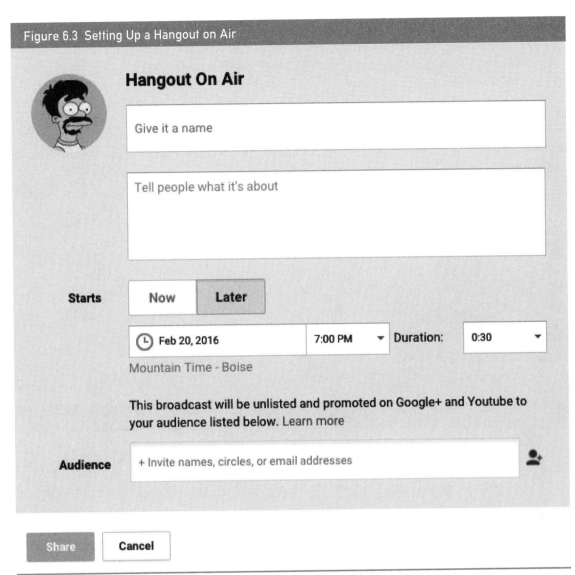

Once GAFE was made available to us in the classroom, I quickly realized that we had a new tool that would allow us to connect with others in a way that was not previously possible.

We have connected with classes within our region, country, continent, and internationally! We have used Hangouts to meet with people who have augmented our learning by providing instruction directly and indirectly. When we started coding, we connected with students studying computer science at the University of Waterloo. They helped excite the students about the endless possibilities that computer programming and coding can offer them. We connected with another Grade 4 class in California who helped us demonstrate our knowledge and understanding in social studies.

Google Hangouts provide us with the ability to interact with people we would not normally be able to connect with. As long as we are connected to the Internet, we can bring people into our classroom no matter where they are geographically located. Thanks to Hangouts, we have adopted a Canadian athlete who we would never have been able to get to know. Whether she is out of the country for training purposes or on the other side of the country for competition, she has been able to come into our classroom to share her experiences and help us with our learning. Our Hangouts with her led to a wonderful media literacy assignment combining a variety of curriculum connections (http://newfluencies.blogspot.ca/2015/06/a-mixture-of-edtech-gafe-and-social.html), none of which would have been possible had we not connected with her via Hangouts.

I look forward to continuing to use Google Hangouts to benefit my learning as well as that of my students. Thanks to Hangouts, we can travel anywhere around the world and meet with whoever we want without even leaving our classroom.

## BIOGRAPHY

Rolland Chidiac

Waterloo Catholic District School Board, Ontario, Canada

Classroom Teacher

Twitter: @rchids

Website: www.newfluencies.blogspot.ca

### More Ideas for Going Google

- Schedule Google Hangouts as a part of Google Calendar events. In the details for your Google Calendar event, you add a video call to be part of the event. This is a great way to get your Hangout set up and provide the members of the group easy access to the video chat.

- Use messaging in lieu of some meetings: Wouldn't it be great if less of our time was spent in face-to-face meetings? Add the other members of your PLC or department, and address important issues immediately in a live chat session. If you need to view a document or share a video, you can easily turn your IM chat into a video conference with the click of a button.

## TIPS FOR THE GOOGLE CLASSROOM

- Create video tutorials: Using Hangouts you can create step-by-step tutorials that can be saved using Hangouts on Air. Simply send your audience to the archived link, and they can watch you share your screen in an online tutorial!

- Encourage modern pen pals: Instead of using traditional pen pals, which can take weeks for a correspondence, use Google Hangouts, and communicate immediately. Teachers will need to connect with other classrooms looking for partner schools—a great place to start is in the communities of Google +.

CHAPTER 7

# Google Classroom

## FIVE Things to Know About Google Classroom

1. Google Classroom is only available for GAFE accounts.

2. Google Classroom links together with Google Drive as a way for students to work on and submit assignments.

3. Google Classroom provides teachers with an online home for announcements, assignments, surveys, and more.

4. Teachers can grade assignments within Google Classroom. Grades can be exported for use with the school grading program.

5. Assignment dates from Google Classroom can be displayed in Google Calendar.

Over the past several years, we've seen a bigger and bigger push to move our classrooms into an online environment. It provides an opportunity to share information with students and provide them with necessary resources for learning content and completing assignments. The problem is that most teachers don't really want to create and maintain a website. They either don't have the time or the skill set to make this a feasible option.

Enter Google Classroom.

Google Classroom provides teachers with an online classroom complete with the ability to post announcements and assignments. As part of this virtual classroom, educators can use tools like Google Drive and Google Calendar for student assignments.

### ISTE T Standard 2 Objective d

*Develop technology-enriched learning environments that enable all students to pursue their individual curiosities and become active participants in setting their own educational goals, managing their own learning, and assessing their own progress. (ISTE, 2008)*

Teachers love Google Drive as it is an amazing tool to help them and their students collaborate on and share documents back and forth. Although it's always been easy to share the files, the problem lies in managing the projects in any type of organized system. If a classroom full of students all shares a Google Doc with their teacher, you'll find 30 or more new documents are all cluttering up that teacher's Google Drive. Perhaps the teacher goes in and organizes the documents into folders, but there's still an issue with permissions. There hasn't been an easy way to turn off student access to assignment written in Google Drive once the due date has passed.

Google Classroom gives teachers the ability to control the flow of project documents back and forth with the students.

Prior to Classroom, students could share documents with teachers, but it was a fairly complicated system of permissions with the instructor having the responsibility of managing a file for each and every student. Imagine trying to keep track of 180 files if you teach secondary!

As Amanda Hart, a high school FACS teacher recently stated, "Google tools have made it SO MUCH easier to distribute and collect materials. I have gone 99 percent paperless by using Docs, Sheets, and Google Classroom."

## ADVANTAGES OF GOOGLE CLASSROOM

It's a one-stop shop—Teachers really have everything they need for students to create and submit their projects in their online classrooms. After students submit assignments, teachers have everything they need to provide feedback and grade student work. Google Classroom is streamlined, so it isn't as cumbersome as many online management tools—teachers and students have just the features they want and use most often.

Permissions are managed automatically—Once the teacher assigns a due date for a project, Google Classroom changes student permissions from edit mode to view mode at the appropriate time. Once the teacher evaluates student work, the permissions can be changed automatically, giving the student back his or her editing rights—perhaps for a second draft of a paper.

Folders are created immediately—As an instructor, this takes a lot of the time and effort out of managing your digital classroom. You simply create an assignment using Google Drive, and the folder structure is developed at the same time. When you look in your Google Drive, you'll simply find a folder for each assignment with the student documents already inside!

### Project Idea: Building an Online Class

#### Getting Started

- To create your own classroom—go to www.classroom.google.com.
- Click on the **+** button located in the top right of the screen.
- You'll find two options to continue—**Join Class** or **Create Class** (see Figure 7.1).

- Select **Create Class**.
- At this point you'll be prompted to enter a name and section for your new class.

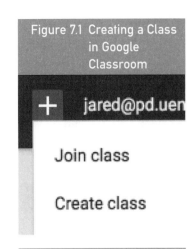

Figure 7.1 Creating a Class in Google Classroom

© 2016 Google Inc. used with permission. Google and the Google logo are registered trademarks of Google Inc.

Tip—You'll want to think about how you plan to create your classes as naming plays a part in your course structure. For example, if you are a secondary teacher, one naming convention is to create a different class for each period that you teach. For elementary, you may only make one class.

## Adding Students to Your Google Classroom

There are two main ways for adding students to Google Classroom. One is to manually enroll students into your class using their email addresses. The other option is to distribute a unique class code that students can enter into Google Classroom.

### Manually add students in your Google Classroom

- Click on the **Students** tab in your Google Classroom.
- Click on the **Invite** button.
- You'll be taken to a window where you can select student email addresses available to you through your student information system.
- Once you select the desired students, click the **Invite** button at the bottom of the window.

Tip—To speed up this process, you can create a Google Group and place all of your students in the group. When it's time to add students to your Google Classroom, you can simply add the group.

### Using the Class Code

- Click on the **Students** tab in your Google Classroom.
- On this page you'll find a **Class Code** located at different locations. This code is case sensitive and is unique to your specific class.
- Students can enter the code when they login to classroom.google.com with their school Google account.
- Student should click on the + button in the top right corner of the screen.
- In the pop-out menu that displays, students should select **Join Class**.
- Here is where they enter the unique Class Code you provided for them.
- To finish they will click on the **Join Class** button.

Once your class is created and students are added you'll want to start working on a few key elements.

### Classroom Stream

The Classroom Stream is the communication hub of your Google Classroom. In the stream you'll post information about your classroom, assignments can be created, surveys can be distributed, and more (see Figure 7.2).

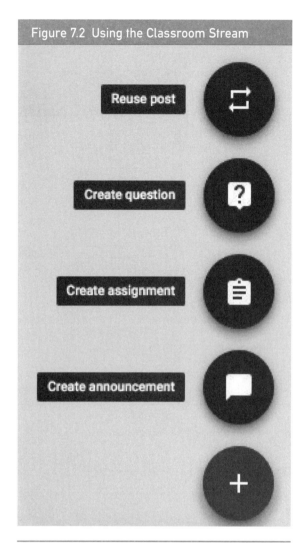

Figure 7.2 Using the Classroom Stream

Reuse post

Create question

Create assignment

Create announcement

*Announcements*—This tool allows teachers to post quick bits of information for students. Announcements are basically text boxes that provide a space to type messages. Additionally, teachers can attach a variety of files to the announcements. For example, an announcement about an upcoming field trip can have a permission form for the field trip attached.

Attachments to your announcements can come from Google Drive files, uploaded files, YouTube videos, links to other websites, and more.

*Assignments*—This is the key feature that makes Google Classroom a must-have. Using the Create assignment option you can create Google Drive files that are immediately shared with your students. These files will appear in a students' Google Classroom as well as in their Google Drive Library.

Assignments can be assigned a point value, and teachers can grade the work from within Google Classroom. In fact, Google Classroom will take all scores and put them into a gradebook that downloads as a CSV file.

As with Create announcement, there are several different choices for attaching files to an assignment in Google Drive. Attachments again include uploaded files, YouTube videos, **URL** links, and more.

*Questions*—Using Create Question allows teachers the power and function of Google Forms within Google Classroom. Teachers can create quick surveys to assess student opinions about classroom activities, or they can develop assessments to determine student understanding.

Questions provide educators with a quick question—something they want to learn from students. Perhaps you want to get the pulse of your students on yesterday's assignment. At the end of the day, you can ask direct questions to assess student comprehension of topics from class.

*Reuse Post*—Another new feature in Google Classroom is the ability to reuse a post. Content in Google Classroom posts chronologically, meaning newer content goes to the top of the screen, and older content moves further down.

## Customize Classroom

To customize your header image in Google Classroom, you have two choices:

*Select Theme*—Choose from more than 50 different images or patterns. Simply click on your desired theme, and choose the **Select class theme** button.

*Upload Photo*—You can upload your own image to use as a header for your classroom. The image will be stretched to fit the header box, so a larger photo typically works better versus a low-resolution image. Drag your photo into the upload window, or search using the provided tool.

## Assignments

Creating and collecting assignments in Google Classroom is probably the tool's best feature. Gone are the days where files are created and shared manually, filling up your Google Drive account or that of your students. Students will love the simplicity of clicking on an assignment in Google Classroom and simply having a doc, sheet, or presentation open where they can immediately get to work.

### Creating an Assignment

Using the Classroom Stream, creating an assignment is a quick and easy process. Let's take a closer look at the simple steps for developing an assignment.

- Click on the **+** button in bottom right corner of your screen.
- Choose the **Create assignment** option.
- Provide a title and some instructions for the assignment. You may need more space for your assignment information. You can attach a handout, a video, a link, or a Google Drive file to add extra details.

Create a due date. Using the ***drop-down menu*** under **Due**, you can select a future day and time for the assignment to be completed.

Finally, you can select which of your Google Classrooms to send the assignment. This is great if you have more than one class that will receive the assignment. Simply check the box to assign the project to multiple classes (see Figure 7.3).

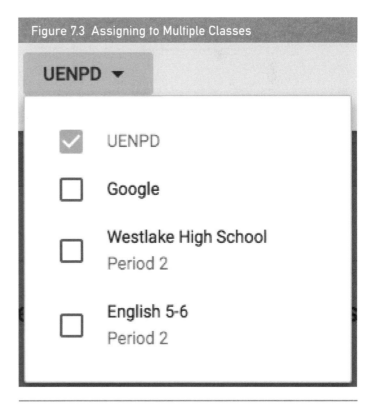

Figure 7.3 Assigning to Multiple Classes

### Submitting Assignments

Students have two basic options for submitting their assignments in Google Classroom: Upload and attach an existing file, or create a new Google Drive file.

Adding an existing file for students is the same process as attaching a file to an email. Get started by clicking on the **Add** button for the new assignment. You can select a file using the provided button, or simply drag and drop a file into the submission window. Click **Done** to complete the process.

Creating a new Google Drive file is also handled with a single click. Students will find the option **Create** at the bottom of the new assignment. A pop-up menu will appear providing the students with a list of different Google Drive files they can create. Once they select the appropriate tool, Google Drive will open, and students will be inside the new file.

Once students complete the Google Drive file, they will find a **Turn it in** button in the top right corner of their assignment.

## Grading Assignments

Grading assignments in Google Classroom is a streamlined process that is quick and easy to complete.

As you click on a specific assignment in your class, you'll notice two choices for student work—either marked as **Done** or **Not Done**. There isn't another option.

To grade an assignment the teacher simply needs to click on an individual student's name. Once a student is selected, the point value for a given assignment will be available. The teacher just adds the point total for each individual student.

If the teacher feels like the assignment needs additional work, there is an option to **Return** a project back to the student. This will allow the student to continue working on an assignment and then resubmit it in Google Classroom.

Once the teacher grades assignments, a student will find his or her scores are now available. The easiest place to find the scores is by using the dashboard menu (three bars in the top left corner of the screen). Here students will find a **Work** menu choice. This tab displays all of their work and allows students to read teacher comments and find their grades for the assignment.

Once assignments are graded instructors can download scores as CSV files or send scores to a Google Sheet. This provides teachers will the ability to import scores directly into most school grading programs, saving educators a ton of time by not duplicating work.

## Calendar

One of the best features of Google tools is their ability to integrate with one another. The Calendar feature in Google Classroom is just another example of blending several tools together seamlessly.

To access Calendar in Google Classroom, click on the **Dashboard** drop-down menu in the top left corner of your screen. Select the **Calendar** option.

Here, students will find a color-coded calendar with all of the upcoming assignments and any scheduled due dates (see Figure 7.4). Click on an entry, and you'll open the assignment for completion.

In addition to using the Calendar option, you can also open all assignments from Google Classroom inside of Google Calendar. To open events in Google Calendar, click on the **About** tab and choose **Open in Google Calendar**.

Using the Google Calendar option gives students and teachers more options for accessing information using your mobile device. Because Google Calendar can be enabled with SMS notifications,

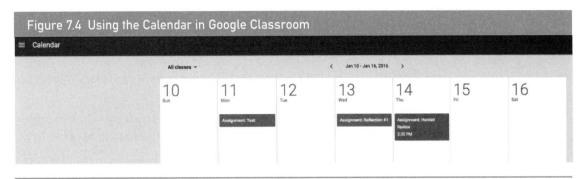

Figure 7.4 Using the Calendar in Google Classroom

students can now get text message updates for future assignments. This is a great option for keeping students up-to-date.

## FROM A GOOGLE GURU

I have found that I am better able to provide feedback than with a traditional assessment. I can work with students throughout the entire project and provide them with precise comments to help them through the projects in class.

As other teachers in my building have observed my classes using Google Classroom, they've looked to adopt the platform as well. Once they see how easy it is to manage student work and provide feedback, the teachers in my school have started to migrate their course work into Google Classroom.

I love the control that Google Classroom provides me in managing student projects. With 375 students it has been overwhelming in the past to set up an adequate system for interacting with students' work. With Google Classroom, I can create an assignment, and it's automatically dispersed to all of my students and uniquely identified with each of them. Google creates folders that house all of the assignments on my end, and they're already organized into class periods. I don't have to hunt around for a project anymore!

The administration has been very supportive in our decision to go paperless using Classroom. At first we had to educate parents about the changing digital nature of our grading and feedback, but once parents realized how much information I could share with the students using the Announcements tool, they quickly jumped on board with Classroom.

## BIOGRAPHY

Diane Valencia
Albion Middle School, Cottonwood Heights, UT, US
CTE Teacher
Twitter: @MsVCTE

- Using the About page in your Google Classroom, you can upload and share important files with your students. Think of this option as a way to create a repository of your important content.

- Be sure to archive old classes to keep them from cluttering your Google Classroom dashboard. You can always restore a class that's been archived if you need to retrieve old content.

- Google Classroom also provides you a great space to display student projects. Once you have access to Google Slides or other programs, you can embed the files in your Classroom.

## TIPS FOR THE GOOGLE CLASSROOM

- You can invite other teachers to be part of your Google Classroom. This is a great option for any of you with a student teacher or those who have a teacher's aide. The class will show up in both of your accounts. Add another teacher from the About tab, and click on the **Invite Teacher** button.

- Students and teachers can access Google Classroom assignments in Google Drive. Once an assignment is created, both groups will find that all the necessary folder structure is automatically created in Google Drive. This makes it very convenient to find and edit any projects within Google Drive.

## CHAPTER 8

# Google Voice

## FIVE Things to Know About Google Voice

1. Google Voice is a phone number that can be assigned to any of your phones.

2. Google Voice transcribes your messages and can be set up to send you emails or texts of your voice mail.

3. Google Voice sends calls out using the new Google Voice number, even if you're calling from a cell phone.

4. Google Voice can record phone call interviews and save them as MP3 files.

5. Google Voice allows you to text to mobile phones without using your cell phone number.

Communicating with parents and students is a challenge for teachers in the digital age. That statement may sound unbelievable as there have never been more phones on the planet than today. As of 2014, it is estimated that there are 7.22 billion mobile phones with a mere 7.19 billion people on Earth (Boren, 2014). Still, for many teachers, communicating with parents often requires a loss of privacy that most educators aren't willing to sacrifice. I mean, who really wants to give out their personal cell phone number to kids or parents!

Google Voice changes the way in which we communicate using digital devices. Rather than using your personal cell phone number as a primary contact, you can now create an alias phone number. What does this mean for teachers? Now they can have contact with parents and students without needing to give out their personal contact information.

> **ISTE T Standard 2 Objective c**
>
> *Communicate relevant information and ideas effectively to students, parents, and peers using a variety of digital age media and formats. (ISTE, 2008)*

## GETTING STARTED

Go to voice.google.com and sign up for a new Google phone number. This number will be assigned to your email address, not to a specific phone. This means you can make and receive calls and messages from a variety of devices.

When you first enroll in Google Voice, you'll be prompted to share an existing phone number you have. This will be the number that links to your Google Voice account. You can always disable the number from receiving calls using Google Voice, but you need to have an existing number in the system.

Next, you'll be prompted to select an area code, zip code, or city for the new Google Voice number. You can also provide a word or phrase you'd like Google to use if it's available. Be patient—you might have to try a few different options to find an available number.

Once you've selected a new number and you've connected that number to other devices, you're set. You'll want to adjust a few other basic setting, but you can now use Google Voice as a new way to communicate with parents and students.

## GOOGLE VOICE FEATURES

- Calling: Calls are registered to your Google Voice number, so that's what shows up on caller ID for a parent or student. All domestic calls are free, so there's no need to worry about a per-minute charge.

- Texting: Sending text messages with Google Voice is quick and easy. Again, text messages come from your Voice account, so you can use any device to send messages— even your computer!

- Phones: You can attach your Google Voice number to a variety of different devices including landlines, mobile devices, and even computers—yes, you can even make calls from your computer using Google Hangouts!

- Messaging: Using the messaging feature teachers can create voice mails that provide assignment prompts for students. Messages can be customized for different purposes and audiences—it's up to you.

### Setting It Up for the Classroom

Whereas there are a ton of different settings to choose from in Google Voice, what follow are some of the most important for educators. To access the settings, click on the small gear icon in the top right corner of your Google Voice screen.

- *Voicemail Transcripts:* Using this setting will actually create a transcription of your voice mails and then send them to you either using your Gmail or as a text message. The transcription isn't always verbatim, but this is a nice option for you to read your message at a glance.

- *Do Not Disturb:* This is a nice option to avoid getting calls during your teaching day. You can set a period during each day where the phone simply won't ring, rather it will go straight to voice mail. You can also enable Do Not Disturb for a specific window— say the next two hours.

- *Call Options:* This feature allows you to take advantage of some of Google Voice's hidden powers. Here are three of the best options:
  - *Call Recording*—When you place a call, simply press the 4 on your Google Voice keypad, and you'll start recording the call. This is a great option for students conducting an interview or for a teacher who needs to document a call home to a parent.
  - *Call Screening*—In Google Voice you can pick up calls after they've gone to voice mail. This means you have new powers to screen calls. Say, for example, you're getting a call you don't really want to take. By enabling Call Screening you can send that call straight to voice mail and listen in while the message is being left. If something important comes up and you want to pick up the call, simply press 2, and you'll be live in the call.
  - *Conference Calls*—Getting into a conference call couldn't be easier in Google Voice. Simply have the different parties call your Google Voice at the established time. Once you're in the call, you'll be prompted to add each new caller with the click of a button.

## Project Idea: Use Google Voice for Vocabulary and Fluency

Google Voice can provide a great way to assess your students' reading levels and vocabulary fluency.

*Reading Level*—An effective option to work with younger students or struggling readers is to record them as they read. Using Google Voice you can simply have students (or their parents for younger readers) call your number, and you can record their reading. This audio file can then be downloaded as part of your assessment information.

**ISTE Standard 6 Objective b**

*Students create original works or responsibly repurpose or remix digital resources into new creations.* (ISTE, 2016)

By using the recording you can target specific strategies to help the student improve his or her reading level. Repeat the process after working on reading fluency, and you'll be able to play both recordings to compare progress.

*Vocabulary Fluency*—Google Voice has become hugely popular with foreign language teachers. They simply provide students with a paragraph they need to assess and have student phone in and provide the recitation in the foreign language. Again, by recording the student recitation, it provides the teacher with areas of focus to help students who are struggling.

## FROM A GOOGLE GURU

### Student-Led Interviews and Podcasts

Using Google Voice's recording feature, have your students conduct interviews and turn them into podcasts. Here's how that could work:

The teacher could give students a speaking prompt. For example, students could talk about freedom of speech and how it affects schools. Students could prepare their responses, either word for word on a script or with a list of bullet points. They could also respond impromptu with no preparation time. Students could call in and record their responses on the teacher's Google Voice account.

When they're finished, the teacher could download all of the student responses as MP3 files, creating file names with the students' names when saving. When they're all downloaded, the teacher or students could drop those MP3 files into Audacity. The teacher or the student could pretend to be a radio talk show host, introduce the show at the beginning, and then take the first "call" (a student's recording from Google Voice). The host could react to that "call" by recording into Audacity afterward.

The host could continue playing calls and reacting to them until the show is over, when he or she could sum it all up and sign off. It would be interesting for students to hear each other's voices in the podcast. *Personalization equals engagement!* If the teacher produced the show, he or she could play it in class for the students or upload it to a class website or audio file hosting service for students to download and listen to on their own. If the student produced it, the student talk shows could be uploaded to a class website for other students to listen to or to be shared with a global audience through social media, the school website, or email.

## BIOGRAPHY

Matt Miller

K–12 Trainer

Twitter: @jmattmiller

Website: www.ditchthattextbook.com

## TIPS FOR THE GOOGLE CLASSROOM

- Group message your class or group. Using the combined power of Gmail and Google Voice you can establish Contact Groups and message everyone at once. The first step is to create a contact group for your class or school club. Be sure to include phone numbers as part of each contact. Once you've got the group established, simply use the group name in Google Voice when sending a text. Everyone in the group gets the message, and you don't have to type in 30 different phone numbers!

- Be sure to add the Google Voice app to your smartphone. This is an easy way to use all the great features on your primary phone. The best part is that Google Voice will integrate with your existing messages, so you won't have to check both voice mail boxes or text messaging apps. Google Voice messages will forward to your regular cell messages.

## ANOTHER IDEA FOR THE GOOGLE CLASSROOM

- Create a scavenger hunt. As part of a class scavenger hunt, provide some of the clues using Google Voice. You can do this by recording a different message each day that provides the student with a necessary clue. The only way for the students to get the clue is by calling your voice number. You could do this each day for a week and have fun making up the new recordings each day.

# PART II

# Creativity and Innovation

Today's students are speaking out to their teachers loudly and clearly: They want activities and assignments in school that allow them to create content and share it with others. Unfortunately, kids still find that much of school involves passive learning. It is time spent listening to teachers lecture from the front of the classroom.

> So much of school is still talking to kids. Presenting, telling, explaining to the whole class and when kids hear that they just fall asleep. What the kids want to do is the group work, it's the project work, and it's the casework. They want to share things. (Prensky, 2010)

As we move into 21st century classrooms, our curriculums must reflect the changes technology affords us. Worksheets and reports still have a place in today's classrooms, but they need to be supplemented with multimedia projects. Activities involving digital images with Picasa, video creation and distribution with YouTube, and innovative multimedia tools like Google Earth move students along the levels of Bloom's Taxonomy and encourage high levels of creativity and critical thinking. Projects provide students with the opportunity to show what they know.

In looking at 21st century learning skills, student projects that involve multimedia encourage students to think creatively, utilizing a wide array of tools to create and innovate. Students may not always readily admit it, but they want to be challenged. When kids are given opportunities to grow and develop their ideas, they want to do these kinds of things:

- Create new and worthwhile ideas (both incremental and radical concepts).
- Elaborate, refine, analyze, and evaluate their own ideas to improve and maximize creative efforts.
- Develop, implement, and communicate new ideas to others effectively.
- Demonstrate originality and inventiveness in work and understand the real-world limits to adopting new ideas (Partnership for 21st Century Skills, 2004).

## GOOGLE'S IMPACT ON CREATIVITY AND INNOVATION

*Authentic assessment requires global distribution.*

—Tyson (2009)

I heard this statement from Dr. Tim Tyson, and it stopped me in my tracks. Why global distribution? American schools don't really have a global perspective, so his comment challenged my way of thinking. As I pondered on his intent, it really hit home with me.

Kids want to create projects and share them with an audience. In schools, it is usually an audience of one—the teacher. This really doesn't provide much motivation. Think about it: You put tons of time into an assignment, and the only person who sees it isn't one of your peers; it's an adult. The only type of validation you get from the hours of work is a grade? An A doesn't really mean anything to some kids.

Now, let's look at what the kids are doing when they aren't in school. Many spend countless days and nights working on a video, a song, or a dance, and the minute they think they have it perfected, where does it end up? YouTube. Why? So everyone they know can see it. Even perfect strangers can view the video and make comments about it. Kids feel important, and they know they are making a contribution that's valued. Remember, authentic assessment requires global distribution, and Google tools provide just that platform for kids.

## DOES SCHOOL REFLECT THE "REAL WORLD"?

So much of students' experience outside of school differs from what life is like in the classroom. Whereas technology dominates much of our kids' attention at home, school seems to be a vacuum—a place where students' experience and know-how seem to be devalued. This fact isn't lost on our leaders. In the National Education Technology Plan (NETP) 2010, the problem is addressed as follows:

> Many students' lives today are filled with technology that gives them mobile access to information and resources 24/7, enables them to create multimedia content and share it with the world, and allows them to participate in online social networks where people from all over the world share ideas. (U.S. Department of Education, 2015)

Students need to be able to share their multimedia projects with others. It doesn't always have to be on YouTube or Facebook, but there needs to be a forum where students feel their work matters. Technology is a great facilitator of sharing content, and Google tools make creating and sharing projects easier than ever.

In this section, we'll focus on three tools that promote creativity and innovation: Google Earth, Picasa/Google Photos, and YouTube. Each of these programs provides opportunities for project-based learning and encourages students to creatively develop innovative assignments.

## CHAPTER 9

# Google Earth

## FIVE Things to Know About Google Earth

1. Google Earth uses aerial maps to create a free interactive map of the world.

2. The Layers panel provides access to multimedia content from around the web.

3. Google Earth provides *real-time data* from places around the world.

4. Students can create multimedia virtual tours of locations all over the globe.

5. Google Earth files are known as KML or KMZ, and they can be found using a Google Advanced Search.

Google Earth dramatically transformed the way in which we see the world. It brought maps into the foreground on our computers and made cartography seem somewhat cool. You didn't need to know the names of tiny countries to be able to find them in Google Earth. You could simply search for a region and fly in to all the amazing sites from around the globe. Instantly, kids were playing with maps—can you believe it?

Google Earth utilizes aerial photos of the entire world to create a new kind of map, a digital map—a map that allows you to zoom in to almost any location on Earth and virtually experience the world from a first-person point of view. But Google Earth is more than just a basic map; it provides the user with a realistic look at places from the ground as well as the air. Google Earth gives such an incredibly detailed view of the world that you may never need a passport again!

For teachers, Google Earth has been a revelation—a free tool that provides content and images of countries around the globe. Because it is such a visual program, it can be used by students of all ages. Before Google Earth, kids saw maps as old and boring—typically, something controlled by the teacher at the front of the room. Once Google Earth was developed, an innovative pedagogical shift occurred. Now it was the *students* in control of what they looked at on the map. They literally could see the world, and they loved it.

One of the biggest misconceptions about Google Earth is that the tool is really only valuable for geography and social studies teachers. This couldn't be more false. Teachers from almost any discipline can use Google Earth as a way to open the real world to their students. Anne Brusca, a library media specialist from Center Street Elementary in New York, noticed how engaged all her fifth-grade students were when they used Google Earth to take a virtual tour of locations from the book *Orphan Train*. "I've never seen them so intent," she says. "This got them to deeper learning" (quoted in Boss, n.d.b).

## GETTING STARTED WITH GOOGLE EARTH

Unlike many of the tools we've examined thus far, Google Earth has both an online and a download version. The online version of Google Earth is fairly new. It utilizes the same search feature as the download version, but most classrooms focus on using the original download version of the program because there's so much more information available. For the purposes of our discussion, we're going to focus on the download version of Google Earth, but feel free to check out the online version at http://maps.google.com—click on the link for **Earth** in the upper right corner of the screen.

To download Google Earth, follow these steps:

1. Go to http://google.com/earth.

2. Click on the big blue **Download** button.

3. Because Google Earth is a program you run and store on your computer, you'll need to be sure your computer meets the system requirements. Basically, you need to be running Windows XP or later if you're on a PC and Mac OS 10.6 or later if you're using a Mac. For a complete list of system requirements, check out http://earth.google.com/support/bin/answer.py?hl=en&answer=20701.

4. After the download, the installation is no different from any other program. Follow the wizard, and within a few minutes you'll be up and running on Google Earth.

## GOOGLE EARTH BASICS

### Navigation

Google Earth has a set of navigation controls going down the right side of the screen. Now, you may not see these tools all the time. When not in use or in contact with the cursor, the navigation controls actually disappear into the background of the program. How cool is that? To make the navigation reappear, just hover your mouse over the top right corner of the screen. Here are a few basic tools in the navigation controls (see Figure 9.1).

- Look Joystick: This tool allows you to look at a location from different perspectives. You'll notice the control has an eyeball in the center of it, giving you the impression that you should use this tool to look around the screen. By clicking on any of the arrows on the joystick, you'll be able to change your vantage point.

- Move Joystick: Use this when you want to move around the screen. Located below the Look Joystick, this tool allows you to slide around on the screen. You can use the arrow keys along the outside of the dial, or you can use the arrows keys on the keyboard directly. One other trick is to left click on the screen and drag your cursor to another location on the map. This will center that location on the map.

- Zoom Slider: This slider allows you to zoom in on a location. You can go from a global perspective looking straight down to looking at an individual house from street level. In addition to using the slider, you can also narrow or broaden your focus by using the scroll wheel in your mouse. Zooming is an effective way for students to narrow their attention and bring different elements into focus.

Figure 9.1 Navigation Controls in Google Earth

## Search

Google Earth has three major search tools to help you navigate around the world. Let's take a closer look at how each one works (see Figure 9.2).

- Fly To: This is how you and your students will travel to locations around the globe.

  - Enter a landmark, an address, a city, a country, or even latitude and longitude coordinates if you know them.

  - The more detail you provide, the better chance you have to reach your destination.

  - Once you've entered your desired location, click on the magnifying glass, and you should be "flying."

- Find Businesses: Using this feature, students can locate all the different services available near a desired location. This is great if you're having kids identify local businesses they have access to when studying a location. One local teacher created a great activity where her kindergarten students found the community services (e.g., police station, fire station, and supermarket) they had recently visited as part of their class field trips.

- Directions: Type in two locations, and Google Earth will calculate your trip and travel time. The information is based on turn-by-turn driving directions. You may never get lost again! Directions is a fun feature to help students understand distance and location.

  - An effective activity for younger students is to have them find a safe walking route to school from their homes. The kids can look at the names of the different streets as they virtually travel from their houses to the school.

## Places

Places is Google Earth's storage bin for saved locations on the map. You can create your own saved locations using the tools in Google Earth, or you can download saved location files from the

Internet and add them to your own version of Google Earth. Once a location is either saved in or added to Google Earth, you'll find it in the Places menu. Let's look at taking an interactive field trip in Google Earth using the Places section.

1. Go to the **Places** section of the menu.

2. Click on the drop-down arrow to the right of the **Places** folder.

3. Here you'll find the **Sightseeing** folder. It contains premade trips to some of the world's most amazing locations. Click on the **Sightseeing** *drop-down menu,* and browse the available choices.

4. Double-click on the name of your desired location, and you'll fly to that destination.

You'll find everything from the Grand Canyon to Red Square as possible travel destinations. This is an amazing way to view areas up close and personal. Instead of simply looking down on the Grand Canyon, you'll literally be flying in between the rock walls along the Colorado River. It's as close as you'll come to the canyon without going there and hiring a tour guide! Can you imagine guiding your class of second graders through the Grand Canyon while exploring the various types of rock you'll see on your journey? Talk about real-world activities!

"We go to places like Mount St. Helens, so we can see the devastation there," says Diane King, a fifth-grade science teacher at Lakeview Elementary School in St. Cloud, Florida. "We go to the Grand Canyon. We fly over the San Andreas Fault, and you can actually see the fault line. Anything we're learning about, we'll just fly there" (quoted in Standen, n.d.).

Places is also the primary folder for any locations you choose to save in Google Earth. We'll get more into this in a bit, but Google Earth allows you to mark and save locations around the globe for a customized view of your world. Once a location is saved, you'll find the information in the Places folder.

In addition to saving your own locations in Google Earth, you can download locations others have marked and save them in your Places folder. For teachers, this means you can search for locations dealing with various curriculum topics you teach.

Figure 9.2 Using Search in Google Earth

▼ Search

Search

ex: Hotels near JFK

Get Directions   History

## FINDING LOCATION FILES OR VIRTUAL TOURS FOR GOOGLE EARTH

None of us has enough time to find or create all the resources we need in the classroom. This is particularly true when using Google Earth. To make it easier on yourself, rather than creating an interactive tour for each of your lessons, try searching the Google database for Google Earth tours and location markers your teaching colleagues have already created.

When trying to find educational virtual tours for Google Earth, there are three primary methods: Advanced Google Search, the Google Earth Community, and the Google Earth Gallery. Let's look at each of these tools.

## Using Google's Advanced Search

1. Go to the Google homepage at www.google.com and perform a basic search on a desired location.

2. Click on the **Options** button in the top right corner of the screen and choose **Advanced Search** from the menu that appears.

3. Scroll down the options look for the field titled **File type**. Here you'll find a drop-down menu that provides you with a list of various types of searchable files.

There are two Google Earth file types you can find online, KML and KMZ. Both types of files can contain locations, descriptions, and embedded information in online content; the key difference between the file types is that KMZ files are compressed into a zipped format, so there can be more stored information and multiple locations.

## Using Google Earth Community

1. In Google Earth, click on the **Help** menu.

2. Select the **Google Earth Community**.

In the Google Earth Community database, you'll find a direct link to the vast amount of information the community provides. A great part of the Google Earth Community for teachers is that there is a dedicated area specifically for education.

In addition to having numerous educational virtual tours stored in it, the Google Earth Community provides teachers and students with a forum to share ideas for implementing Google Earth in their assignments. There are also many available educational tools in Google Earth found in the Google Earth Community.

Remember, the education world has tons of tools just waiting for you to access. Once you know where to look for them, Google Earth can transform from a basic search tool into a multimedia treasure chest.

## Using the Google Earth Gallery

1. In Google Earth, click on the **Layers** panel.

2. Select the **Earth Gallery** link.

Another good place to find Google Earth resources is in Google Earth itself. Located at the top of the **Layers** panel, the **Earth Gallery** link takes you directly into the public gallery on earth.google.com. There are several different galleries available at this site, but the best one for our purposes is the **Educational Gallery**.

In the Educational Gallery, you'll find KMZ files covering a variety of subjects and curriculum areas, such as the following:

- Science: Find information about topics including real-time earthquakes, global climate change, and oil spills.

- Social Studies: Access information about historical sites, census data from around the world, and political campaign results from recent elections.

- There are also biographical sketches of some famous people, and you can take a peek at the different Major League Baseball stadiums. The gallery is constantly growing, and it's a good starting point for a fun Google Earth research project.

## LAYERS

The Layers panel is the hidden gem of Google Earth. This is the section that turns Google Earth from a normal 3-D map into an interactive information center. As you "turn on" various layers, you have visual access to information from tons of different sources, utilizing multiple areas of the core curriculum (see Figure 9.3).

Each of these layers will display on your Google Earth map, and they provide unique content about sources from around the globe. As a teacher, this provides you with the opportunity to share information, and it allows your students to draw connections to the content they are learning in class.

"It has kids make realizations based on observations they make," says Aidan Chopra, an education program manager at Google, "and that's really the gold standard in education. There are no conclusions in Google Earth; there are trillions of pieces of information out there that students can use to form their own conclusions. A good teacher can then build on those observations and guide them to meet the class's learning objectives" (Standen, n.d.).

Let's take a closer look at some of the "layers" in Google Earth and explore the various ways in which you can use this information as part of your curriculum. Access the **Layers** panel at the bottom of the menu toolbar along the left side of Google Earth.

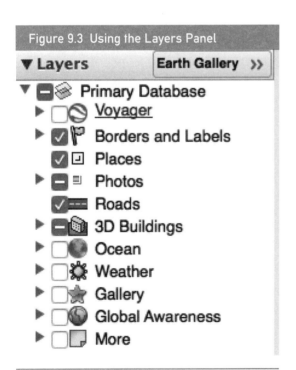

Figure 9.3 Using the Layers Panel

### Finding Your Way Around

There are a few layers specifically designed to help with identifying places on the map. These include **Borders and Labels**, **Places**, and **Roads**.

- Borders and Labels: This layer will display geographic boundaries such as state lines and country borders as well as geographic features like rivers, mountains, lakes, and so on.

- Places: This layer displays city, state, and country names.

- Roads: Turning on this layer helps students find their way around on the local level by displaying the names of roads on the map.

For a fun look at the White House, be sure and turn on the Roads layer to ensure the address really is 1600 Pennsylvania Avenue!

Enabling the Roads layers can also help younger students recognize areas around the school. We mentioned earlier the idea of having students create a walking route from their homes to the school. You can do that far more easily using the Roads layer.

## Viewing the World Differently

Google Earth has several layers that can help your students see the world around them using innovative model, photo, and video layers. Let's explore a handful of these visual layers including 3D Buildings, Street View, Photos, and Gigapan/GigaPixl. As you turn on these different layers, Google Earth will display a wide array of visual content to help your students view their world differently.

3D Buildings turns Google Earth from an average mapping program into a transformative tool, one that changes the way in which we view our world. Imagine scrolling across the countryside and then encountering the Coliseum rising from the ground in the heart of Rome. Take a trip to New York and have your students view the Statue of Liberty for the first time.

Google Earth has hundreds of three-dimensional models you can access by using the Layers panel. In the 3D Buildings layer, your students can access models of local buildings, including government and civic centers, but also famous landmarks and cultural icons. Now, much of this content is user created, so you won't find a 3-D model of everything you'll see in reality. Still, your students can get up close to landmarks such as the Golden Gate Bridge, the Great Wall of China, the Eiffel Tower, and many others.

I'm always amazed when using Google Earth to take students to Washington, DC, to look at the White House for the first time (see Figure 9.4). The aerial photos are impressive at first glance, but there's something magical about turning on the 3-D layers and having students look around the building as though they were there. (Trust me, you can get a lot closer to the White House in Google Earth than you'll ever get on the public tour!)

> **ISTE S Standard 1 Objective c**
>
> *Students communicate complex ideas clearly and effectively by creating or using a variety of digital objects such as visualizations, models, or simulations.*
> *(ISTE, 2016)*

## Project Idea: Have Students Create a 3-D Model Using Google SketchUp

I mentioned earlier that 3-D models exist due to contributions from Google engineers as well as user creations from around the world. So, just how do people make the models? A few years ago, Google released Google SketchUp, a free three-dimensional drafting program. Google SketchUp is a fantastic program that allows students to make their own models of buildings from around the world.

A popular activity in secondary schools is to have students create models of local buildings or attractions they're studying. Imagine having your students create models of your school building or the town hall. Creating 3-D models of your world is a great example of real-world projects for students using Google Earth and Google SketchUp. You can get started at https://www.sketchup.com/3Dfor/k12-education.

Street View is another Google Earth innovation. One of the minor complaints in the early days of Google Earth was that aerial photos could only provide users with one angle of the world. Seeing places from above was helpful, but we wanted more. People wanted to experience what areas would look like from the ground. The Google Earth team responded. Starting in 2007, maps became three dimensional as Google staff traveled the globe to take pictures of places from the street view. Now you could see locations in Google Earth just as you would if you were standing in the actual spot. It gave users a sense of realism that was difficult to achieve otherwise. Before Street View, teachers could have students travel to locations and look down on the areas; now activities could actually take place at the locations.

Street View not only allows you to look at a location, but you can actually travel along the streets and pan around to see everything that's around you (see Figure 9.5).

- To move up and down the street, click the arrows on the road. This will change the photos to simulate movement.

- To "look around" on the street, use your mouse and click on the area of the photo you wish to view up close. Google will shift your perspective and give you a 360° view of the area.

Earlier, I shared the idea of having kids trace their walking route to school using directions. Now, combine that with Street View, and you can actually have kids take an exact path between home and school. The students can pan around the screen and see places they are familiar with. For younger children, the line between virtual and reality is nearly nonexistent.

Google Earth provides some of the most realistic photos you'll find depicting various locations around the world. To enhance the aerial photos in the program, try turning on the Photos layer. In this layer, you'll encounter user-submitted photos from Panoramio, a partner site with Google Earth (see Figure 9.6). Photos allows you to see places in the world through the eyes of people who've been there before. Let's say your students are using Google Earth to explore Mount Rushmore. You want to look around the monument, so you turn on the 3D Buildings layer; the problem is that the model doesn't really provide you with a great view of the huge sculpture.

Now you turn on the Photos layer, and instantly, dozens of tiny blue squares appear on the map. As you click on each of the icons, an image appears showing you various aspects of the incredible edifice. Your students can see firsthand several different angles showing the monument. Each of these images was provided by someone who had traveled to Mount Rushmore and shared their experience by uploading their photos to the website Panoramio (see Figure 9.7).

The Photos layer isn't the only place where you can find quality images in Google Earth. There are actually three other layers containing high-resolution images of various locations: Gigapan and Gigapixl photos and Cities 360. All of these collections are found within the Gallery folder.

Gigipan/Gigapixl and Cities 360 use panoramic photos to show details of landmarks and locations that you can't find in your average photo. Take a trip to China, and you'll certainly want to visit the Forbidden City. With the Gigipan Photos layer on, your students can experience the same amazing architecture using an incredible image on the screen that you actually "fly into" to see up close. Using the scroll wheel on your mouse, you can get up close to various aspects of the photo. Because it is a high-resolution photo, the image won't blur or degrade as you zoom in.

## USING REAL-TIME DATA WITH WEATHER, OCEANS, AND SUNRISE/SUNSET

Because Google Earth utilizes a high-speed Internet connection, it has the power to access real-time data in ways that other information sources cannot.

Figure 9.5 Looking Around in Street View

**Figure 9.6 Panoramio Layer Provides Photos**

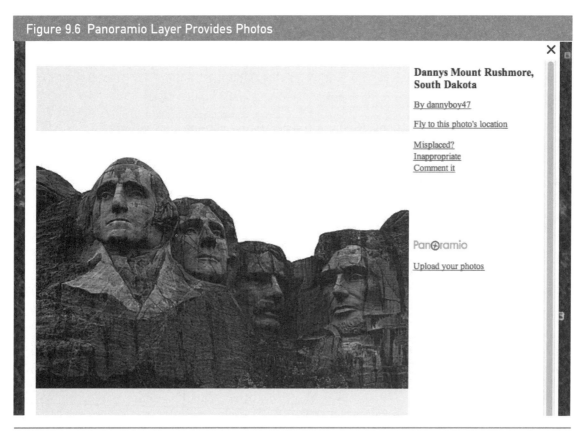

**Figure 9.7 High-Resolution Photos in Gigapan Layer**

Take the Weather and Oceans layers in Google Earth. Each of these layers ties into international databases of information to provide users with real-time information on a variety of science-related topics. Over the course of a lesson, students, using the Weather layer, can actually see evidence of how temperature or radar patterns have changed in a given location.

## Weather

Even though this layer isn't new to Google Earth, it keeps changing and adding new features. In the latest version (Version 6) of Google Earth, the Weather layer "projects images of rain and snow over the areas with those weather patterns as it's actually happening" (Melanson, 2010).

Can you imagine looking at your area in Google Earth, noticing that it's snowing in the Weather layer, and then having your elementary students look out the nearest window to confirm the current weather (see Figure 9.8)? Think of having your secondary school students track a tropical storm as it is moving across the ocean toward land. The Weather layer provides students with basic tools to help them identify weather patterns and make predictions. This is using real-time data at its best!

Having students explore weather patterns is a great way to have them explore information on deeper levels. The kids can make predictions, evaluate patterns, and identify changes—all by watching temperature and radar patterns in Google Earth.

Figure 9.8 Watching Snow Fall in Google Earth

© 2016 Google Inc. used with permission. Google and the Google logo are registered trademarks of Google Inc.

## Oceans

This layer is still relatively new in Google Earth, but it didn't take long for its impact to be noticed. Using the Oceans layer, you'll find information from tons of different sources (see Figure 9.9). There's everything from videos by the Cousteau Ocean World to historical information about ancient and modern shipwrecks. You can even learn about endangered species using several different layers.

One of the best ways to have students explore the oceans in an innovative way is by turning on the Animal Tracking layer found inside of the Oceans layer. Here, you'll be able to swim along with

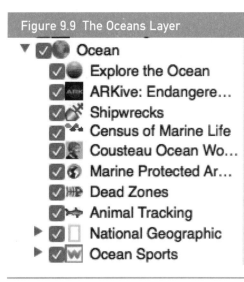

Figure 9.9 The Oceans Layer

▼ ☑️🌐 Ocean
   ☑️⚫ Explore the Ocean
   ☑️ ARKive: Endangere...
   ☑️ Shipwrecks
   ☑️ Census of Marine Life
   ☑️ Cousteau Ocean Wo...
   ☑️ Marine Protected Ar...
   ☑️ Dead Zones
   ☑️ Animal Tracking
 ▶ ☑️ National Geographic
 ▶ ☑️W Ocean Sports

dolphins, sharks, and whales as they cruise through the world's oceans. Hundreds of marine animals have been tagged with tracking devices, allowing us to observe their travel patterns and understand much of their movement beneath the water. As you follow different animals, you can actually turn on time-lapse animations to see their travels up close. What a great way to learn about marine biology!

## Sunrise/Sunset

This isn't really a layer; rather, it's a tool that allows the user to access real-time data to chart the Earth's orbit and rotations by checking the sunrise and sunset. Located on the toolbar across the top of the map, the **Sunrise/Sunset** option provides users with the ability to watch the sun rise and set in a given location.

Using the Sunrise/Sunset tool is a great way to teach younger students about the differences between night and day (see Figure 9.10). Here's how it works:

1. Find the toolbar across the top of your map in Google Earth.

2. Turn on the tool by clicking on the image of a sunrise.

3. Use the time slider to see how the sun travels across the world turning day into night and back again.

The kids will see how the sky gets lighter as the sun rises in that area. As you zoom into a city and change your perspective from overhead to across the horizon, you'll actually see the sun rise in the east and set in the west.

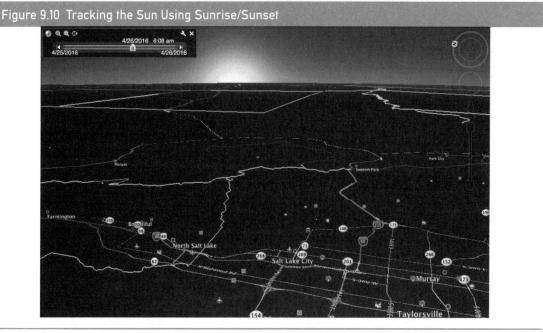

Figure 9.10 Tracking the Sun Using Sunrise/Sunset

SOURCE: **2011 ©INEGI.**

With older students, you can use the Sunrise/Sunset feature to have them make predictions about the way in which the time of year impacts the sunrise and sunset and the length of the day. It's another interesting way to have kids interpret real-time data to make conclusions about the world.

## Project Idea: Measuring the World Around You

I mentioned earlier in this chapter that a common misconception about Google Earth is that you'll only use it for teaching social studies. Let's take a look at a potential math application in Google Earth. This can be used for a variety of grade levels, but we'll focus on elementary math in this example.

One of my favorite tools along the top toolbar of Google Earth is the **Measurement** tool (see Figure 9.11). The icon for this tool is a blue ruler, inconspicuous enough that you might overlook it if you're not paying attention. Here's how it works.

The Measurement tool has two options:

1. Line: measures the distance between two points
2. Path: measures distances between more than two points

Here's an example of using the line tool that involves using estimation and then gathering data to test that estimate. If I want my students to understand distances and units of measurement, I could give them some standard story problem from a math textbook. Or, using Google Earth, I could take the students to Fenway Park in Boston and have them estimate the distance of a home run to dead centerfield. Which do you think would be more engaging for fifth graders?

Using the Measurement tool in the line mode, students can mark home plate and drag a line out to centerfield to discover the distance a home run actually travels.

We can extend this lesson by exploring different units of measurement as well. In the Measurement tool, there's a drop-down menu that provides options to display the distance in feet, miles, meters, and more. For our home run example, we wouldn't want to leave the distance in miles; rather, the kids will want to switch the unit of measurement to feet. It's a great way to help kids understand the relationship between various units of measurement in a real-world example they can relate to.

> **ISTE S Standard 3 Objective b**
>
> *Students build knowledge by actively exploring real-world issues and problems, developing ideas and theories, and pursuing answers and solutions.*
> *(ISTE, 2016)*

If I switch to the path mode of the Measurement tool, we can find the perimeter of any building or monument. Imagine using Google Earth to have the kids measure the distance around the school or have them discover just how big the Grand Canyon actually is.

## Project Idea: Google Lit Trips for Language Arts

One of the most innovative ways to use Google Earth as a teaching tool is the creation of a multimedia virtual tour called a Google Lit Trip. When you think about most books we assign our students, the major criticism teachers hear is: How does this relate to the real world? With Google

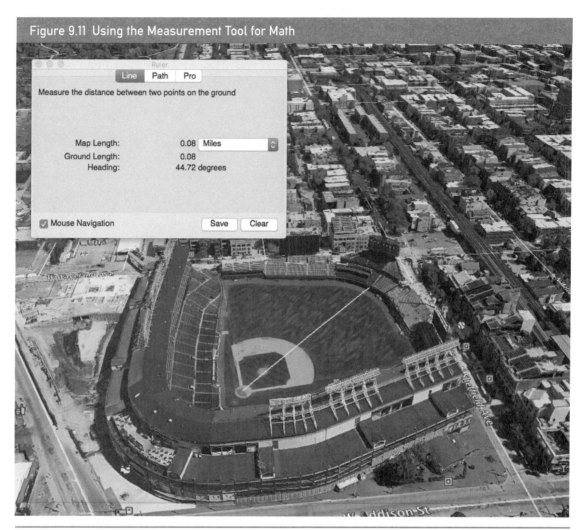

Figure 9.11 Using the Measurement Tool for Math

SOURCE: 2011 ©INEGI.

Earth, you can take your students to the actual places they are reading about in a story and engage them with questions and activities (see Figure 9.12).

The basic idea of a Lit Trip is that you create location markers about different elements of a book. Each marker contains a combination of text and various multimedia elements to provide the users with a virtual field trip related to a book they are reading. Once the tours are compiled, students can literally fly to various parts of the books and experience the sites firsthand. Take a look at a fantastic collection of Lit Trips at www.googlelittrips.com. There, you'll find dozens of trips organized for a variety of grade levels. They range from kindergarten all the way through higher education. Googlelittrips.com is an incredible resource for teachers looking to create virtual tours with their own students.

For example, a kindergarten class can take a tour of the Boston Harbor with the teacher as they explore the different locations found in *Make Way for Ducklings.* Each of the locations in the book is brought to life through text and images that encourage students to think about issues in the book and visualize the events they read about. Check out the tour online at http://www .googlelittrips.org/litTripLibrary/gradesK-5.php.

Lit Trips are a great activity for all ages of student; the older students (Grades 3–12) can create their own Lit Trips, and the younger kids can travel along a tour made by their teacher. The Lit

Trip assignment is highly engaging for students as it encourages them to explore the world through the places they've learned about in class. As we learn from West Yellowstone School librarian and technology teacher Jo Stevens, some students can't get enough of working on the interactive tours: "The students' work ethic was incredible. Some students even came in before and after school [to work on their projects]," Stevens said (as quoted in Tumbleson, 2011).

## Creating a Google Lit Trip

- Search for a location from the book you'll be reading with your class. Using the basic search function in Google Earth, type in the first location from your text. Once you navigate to the proper destination, it's time to mark the location.

Figure 9.12 Google Lit Trip Example

After the Crash

1. What happened to the main character while he was on his trip?

Directions: To here - From here

Image © 2016 CNES / Astrium
© 2016 Google

SOURCE: Used with permission of Google Inc. and Jared Covili.

- Create a *placemark* for your location. The **Placemark** tool is located along the top left corner of your Google Earth map. The icon is a yellow pushpin that marks the latitude and longitude of your current location. Once you drop a placemark on the screen, you'll find that a description window opens, allowing you to add the content for your virtual tour (see Figure 9.13).

- Add and edit text in your placemarks. With the description window open for your placemark, you're ready to customize the marker with details from the book. By default, all placemarks start as Untitled Placemark. Start by naming the placemark with an event from the book. For example, if the location depicts the scene where the animals overtake the farmhouse in *Animal Farm,* "Animal Revolution" may be an appropriate title for the placemark.

After naming the placemark, it's time to add text to the Description field. The Description field is an *HTML*-formatted text box, so you may type whatever you choose and arrange the content using HTML. The type of text is up to you, but a traditional Lit Trip includes a couple of basic elements.

1. Summary of the event from the book—usually, it's not more than a paragraph and may include a quotation or reference from the book.

   For example, from the book *Hatchet,* by Gary Paulson, I would use a summary of a chapter in the book to introduce some guiding questions:

   *Brian encounters a moose, a female with no horns, who drives him into the lake. She is relentless in her attack, and Brian quickly realizes how hurt he is. He thinks the moose has broken his ribs.*

2. Discussion questions or activity—another component of most Lit Trips is an activity prompt or discussion questions. Use these as a way to help guide the students' comprehension of the book by engaging them with various prompts. Again, from *Hatchet,*

   *What do you think will happen next to Brian?*

   *How would you try to start a fire without matches?*

Combining Google Earth with literature study allows teachers to come up with activities that are highly creative for their students. Instead of having students use this powerful tool just to make a plot summary, Jerome Burg, English teacher and technology-integration coordinator, suggests nudging them toward activities that will generate higher-order questions and more analytical thinking (Boss, n.d.a).

I mentioned that the Description field can be formatted using HTML. You may notice that, when viewed, the placemark text all combines into one large paragraph. All of the spacing you provided doesn't seem to be working. This is because you need to format items like line spacing using HTML.

There are lots of different ways to format with HTML, but let's keep this simple.

If you want a single space between your text, use the <br> tag. This means type <br> in between two lines of text, and you'll create a line break.

If you want things double-spaced, use the <p> tag. It should look something like this example from *Hatchet:*

*After all he's gone through, Brian realizes the beauty that surrounds him. He takes a moment to reflect upon how lucky he is to have survived the crash.*

*<p>*

*Discussion:<p>*

*1. Share a time in your life when you've realized something important.<br>*

*2. Why do you feel Brian's attitude is changing?*

Using a few basic HTML tags will help you format the text the way you want. It will make it easier to read for the students, and as an added bonus, you just learned a little web design. Pretty cool, huh?

- Add an image to your Lit Trip. One of the creative aspects of the Lit Trip is the ability to add multimedia to placemarks. It gives the real-world location a tie-in with the book and makes the tour much more engaging.

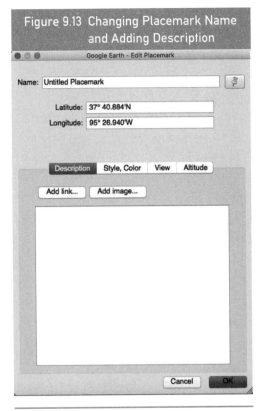

Figure 9.13 Changing Placemark Name and Adding Description

© 2016 Google Inc. used with permission. Google and the Google logo are registered trademarks of Google Inc.

So what types of images are used in a Lit Trip? Generally, the idea is to use images that illustrate the events from the book. You can use images directly from the book, such as if it's a children's book. The images could be digital photos that students took themselves. They can be images that students find on the web. The key to having an image displayed in the placemark is that the image has to exist online or in a digital format already.

To get your images in a digital format, you'll need to use a digital camera or a scanner. If you want to use images directly from the children's book, you can either scan the pages or take digital photos of the pages. Once you have digital images, you will need to get them online, so they'll display in Google Earth. There are several ways to get your digital images online. Because we're focusing on Google tools in this book, let's explore how you store your photos online using your Google account.

Google provides you with 1 ***GB*** of online storage for your digital images. As mentioned earlier, it's called Google Photos, and it's free! Here's how to find Google Photos.

1. Go to http://photos.google.com. After you sign in to Google Photos, you'll land on the **Home** tab. If this is your first time here, there won't be any content. If you're using other Google tools (like Blogger or Google+), you may find that some albums of images already exist as this is the default image storage for Google.

2. To add your photos to the library, click on the **Upload** button.

3. You'll be asked if you want to **Add** the photos to an existing album or if you want to **Create** a new album. Choose **Collections**.

4. Name the album based upon the title of the book you're using for the Lit Trip.

## Uploading Images to Google Photos

After you've set up the album structure, now you're ready to upload the images. You can upload up to five images at a time into the album. Uploading the image is much like attaching a document to an email. Here are the steps:

1. Click the **Choose File** button.

2. You'll be prompted to browse your computer to find the images you'd like to use.

3. Select up to five for upload at a time.

4. Click on the **Start Upload** button, and a few moments later, the images will be online in your Web Album.

## Adding the Image to Your Lit Trip

With your photos in Google Photos, you can now add the images to your Google Lit Trip. Each image has its own unique web address. This is necessary for the image to display properly.

- To access the address for the image, right click on the desired photo.

- Select the **Copy Image URL** or the **Copy Image Address** link in the menu. Selecting this option copies the image's web address or *URL* to the clipboard, so it can be pasted into Google Earth.

- Click on the **Add Image** button, and paste the URL for your image.

## Embedding Video in Your Lit Trip

To incorporate YouTube video clips into your Lit Trip, do the following:

1. Go to youtube.com.

2. Find your desired video.

3. At the bottom of each video in YouTube, find the **Share** button.

4. You want to use the **Embed** option.

5. Just copy that code, and paste it into your placemark. As long as the video remains on YouTube, you'll see it in your Lit Trip.

There are other options for customizing your placemarks using HTML code. I'd suggest checking the Google Lit Trip website (www.googlelittrips.org) for tons of examples. If you're not sure about how to type the necessary HTML code, you'll find dozens of websites that provide examples. A simple Google search for HTML code should move you in the right direction.

## Taking the Tour on the Road

Once you create all the placemarks you want to use in your Lit Trip, it's time to package the entire tour together into a file you can share with others (see Figure 9.14). Up to now, all the placemarks should be located in the Places section of Google Earth. Each has a separate icon and its own location on the map. We need to group all the placemarks together, so they can be saved in one file.

## Creating and Using a Folder for Your Tour

The key to packaging the placemarks is to make a folder. This container will house all the placemarks in one location. Creating a folder is simple.

1. Click on the **Add** menu and select the **Folder** option.

2. Name the folder, and provide a description of the project.

3. Choose **Save** to protect your work.

4. The new folder should be in the Places area near the placemarks. It may help to drag the folder to the top of the Places tab, with all the placemarks beneath it.

5. To add the placemarks, drag and drop each into the folder. Once a placemark is inside the folder, the icon will be indented from the main folder. You can drag placemarks around inside the folder to determine the correct order for your tour. Most start with the first event and work their way through to the end.

6. Our last major step in packaging the Lit Trip is to save the tour. Saving the project as a KMZ file (one with a.kmz extension) allows us to create a portable version of the Lit Trip.

7. To save the project, right click on the folder, and select **Save Project As** from the menu that appears.

You have successfully created a Google Lit Trip.

Now that your trip has been saved to the computer, it can be shared with others in any number of ways. Email it, post it to the web, or even transfer the file with portable storage—it's up to you.

I know this example focuses on using Google Earth to create a Lit Trip, but these virtual tours can encompass any curriculum area. Whether you're exploring volcanoes from around the world, studying a real-world example of Fibonacci's sequence, or visiting the beaches of Normandy, Google Earth is the perfect tool to see these examples firsthand.

Figure 9.14 Packaging Your Google Lit Trip in a Folder

© 2016 Google Inc. used with permission. Google and the Google logo are registered trademarks of Google Inc.

## FROM A GOOGLE GURU

One day early in the school year, I was speaking to my small high school class for students with learning disabilities about my previous experiences as a teacher. I explained to these suburban students how my first teaching job in the South Bronx involved taking a subway and a bus every day. I realized I could show them this with Google Earth, so I did.

Soon, my students were virtually at the Prospect Avenue subway stop (the 2 and 5 lines) and following the bus route to the doors of my old school. This led to the students making tours of their own lives using Google Earth. This helped students with presentation skills and was very meaningful for them. For example, we had a student who left a week early for winter break each year to see her grandmother in Brazil. She was able to show her classmates her grandmother's house and other favorite places in the area. This brought that student's interesting experience to life for her classmates. Students learned about themselves and their families' histories.

Students were able to show on Google Earth where they were born, where they went to kindergarten, and other places that held special significance in their lives. Rather than simply type an autobiography, my students with learning disabilities shared about their lives in a way that was meaningful and relevant to them and their audience, all thanks to Google Earth.

## BIOGRAPHY

Tom Mullaney

Gravelly Hill Middle School, Eland, NC, US

Educational Technology Coach

Twitter @edtechtom

Website: https://tommullaney.com/

### More Ideas for Going Google

**Other Google Earth Project Ideas**

- Use the **Historical Imagery** button to see the changes an area has made over time. This is a great way to see the history of an older school and the surrounding community. Some of the images go back several decades. It's amazing to see the growth in different parts of the world!

- Google Earth can help you explore the heavens as well as the Earth. When you click on the **Google Sky** button, your perspective immediately shifts to outer space. You'll take your students on a journey around the solar system to study the planets, constellations, stars, and National Aeronautics and Space Administration (NASA) space explorations. What an incredible way to teach your students various elements of astronomy during the daytime hours of school. Google Sky uses simulations and photography from a variety of NASA satellites to capture the universe we've only imagined until now.

Not only can you explore the universe as a whole, but Google also provides users with in-depth information on both the Moon and Mars. You'll learn historical information from various lunar expeditions and view aspects of these celestial bodies from a totally new perspective. With image overlays and photos from the Hubble space telescope, you'll feel like you were with the astronauts on one of the Apollo missions.

- Have the students record their journeys around the world. Using the **Video Camera** button, students can create screen recordings of their trips to various locations. Plug in a microphone, and the kids can actually provide their own narratives or unique travelogues to places around the globe. This is a great way for students to create personal reports about countries, states, or even cities. This file can be saved and shared for others to view as well.

## TIPS FOR THE GOOGLE CLASSROOM

- The Layers panel can quickly overtake the screen if you leave all the various data fields turned on. When you move between different layers, be sure to turn off the ones you've finished using.
- As you create placemarks of locations on the map, check to make sure they don't end up in a temporary folder. All the data will be lost if the program crashes or you forget to save properly.
- When searching for a location, the search results will include a variety of advertisements for different companies near that location. You can remove all unwanted search results by selecting the **X** in the lower right corner of the search panel.
- To ensure you have the most recent version of Google Earth, click on the **Help** menu, and select **Check for Updates Online**. Updated versions of Google Earth come out periodically, and it's important to have access to all the latest features.
- Be sure to check out Google Cardboard for a virtual way to take students on field trips using the images from Google Earth. You can access Google Earth directly in Google Cardboard if you're on an Android device.

## CHAPTER 10

# Google Photos

## FIVE Things to Know About Google Photos

1. You can sync your photos from your mobile device or computer to Google Photos.
2. You can have unlimited free storage for your photos in Google Photos.
3. Google Photos has more than 25 different filters for enhancing your images.
4. Google Photos can create movies, collages, and animations.
5. Organize your images into a variety of categories including People, Places, Things, and more.

When multimedia in the classroom comes up as a topic, a discussion of using digital images with students often ensues. Our kids all seem to have access to digital cameras (even if it's only on their cell phones), and they love taking pictures of the world around them. Says Dan Mayer, a teacher at San Lorenzo Valley High School, near Santa Cruz, California,

> I walk around with a digital camera on my phone. As I become more acquainted with my subject matter, I see examples of it everywhere. And the examples are 100 percent of the time better than what my textbook would have me use to introduce a topic. (quoted in Boss, 2008)

In the past decade, digital photo editing and multimedia project creation with these images has become an essential skill. It allows students the opportunity to develop their creativity and see the world through their own lens. It's a skill that, once learned, will be with students throughout their entire education and follow them into the modern workforce. In a recent study sponsored by Adobe, the researchers discovered the role that a creative mind plays in a productive work environment.

> Creativity, in fact, is now becoming a sought-after skill in all walks of life. According to a survey, Creativity in the Classroom, by digital media specialist Adobe, some 77% of employers and higher education lecturers quizzed said that they viewed "creativity"—interpreted

as the ability to generate ideas, developing online content, delivering persuasive, polished presentations or being imaginative problem-solvers—as "an essential or important skill," alongside the basic ones of literacy and numeracy. (Nightingale, 2011)

In this chapter we'll look at Google Photos, an amazing online tool that provides users with free storage for their photos and videos. Additionally, you'll be able to edit and share your images using this incredible tool. Finally, we'll explore some different projects you and your students can create using Google Photos.

## Getting Started With Google Photos

To access your photos in Google Photos in a browser, follow these steps:

1. Go to photos.google.com.
2. Log in with your Google account.

If you've already been using other Google services, you may find that photos already exist in your Google Photos account. Google has migrated your images from different tools such as Google+, Blogger, and Picasa Web Albums into Google Photos.

### Uploading Images Into Google Photos on a Computer

There are three options for adding images to your Google Photos account. You can choose to upload your photos directly into Google Photos, use the Google Photos Desktop Uploader, or add images to Google Photos using Google Drive.

Upload your images at photos.google.com.

1. You can upload new photos directly into Google Photos. Once logged into your account, you'll find a button to **Upload** photos.
2. You'll then be prompted to add the images to an existing album or to create a new album for the pictures. Once you've decided where the photos will be stored, the system works like attaching a file to an email.
3. Browse to find your desired photo, and select the image for upload. You can actually upload five images at a time using the direct upload to the Google Photos. Once you've selected the image(s) for upload, click **OK** for the transfer to take place.

### Google Photos Desktop Uploader

Another common way to add photos to the Google Photos is to sync your images using the Google Photos Desktop Uploader. The process couldn't be simpler.

1. Go to https://photos.google.com/apps. Here you'll find a download for the Google Photos Desktop Uploader. You'll be able to back up your images from your computer to Google Photos.
2. Installation is simple—follow the wizard, which will prompt you to different common photo folders on your computer. Select the different folders you want to sync, and photos will automatically be transferred to Google photos.

3. The last step is to select the upload size of your images. You'll be provided with two options (see Figure 10.1):

   a. High Quality: By choosing High Quality as your photo size option, you'll be given unlimited storage from Google. This does reduce the photo resolution slightly but is the preferred option for maximizing your Google Photos accounts.

   b. Original: Provides you with the highest resolution on your images. You'll be capped on storage capacity with a limit of 15 **GB** of total storage.

**Figure 10.1  Setting Up Your Google Photos**

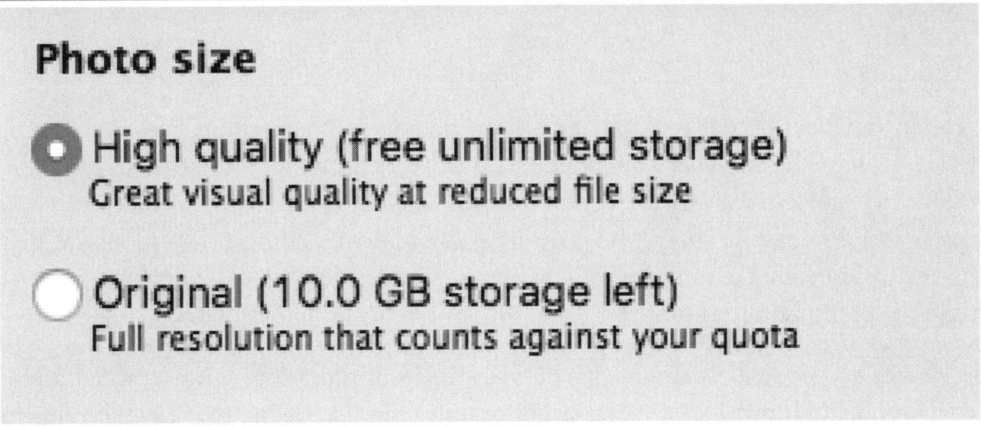

**Photo size**

◉ **High quality (free unlimited storage)**
Great visual quality at reduced file size

○ **Original (10.0 GB storage left)**
Full resolution that counts against your quota

## Uploading Images Through Google Drive

Finally, you can upload your images to Google Drive and place them inside the Google Photos folder. This option allows you to upload your photos one at a time or several in a folder.

- Go to drive.google.com.
- Click on the **New** button.
- Select **Upload File** to upload one image at a time.
- Select **Upload Folder** to choose an entire folder of images.
- With either of these options, you'll want to make sure your photos end up in the Google Photos folder within Google Drive. This will make them accessible in Google Photos.

## Downloading Your Google Photos Back to Your Computer

Google Photos is a great way to back up your photos, but how do you actually get the images from the web to your computer? It only takes a few simple steps to go from computer disaster to enjoying your pictures again.

1. Select the album you wish to download to your computer.
2. Click on the **More Options button** (three dots in the top right corner of the screen)

3. Choose **Download All,** and select your desired location for the download.

4. The photos will download in a ZIP file to your machine.

This not only serves as a form of backup, but teachers and students can use this system as a way to transfer from one computer to another. Just upload the images at home, and you can access or edit them at school.

## Why Use Google Photos?

If the idea of posting photos online seems a bit overwhelming, let's look at the advantages to uploading your images to Google Photos.

### Backup

We've gotten so reliant on our desktops or laptops that a good deal of our lives is stored on their hard drives. Imagine having your computer's hard drive crash with years of digital photos stored within. This is a problem waiting to happen for thousands of us. So, what do we do? Sure, we can burn photos to a disc, or copy them onto our external hard drives, but those solutions are all on-site, meaning they're stored in the same location as our computer. Most people don't have a good system for backing up their photos off-site.

Google Photos gives you a secure site where you can store your pictures and protect them in an off-site environment. It provides a great deal of peace of mind knowing that you'll be able to enjoy your images, even in case of a computer emergency.

### Storage

Google Photos provides you with 15 GB (or more) of free storage for your photos. As previously mentioned, one feature when setting up your Google Photos account that can increase your storage is to allow Google to optimize your photos. Optimized photos have no limits on your storage. This is a great option for backing up your photos from your smartphone!

Even if you choose not to optimize photos, with 15 GB of storage, you should have plenty of room to place your school- and curriculum-related photos as well as many of your personal photos. Don't forget, you can share digital video, too, in addition to your digital images.

### Sharing

One of the fun aspects of having your photos online is the ability to share your images with others. This is one of the misunderstood aspects of storing materials online—everything you store in Google Photos is not actually available for the world to see. *You* decide which photos you want to share publicly and which images you want to remain private.

As you upload your photos to Google Photos, you can choose whether to keep your photos private or share them with others using a secure link. Please be aware that sharing the link provides others access to your photos. Just remember the link isn't tied to a specific email address so anyone with the link can view the photos. Be careful not to share a link to photos on a website or other public forum, unless you don't mind letting others see the photos.

Sharing allows you to provide access for parents to classroom photos that have likely not been seen in students' homes. One of the advantages of sharing the photos online is the chance to let parents see some of the great things their kids are doing at school. Whether it's the term project, group presentation, class field trip, club activity, school athletic team, or even just everyday photos around the halls of the school, sharing photos in a controlled setting builds a sense of community that's amazing to witness.

## Google Photos Basics

### Organizing Photos

One of the best things about the Google Photos is the automatic tools that organize photos into a variety of groups or styles. In Google Photos images are organized into albums. This is a fast and easy way to group pictures together and share them all at once.

## Project Idea: Annotated Albums

Google Photos can be a fun way to share images, but you can also use the Albums feature as an instructional tool. Albums can provide you with an annotated collection of your photos that can be used as part of your online library.

1. Select the **Create** button (+ button along the top of the screen) and choose **Album**.
2. Select your photos for the project. You can select anywhere from two to 2,000 images to use in your album.
3. Be sure to type a title for your album.
4. Choose **Create,** and you'll have a new photo album.

To add an annotation (see Figure 10.2), select your album in your Google Photos Library.

5. Click on **More** menu (the three dots in the top right corner of the screen).
6. Choose the option to **Edit Album**.
7. You'll find the options to reorder images, add more images, add locations, or add descriptions in the top right corner of the screen.
8. Annotate your album using the annotations tool (the letter T in the top right corner). Simply type your text and move it around among images. This will allow you to create an incredible annotated web album of images.
9. Click on the **check mark** in the top left corner to complete your edits.
10. To share your Album, click on the **share icon,** and you can choose from a variety of social media and other tools for sharing.

Google Photos will also take your photos and organize them automatically into a few fun categories (see Figure 10.3). You'll love having your images grouped into People using face recognition software. Places is another fantastic feature as it will organize your images based upon where they were taken. Things takes your images and arranges them into groups based upon some of your favorite activities. You'll even find a category for all your selfies!

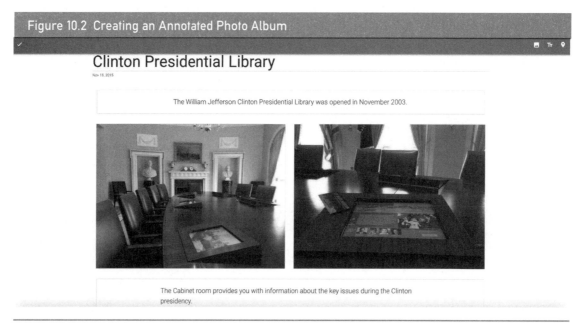

**Figure 10.2 Creating an Annotated Photo Album**

# Clinton Presidential Library

Nov 19, 2015

The William Jefferson Clinton Presidential Library was opened in November 2003.

The Cabinet room provides you with information about the key issues during the Clinton presidency.

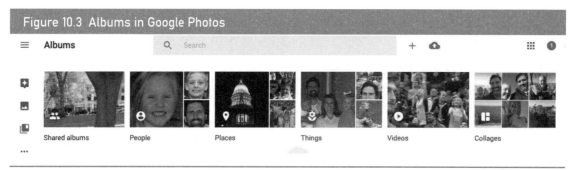

**Figure 10.3 Albums in Google Photos**

☰  Albums        🔍 Search                    +  ☁                    ⊞  ①

Shared albums    People    Places    Things    Videos    Collages

## Editing Photos

Google Photos provides some basic photo editing features that you can perform online. Although there aren't many filters and tools, having a few editing options provides students with a way to edit images in the cloud. This can be particularly helpful when using Chromebooks.

To edit a photo, click on the **pencil icon** in the top right corner of the image.

Edits are found in three different categories: Basic Adjustments, Color Filters, and Crop/Rotate. Although these are limited in scope, they each have tools worth mentioning.

*Basics Adjustments*—With this option you'll find a few tools to help you make corrections to your images in regard to light and color (see Figure 10.4). This tool is simple to use—just adjust a slider to intensify or reduce an effect.

My favorite tool is the Pop function. With Pop, you can adjust the saturation of colors in your photo and make the image more vibrant!

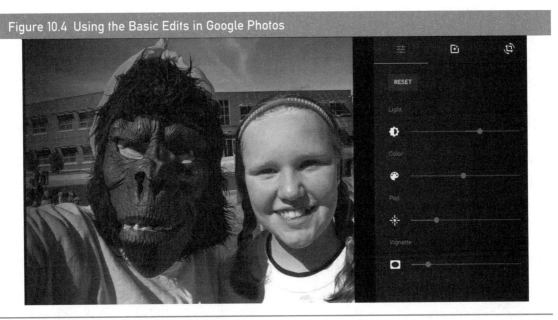

Figure 10.4 Using the Basic Edits in Google Photos

*Color Filters*—This menu provides users with 14 unique presets (all named after celestial bodies) to apply to your photos. Simply chose a filter, and it will immediately apply to your image. If you want to make any adjustments, again there is a slider you can correct. Once you've made an adjustment, you can always select **Compare Photo** to see how it looks alongside the original.

*Crop and Rotate*—These two tools allow you to recompose images and create a better focal subject (see Figure 10.5).

Cropping an image is simple, just click on a corner and drag in toward the middle of the photo. You'll find a select box will adjust to recompose the image.

Rotate allows user to straighten photos that were taken on an angle. After clicking on the **Rotate** button (a box with a curved arrow), just drag the photo into the correct position.

## Sharing Photos

Sharing an album provides parents and students with access to photos you've taken at school. Let's not forget that students can share their digital photo projects with you as well. Students sharing their photos with an instructor can provide a secure way to evaluate their work and manage classroom projects.

To share images with others, follow these steps:

1. Select the album you'd like to share (or have your students select one of their albums to share).
2. Click on the **Share** button.

Figure 10.5 Crop and Rotate Feature in Google Photos

3. Choose the method by which you'd like to share. You can use social media tools like Google+, Facebook, and Twitter, or there is a shareable link you can send through email.

4. Another option for sharing photos is to create a Shared Album. This will actually allow others to add their own photos to the album. What a fun option to create a community photo album. Use this idea at your next parents' night or classroom party!

## CREATE WITH GOOGLE PHOTOS

Google Photos has several creative and innovative tools to help your students visualize concepts and share information. In the past, photos were printed and shared with the class, glued to a poster board or taped to a classroom wall. Once students viewed the images, they were basically forgotten. Google Photos provides teachers and students with a wide array of project options to enhance learning and create lasting memories.

## Project Idea: Create a Custom Animation

ISTE-S Standard 6 Objective b

*Students create original works or responsibly repurpose or remix digital resources into new creations.*
(ISTE, 2016)

A simple photo project you can do with students is to create a custom animation using a few of your photos. This is a great way to illustrate a time lapse, like when you want to demonstrate the way plants grow over the course of several days. You can even bring a photo series to life by turning it into an animated GIF.

1. Click on the **Create** button and select **Animation**.

2. Select your photos for the project. You can select anywhere from two to 50 images to use in your animation.

3. Choose **Create,** and you'll all done!

## Project Idea: Creating a Photo Collage

One of my favorite tools in Google Photos is the Collage tool. This tool allows you to select a variety of photos and create a unique collage. The layered photos can serve to show a topic in a combination of shared images. It is a great way to focus on a subject using several photos to illustrate parts of the concept.

1. Click on the **Create** button and select **Collage**.

2. Select your photos for the project. You can select anywhere from two to nine images to use in your collage.

3. Choose the **Create** button in the top right of your screen.

4. Your collage is automatically created in a mosaic design, with images arranged in a grid with a border surrounding them (see Figure 10.6). Your images will be resized automatically to create a collection of larger and smaller photos.

1. You can make basic changes to your finished collage using the different options in the Edit menu. You'll be able to adjust color and light, crop, and apply filters to your new collage.

2. After creating the collage, a Collage option will be available in under Album menu.

## Project Idea: Creating a Movie

Another fantastic tool in Google Photos is the ability to create a video using your stills and video clips. You can add music and titles to your project, creating a fun and simple way to share your images and clips as a movie.

Movies is currently available only using mobile devices—but you can view and share your movies on any device. Creating a movie takes only a couple of simple steps:

Figure 10.6 Creating a Photo Collage

## Getting Started

1. Open the Google Photos app on your mobile device.

2. Click on the **More** button (three dots) in the top right corner of the app.

3. Select the **Movie** option under **Create New**.

4. Choose your images and videos from within Google Photos. You can select up to 50 images and clips.

5. Once the images are selected, click **Create** and your movie will be built automatically.

*Making Changes to Your Movie Project*

You'll find three different options for editing your movies: Themes, Music, and Timeline.

1. Themes: You can choose several different themes for your movie, including fun filters like Silver Screen, Vintage, and Modern Pop. Themes will provide your movie with a custom flair!

2. Music: There are many different genres of music available for use in your movie project. In fact, you'll find five categories of music with up to nine different songs in each. You're sure to find the right mood for your movie.

3. Timeline: In this option you'll be able to reorder the images and clips in your movie, trim movie clips down to size, and add images to your project (see Figure 10.7).

    a. Reordering your Images or Clips: Simply tap on an image, and drag it into the right spot in your movie timeline.

    b. Using the **scissors icon**, you can trim any video clips for your video project. Simply drag the edges of your clips to reset the start or end points of your video.

    c. Adding Images or Clips: Use the + button to select additional photos and movies to add to your project.

4. Click on the **check mark** when you're finished making edits to your project.

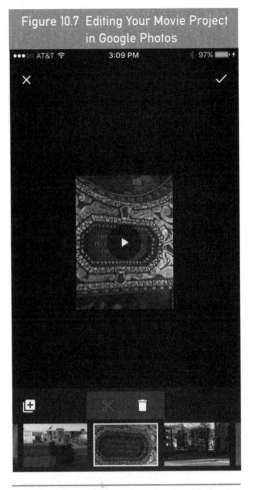

**Figure 10.7** Editing Your Movie Project in Google Photos

## FROM A GOOGLE GURU

Every day in my classroom I take pictures of students and student work. Taking pictures of students helps me to remember their names in the beginning of a semester and remember their work toward the end of a semester and beyond. I take pictures of student work, so I can share their creativity and great ideas with others.

This all sounds magical and beneficial, right? Well, it is—until it takes up all the space on my device and I can't download apps or even take a movie of my own preschooler. Digital clutter is a real problem for a millennial teacher like myself. Enter Google Photos App.

Google Photos and the Google Photos App allow me to sync the pictures taken on all my devices and store them in Google Photo with (currently free) unlimited storage. The app will automatically sync all pictures when your device is connected to Wi-Fi. When the app recognizes your storage is full, it will "offer" to delete all of the photos on your device that it has synced to the Google cloud.

Now, when I use a word like "offer" for an app, it makes it sound more like a person than an app, doesn't it? I talk about the Google Photo App as a person often because the app has a built-in assistant to help you compile your photos and even create GIFs from a group of photos taken at once, stylize photos (think Instagram without the effort), and build stories from groups of pictures. You have the choice to then save your assistant's work or not.

Google Photos allows me to save and organize all the pictures I take of student work or save from students and not have to worry about paralyzing my device with too much clutter. I can organize the work into folders that are easily searchable and, more importantly, findable. As I'm now one of the many people who have multiple Google accounts, I can add all of my google accounts and sync accordingly.

## BIOGRAPHY

Dani Sloan

University of Utah, UT, US

Instructor/Educational Technology Trainer

Twitter: @daniksloan

Google Photos is an amazing tool that is sure to bring out the creativity in your students. When used as part of your classroom, Google Photos can build community among parents, students, and schools. You can engage visual learners in innovative ways. Students see so many incredible things in the world around them, and you can help them visualize their learning both inside and outside of the classroom.

### More Ideas for Going Google

- **Let everyone share in the fun. Inside the shared albums you'll find an option to allow others to add their photos to the album. What a great way to have everyone share photos from a class event or field trip!**

## TIPS FOR THE GOOGLE CLASSROOM

- Be sure to get parental permission when taking pictures of students, especially when planning to use the images online. Your district will have a policy regarding using digital photos of students. Make sure you understand the policy and follow it.

- Take advantage of the cameras the students already have. Many of your students have cell phones in their pockets every school day. With budgetary restrictions and limited resources, it's important to note that those cell phones are digital cameras the students can use for class projects! Again—be sure to follow your district policies for device usage at school.

- A fun way to get the students involved is to have a classroom photographer. Make this a rotating position that gets to use the class camera to document what happened during the period or activity. Kids will see things that adults never imagined (and that's a good thing).

## CHAPTER 11

# YouTube

## FIVE Things to Know About YouTube

1. There is no limit to the number of videos you can upload on YouTube. Initially there is a 15-minute time limit on your first video uploads.

2. Playlists are a great way to organize content and share it with your students.

3. The YouTube Video Editor allows students to create "mash ups" of video content.

4. You can upload video from your mobile device as well as from your computer.

5. There are several ways to backup YouTube videos to your local machine including Save From.net, File Wiggler, and more.

YouTube has truly revolutionized the Internet over the past decade. We now have access to images and stories that we never imagined possible. Students are "firsthand" witnesses to world events, and they have the ability to contribute their thoughts and feelings about what they are seeing to the global community. YouTube has given unprecedented access to the globe and has influenced billions of people. And yet, it is banned in many schools and even colleges across the United States as well as in a number of countries. Why?

It would seem that access to this site is one of the most polarizing topics in school today. No matter where you stand on the issue of open access to YouTube for students, one thing is undeniable—YouTube isn't going away, and its impact will only get stronger. Many educators have embraced the site as another resource that can be used to enhance instruction and help students learn. Video is a tremendous teaching tool, and students are excited by visual instruction.

> Students today do tend to have shorter attention spans than ever before because their minds are bombarded with extraordinary amounts of visual stimulus from a young age. By using their fascination with this medium, and showing relevant course material that both directly and indirectly relates, we as educators can help bridge the academic rift that often stretches between students and their texts. (Graves, Juel, & Graves, 2006)

In this chapter, we'll explore the basics of how teachers can use YouTube to share their own original content for students by uploading their videos to YouTube. You'll learn how creating a YouTube channel can help you organize your content and provide links to other YouTube content. The chapter will show you how to help student create a mash-up video, where they remix existing content into a brand-new movie.

## TYPES OF VIDEOS ON YOUTUBE

**Current Events:** The media maximize YouTube as an outlet for sharing current news stories. You'll find the latest international news stories as told by Reuters, the AP, the BBC, *New York Times*, and more. National news outlets using YouTube include CNN, ABC, NBC, CBS, PBS, Fox News, and so on. It isn't just the media outlets either—national and local governments also share their messages using YouTube. Go check the White House Channel, and you'll be able to view behind-the-scenes content from President Obama and the White House staff.

However, news isn't just being reported by the professional sources; everyday people like you and me are recording firsthand accounts of history and sharing it through YouTube. Often, eyewitness accounts are shared across the globe as individuals upload their cell phone videos on YouTube.

**Inspirational:** Teachers understand the role that video can play in helping inspire students. On YouTube, you'll find all kinds of inspirational clips—everything from true-life stories of people overcoming challenges to historical speeches that stirred the nations.

**How-To Videos:** This is one of the best things about YouTube. With so many students (and teachers) considering themselves visual learners, YouTube is an amazing repository of 3- to 5-minute tutorials about a limitless number of topics. When it comes to technology and software instruction, you can find videos on all of the tools you have access to in your classroom. Want to learn how to use PowerPoint? What about building a classroom website using Dreamweaver? There are hundreds of training videos being created by users for users.

**Google Tools Videos:** Google has several different channels on YouTube that can help you learn directly about their tools. You'll find information on using Google Docs, Google Earth, Picasa, Blogger, Google Search, iGoogle, Gmail, Google Calendar, and more. These videos are professionally created, and they provide skill development from the very basic to the most advanced.

**Student Showcase:** Because YouTube is part of one's Google account, users are invited to share their videos with the public. This makes it a great venue for students to share their school projects with peers, teachers, and parents.

## ADDING VIDEOS TO YOUTUBE

Finding useful videos on YouTube is terrific, but you'll uncover the real influence of YouTube when you and your students share your own content with peers, parents, colleagues, and—potentially—the world. You and your students will need Google accounts to upload your videos to YouTube. The process is then fairly simple:

1. Go to YouTube.com. Sign in with your Google account.

2. Click on **Upload**.

3. There are two major ways to add video to YouTube. One is by uploading a completed video using the **Upload Video** button. The other option is to record a video using a webcam. YouTube has buttons that will guide you through each of these choices.

When uploading a video there are a few guidelines to consider:

- Videos being uploaded to YouTube can be no longer than 15 minutes and no larger than 2 *GB* in size.
- Videos can come from a variety of formats, but the most common file types include MPG, AVI, M4V, MOV, and WMV.
- Videos must not contain any commercial content that one does not have permission to share. This includes movies, TV shows, music, and live concerts.

To upload a video, do one of the following:

1. Drag and drop the clip into the upload window.
2. Or you can browse to your desired video using the **Upload Video** button.

Once you find the video and select it, an upload screen will appear. The video should already be uploading to YouTube, but you'll need to provide some basic information about the content. Some of the elements you'll add to your videos include name, description, tags, category, and privacy setting. You can control all of these settings, particularly the privacy setting. Your three choices for privacy include these:

- Public—the video is available to all YouTube users.
- Unlisted—the video is only available to those with the *URL*.
- Private—the video's owner provides access to the video by adding selected viewers.

## YOUTUBE CHANNEL

Once you start adding videos to YouTube, they become part of your YouTube channel. This is a repository of all your uploaded content. This is a great way to back up your videos, and it also becomes a convenient way to share that content with parents, students, and colleagues. Perhaps the easiest way to share related content is with a playlist from your YouTube channel (see the following section).

Here are a few things to remember about your YouTube channel:

- Your channel can be public or private (see Figure 11.1). The default setting is public, but if you want to keep the channel unavailable, choose **no** on the **Make Channel Visible** option in the **Settings** tab.

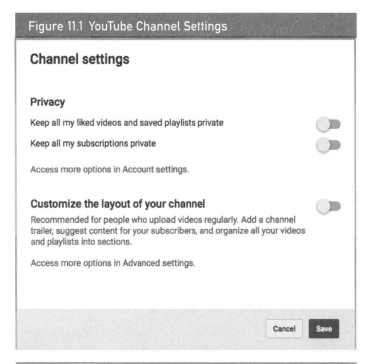

Figure 11.1 YouTube Channel Settings

**Channel settings**

**Privacy**

Keep all my liked videos and saved playlists private

Keep all my subscriptions private

Access more options in Account settings.

**Customize the layout of your channel**

Recommended for people who upload videos regularly. Add a channel trailer, suggest content for your subscribers, and organize all your videos and playlists into sections.

Access more options in Advanced settings.

Cancel  Save

- As a teacher, a fun option for your channel is to declare yourself a "guru," thus letting people know of your educational background. If you aren't interested in that label, the basic status is "user."

- You can choose what content to display on your channel. Playlists, subscriptions, favorites, and comments are all possible content for your YouTube channel.

## Creating a Playlist

Once you have your YouTube channel filled with content, a nice way to manage your videos is by organizing clips on a topic or concept into a specific playlist. With the average video in YouTube being 3 to 5 minutes long, playlists are extremely valuable to help keep a series of video tutorials together in one location. Another advantage to playlists is that they can be shared or embedded on a website. To create a playlist from your YouTube channel, follow these steps:

1. Choose the desired video from your **Uploads** or your **Favorite videos** from your YouTube channel.

2. Select the **Playlists** button from below the **Preview** screen on your YouTube channel.

3. Create a new playlist by typing a **Playlist Name** in the provided space.

4. Click **Create Playlist**.

5. You can add a video to an existing playlist by choosing the appropriate playlist and clicking **Add to Playlist**.

## Downloading a YouTube Video

I know, I know. How can I write a section about downloading a YouTube video with so much debate about access to YouTube while at school? There are some ways to avoid the debate and to use the great materials found on the site. Let's look at a few different downloading tools that can help you show educational videos to your students.

### Savefrom.net

One of the best ways to download a YouTube video is also the easiest way to download a YouTube video. With one small change to the URL of any video on YouTube, you are immediately taken to a separate site with downloading options—who knew downloading a YouTube video could be so simple? Here are the steps:

1. Type in the URL for YouTube video in the browser bar or search for the video in YouTube.

2. Once you're on the video, simply enter the letters **ss** in front of the **Y** in the YouTube URL. For example—if your URL is https://www.youtube.com/watch?v=zbsa6trTs90, add the letters **ss** to the front of the address, and you'll have https://www.ssyoutube.com/watch?v=zbsa6trTs90.

3. On this page you'll have different download options from which to choose. The most common option is an MP4—either in high definition (HD) or standard definition (SD).

4. Click the **Download** button, and your movie will download to your computer.

### File Wiggler

Filewiggler.com is a free website that allows you to download a YouTube video to your computer. You'll need to copy the URL for the video in YouTube and then go to filewiggler.com. It takes just four steps to set up your conversion.

1. Paste the URL for your YouTube video in the space provided.

2. Choose the format you plan to use for the conversion. There are several options to choose from, and they include both desktop and mobile platforms.

3. Provide an email address to File Wiggler, so they can notify you when the conversion in complete.

4. Agree to the terms, and submit the conversion.

A few minutes after you submit your YouTube version for download, you'll receive an email address that contains a link for your video. Follow the link, and download your video.

### YouTube Downloader Extension in Firefox

Another great downloading tool is found in the browser Firefox. To install this extension, you'll need to be using the Firefox browser. (It's a free download if you don't already have it on your computer.)

1. Open Firefox, and click on the **Tools** link along the top of your screen.

2. Select the **Add-ons** option from the *drop-down menu*.

3. Under the **Get Add-ons** tab, and search for **YouTube Downloader**. There are several different downloading tools available. The one I prefer is the Flash Video Downloader (YouTube Downloader)—you'll recognize it by the blue download arrow (see Figure 11.2).

4. Once you install the downloader, it will appear in your toolbar in Firefox. The arrow will be grayed out until you arrive on a video in YouTube. The arrow will turn blue once a video becomes available.

> **ISTE S Standard 6 Objective b**
>
> *Students create original works or responsibly repurpose or remix digital resources into new creations.*
> (ISTE, 2016)

5. The downloader will provide you with different options for saving the file. The primary option for playback on your computer is the MP4 file type.

6. Click the **Download** button, and a few seconds later you'll have a downloaded copy of the YouTube video.

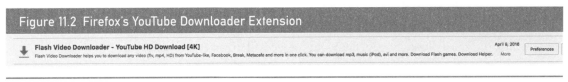
## Project Idea: Creating a Mash-Up Video in YouTube

Much of the content on YouTube is only viewable, but students can use video to *create* new content. One of the lesser-known tools in YouTube is the Video Editor. The Video Editor is a free tool in your YouTube account that allows you to edit various clips and produce an entirely new mash-up. The Video Editor allows you to do the following:

- Combine multiple videos, thus creating a mash-up of your clips.
- Edit the video by trimming the beginnings or endings of your clips.
- Add a music soundtrack from YouTube's AutoSwap collection of songs.
- Create new videos that can be published to your YouTube account.

### Getting Started With the YouTube Editor

The easiest way to access the YouTube editor is by going directly to www.youtube.com/editor. You can also access the editor through your account settings, but we won't worry about that right now. To create a mash-up video, you'll need to have the clips already uploaded to your YouTube account.

### Adding Video to Your New Mash-Up

1. In the **Media Picker**, select the clip(s) you'd like to edit.

2. Click the **plus icon** (+) on the side of the clip. This will add the clip to the storyboard. You can also drag and drop the clip down to the storyboard (see Figure 11.3).

3. You can add from one to seven clips to your new video.

### Editing Your Clips

There are three basics edits you can perform in the YouTube Video Editor: trimming, rotating, and brightness or stabilization (see Figure 11.4). One of the basic edits dealing with digital video is trimming. This allows you to pick the start and end points of any of the clips you plan to use in your mash-up.

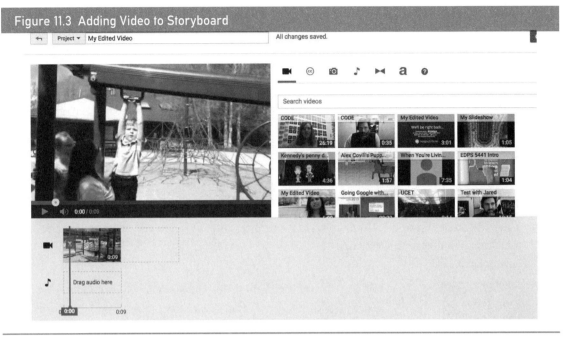

**Figure 11.3  Adding Video to Storyboard**

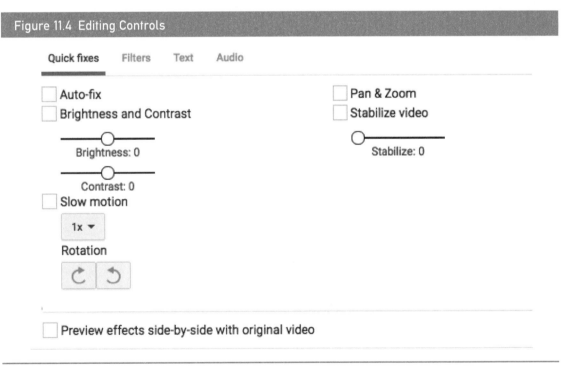

**Figure 11.4  Editing Controls**

To trim a clip in Editor, follow these steps:

1. Hover over the clip and click the **Scissors** or **Trim** icon.

2. An editing window will appear.

3. To shorten the clip, select the **Clip Trimmer** at the beginning and/or end of the video's frames (see Figure 11.5).

4. Drag the gray trimmer to your desired start or end point of the clip that you'd like to trim.

5. Once you've cut your clip, click the **Save** button. This will store your changed clip and send you back to the main editing screen.

You can edit all the clips that are currently in the Clip Trimmer. Remember, each clip is edited individually, and you'll need to click the **Save** button when you've finished trimming a particular clip.

### Clip Trimmer Basics

- The inside of the gray bar is the point of the actual edit. Don't worry about the outer edge of the Clip Trimmer; it's the inner edge that determines your edit points.

- You can trim a clip to a 15th of a second. For longer videos, if you click the **Nudge** buttons, this will nudge the trimmer forward or backward a 15th of a second from its current position.

Figure 11.5 Using the Clip Trimmer

- When you add a video clip to the storyboard, the video that appears in the player is the *actual* video from YouTube.com. This video loads and plays like any YouTube video.

Beyond trimming your clips (see Figure 11.5), the YouTube Editor also allows you to *rotate* your clips. Click on **the curled arrow** icon, and you'll be prompted to rotate the video clockwise or counterclockwise.

If your clips are shaky and difficult to watch, the YouTube Editor has a *stabilize* option. Click on the **magic wand** icon, and you'll find a check box for stabilization. You can adjust the level of your stabilization by using the slider provided.

### Adding an Audio Soundtrack

You can add a new audio track to your video in the Video Editor (see Figure 11.6). Here's how:

1. In the **Media Picker**, click the **Audio Tab**. You'll then see audio options appear. These audio tracks come from YouTube's **AudioSwap Library**.

2. Browse the AudioSwap tracks by genre and artist, or by typing a query into the **AudioSwap** search bar.

3. To preview the listed audio tracks, hover your mouse over the audio track in question and click the **Play** button. A preview will then play for you.

4. You can add an audio track to your clip in one of two ways: One way is to click the **plus** icon (+) on the audio track. Alternatively, you can drag and drop the audio track into the audio section of the storyboard.

5. The audio track cannot be trimmed in the YouTube Video Editor. This means you cannot select portions of the soundtrack; the audio will start at its beginning and end when the video ends.

6. Deleting an audio track is simple. Just click the **X** icon on the audio track in the storyboard. You can also replace the audio track by dragging another track from the clips down to the storyboard. The new track will immediately replace the old track.

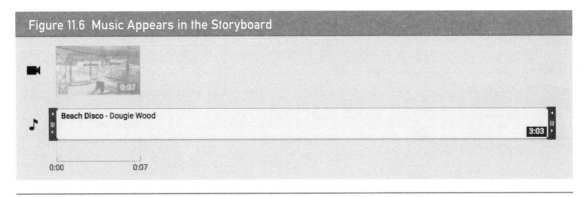

7. The video has its own audio as well as a soundtrack. You can adjust the volume to play only the soundtrack, to play just the video's audio, or move the slider somewhere in between for a mixture of both inputs.

## Creating Transitions

Because we're combining two or more videos into our mash-up, adding transitions is an effective way to blend the videos together (see Figure 11.7).

1. Click on the **Transition** icon along the top set of tools. It resembles a bow tie.

2. Choose your desired transition from the list that appears.

3. Drag the transition in between the two clips in the storyboard.

Figure 11.7 Transition Option

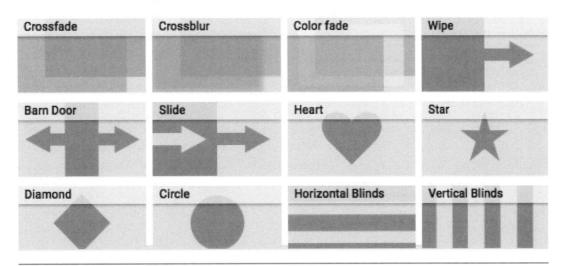

## Publishing Your Final Video

The final steps in creating your mash-up video involve naming the new project and publishing the video to your YouTube channel (see Figure 11.8). The controls for this are found in the top right corner of the editor.

1. Type the name for your mash-up video in the window provided.
2. Click the **Publish** button.

Depending on the new video's length, it may take a few minutes to process. You can check on the video's processing status on the My Videos page of your account. Once completed, the new video you created will have an entirely separate URL of its own.

### Figure 11.8  Publishing Your New Video

© 2016 Google Inc, used with permission. Google and the Google logo are registered trademarks of Google Inc.

## Project Idea: Creating a Photo Slideshow

The Photo Slideshow feature in YouTube combines two of Google's most creative products, Google Photos and YouTube. Imagine having your students tell stories using great images and music.

1. Go to https://www.youtube.com/upload. On the right side of the screen, you'll find an option for **Photo Slideshow**.

2. Immediately, you'll be asked to select images from your Google Photos albums. You can choose images from as many different albums as you would like.

3. The settings on your slideshow are pretty basic; in fact, there are three editing controls: Slide duration, Slide effect, and Transition.

4. Additionally, you can select a background audio track for your slideshow. There are more than 150,000 songs to choose from with music from a variety of genres. Unfortunately, there isn't an option to upload your own music—but this also means that students won't have to worry about any form of copyright violation as well.

5. Click **Upload**, and you're done (see Figure 11.9). Your video will appear on your YouTube channel within a few moments.

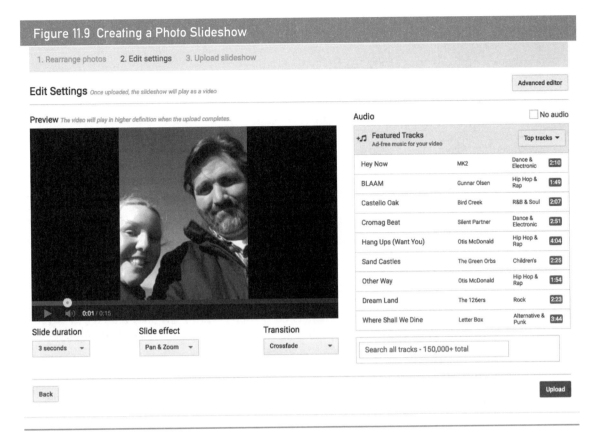

Figure 11.9 Creating a Photo Slideshow

## FROM A GOOGLE GURU

In the Tintic School District at Eureka Elementary, there has been a Christmas tradition of staging an operetta where every student performs, with the sixth grade having all the speaking parts. This tradition has gone on for about 100 years and has grown in size. The elementary does their production at Tintic High School. They put on a dress rehearsal where the high school students can watch and also parents who can't come to the evening performance. The dress rehearsal though has become very popular, so it was decided that both the elementary and high school students would not be able to go but would have to watch the performance via streaming.

As the technology director, I was unfamiliar with how to create a streaming event. I looked at USTREAM and a couple of other programs but then saw a live streaming event from *Salt Lake Tribune* done over YouTube. I then checked my account to see if I was able to stream and found out that I had to apply to do that, so I applied, was accepted, tested my streaming capability on my Mac computer, purchased a webcam, set up the webcam, tested it during a practice rehearsal, found out it worked, and set up and broadcast the operetta via streaming on YouTube. During the performance we had up to 16 connections, which accounted for seven classrooms watching and an additional nine connections for people outside of our school also watching. After the event, the operetta was posted on YouTube, and in the past month there have been 442 additional views—not bad for an elementary school with only 90 students.

## BIOGRAPHY

Tom Nedreberg

Tintic School District, Eureka, UT, US

District Technology Director

Twitter: @tom_nedreberg

**More Ideas for Going Google**

Other video projects can include these:

- YouTube has a repository of videos just for students and teachers. Go to www.youtube.com/education, and you'll find a collection of videos in the primary and secondary education categories. Here you can find video tutorials from sources like Khan Academy. You can also find resources from PBS and TedEd.

- Check out Zaption or Edpuzzle as third-party tools that can enhance your YouTube videos. Both of these tools provide teachers with options to add a variety of assessments as "wrappers" to the video content. For example, you can have multiple-choice questions appear alongside your YouTube video. Charts can also be embedded into a project as a great option to expand learning.

- Subscribe to other educators' YouTube channels. Part of the allure of YouTube is the social side of sharing videos. By finding and subscribing to other teachers' YouTube channels, you'll be developing a PLN with educators from around the globe. These relationships can be very beneficial as your PLN can help you find additional resources.

## TIPS FOR THE GOOGLE CLASSROOM

- Preview videos before using them to determine appropriate and relevant content. Many YouTube videos get right to the point, but others may need to be scanned to ensure you only show the relevant content to strengthen your curriculum. Even though students like watching videos, no one wants to watch a long clip that doesn't relate to what he or she is learning.

- Downloading a video before showing it in class provides you a security net with your local network. Rather than relying on the Internet to be up and running at the very moment you need it, downloading the videos in advance provides you with the assurance that you'll have access to your clip.

- Be sensitive to the guidelines and policies of your local school or district. Although there are many good things about YouTube for education, there are also many justified concerns that local officials have about opening up a public video service to young people. Be an advocate for effective instruction using video, but don't be overbearing with demands for access.

# PART III

# Critical Thinking and Problem Solving

Modern learners have access to so much more information than previous generations. One of the biggest challenges to students today isn't finding information; it's evaluating the information they've found. This is reflected in the following guidelines for 21st century learning skills.

Students should be able to

- Effectively analyze and evaluate evidence, arguments, claims, and beliefs.
- Analyze and evaluate major alternative points of view.
- Synthesize and make connections between information and arguments.
- Interpret information and draw conclusions based on the best analysis.
- Reflect critically on learning experiences and processes (Partnership for 21st Century Skills, 2004).

As we work with students it is more important now than ever before that we help them uncover information rather than simply trying to cover your material. This is reflected in the following quote from *Teaching the 21st Century Learner:*

> With the rate of information growth continuously accelerating, higher education today must place less emphasis on the amount of material memorized and more weight on making connections, thinking through issues, and solving problems. We must discard the notions that schools can teach everything every student will need to know. (Rogers, Runyon, Starrett, & Von Holzen, 2006)

## IS GOOGLE MAKING US STUPID?

Google's primary focus since its inception has been that of searching. Google is a place to find information. Although Google's search engine has helped students find a great deal of content on the Internet, one of the largest issues surrounding its use in education is the notion that the search engine is "making us stupid" (Carr, 2008). Many in education feel that Google searches have halted our students' ability to think critically and to solve problems. Take this example of author Nicholas Carr (2008), reflecting upon his ability to process new information in the Google era.

> Over the past few years I've had an uncomfortable sense that someone, or something, has been tinkering with my brain, remapping the neural circuitry, reprogramming the memory. My mind isn't going—so far as I can tell—but it's changing. I'm not thinking the way I used to think. I can feel it most strongly when I'm reading. Immersing myself in a book or a lengthy article used to be easy. My mind would get caught up in the narrative or the turns of the argument, and I'd spend hours strolling through long stretches of prose. That's rarely the case anymore. Now my concentration often starts to drift after two or three pages. I get fidgety, lose the thread, begin looking for something else to do. I feel as if I'm always dragging my wayward brain back to the text. The deep reading that used to come naturally has become a struggle.

Is this the case? Is Google at the root of our students' inability to focus on in-depth information and to solve problems using the data found in a typical search?

In a 2008 research study, Dr. Gary Small (quoted in Dretzin, 2010) of UCLA explored the amount of brain activity someone has while conducting a Google search. The findings were staggering. There was almost twice as much brain activity from researching on Google versus reading a book. Small noted that there is a great deal of activity taking place in the frontal lobe of the brain. "This is the decision-making part of the brain. It makes sense because we know we're making lots of decisions when we're searching online."

So, maybe Google isn't really making our students stupid. Rather, it looks like students make hundreds of decisions during the time when they are conducting searches. Students are using the search results to determine relevance to their topic; they are establishing relationships between various sites' content. Google is helping our students reach additional skills for 21st century learners such as the following:

- Use various types of reasoning (inductive, deductive, etc.) as appropriate to the situation.
- Analyze how parts of a whole interact with each other to produce overall outcomes in complex systems (Partnership for 21st Century Skills, 2004).

In this section, we'll explore how Google can play a role in developing critical-thinking skills and help students solve problems. We'll look at how Google can be used to access information and utilize it to improve their researching for school. As part of our discussion, we'll focus on Google's search engine and aggregating information with Google.

## CHAPTER 12

# Google as a Searching Tool and Advanced Search

## FIVE Things to Know About Google Search

1. Using Google's Advanced Search will improve and focus search results.

2. Google can search for specific types of files including images, PowerPoints, PDFs, and more.

3. Google Translate translates between dozens of languages.

4. Google Custom Search can provide teachers with a content search on specific teacher-selected websites.

5. Google's time-saving searches can help your students find quick reference material on the Internet.

It's the number one way in which you use Google. Before there was Gmail, Docs, or Earth, there was Google's search engine. Google is one simple site that changed everything we do on the web on a daily basis.

It is estimated that Google performs more than 40,000 search queries every second on average, which translates to more than 3.5 billion searches per day and 1.2 trillion searches per year worldwide (Google Search Statistics, n.d.).

So the question is, why? What makes the Google search engine the first choice for finding information for millions of people every day? According to ConsumerSearch (2011), Google remains the world's number one search engine for a number of reasons.

> **ISTE S Standard 3 Objective b**
>
> *Evaluate the accuracy, perspective, credibility, and relevance of information, media, data, or other resources.*
> *(ISTE, 2016)*

Google remains the favorite choice of both users and expert reviewers, who praise its speed, relevant results and ease of use. Google has such cutting-edge features as the ability to search images, videos and blogs, and one can use Book Search to preview text from Google's selection of digitized books.

We love Google for the same reasons as our students: It's easy to find information quickly, from a variety of sources, and in several different media types. With one search engine, we can find websites, PowerPoints, images, videos, blog posts, maps, and more.

Google Search has empowered us as teachers, but more importantly it has transformed our students into knowledge sources as well. Before the Internet and, specifically, before Google, knowledge was the primary domain of the teacher. Now, our students are capable of finding information quickly and contributing more to the classroom conversation.

We have the opportunity with today's technology to access a great deal of information, and quickly. You can be sitting there watching TV and somebody might bring up a comment and you can say, "Let me check that, let me verify that," and instantly we Bing it or Google it. (Bulley, 2011)

The next few sections will explore some of the hidden tools included in Google's Advanced Search and Google Custom Search. Each of the tools can help you and your students find the right information on the Internet.

## ADVANCED SEARCH

As people search with Google, a common complaint is the number of unrelated searches that come back with the results. When we search, we want to know how to find the most relevant information and how to filter out a lot of the unwanted material that comes in a normal search. Google wants to help you access the content you're looking for while minimizing unnecessary results. I mean, come on, who really needs access to over half a billion search results about the food product Spam (see Figure 12.1)?

Boolean searches are a possible solution, but who wants to remember to use plus signs or how to exclude terms from one's search? Google has built in a great solution for maximizing results—the Advanced Search option.

After you conduct your next basic search on Google, click on **Advanced Search,** located in the settings (small gear icon) *drop-down menu* in the top right side of the screen.

Let's look at how you can reduce search results and find better resources using the Advanced Search feature and a recent national news story. If a student types "Joplin" into the basic Google Search box, the results in Figure 12.2 are what come up.

Like many Google searches, you'll find that mixed in with information about the town of Joplin, Missouri, and the disaster from a tragic tornado, there are references to Scott Joplin and Janis Joplin—great topics but not the information you were looking for with your search.

With a basic Google search, any reference that includes the term "Joplin" is part of the results. That's why Janis and Scott Joplin make the list and why you get frustrated with the 26,400,000 other items that returned with the search. We need to get more specific and use better search techniques to help us refine our results.

Now, let's conduct the same search but using the Keywords feature of Advanced Search to help us get the results we're looking for (see Figure 12.3).

Figure 12.1 Example of Millions of Search Results Using Google

Figure 12.2 Standard Search Results in Google

Figure 12.3  Advanced Search Will Build Your Search With Keywords

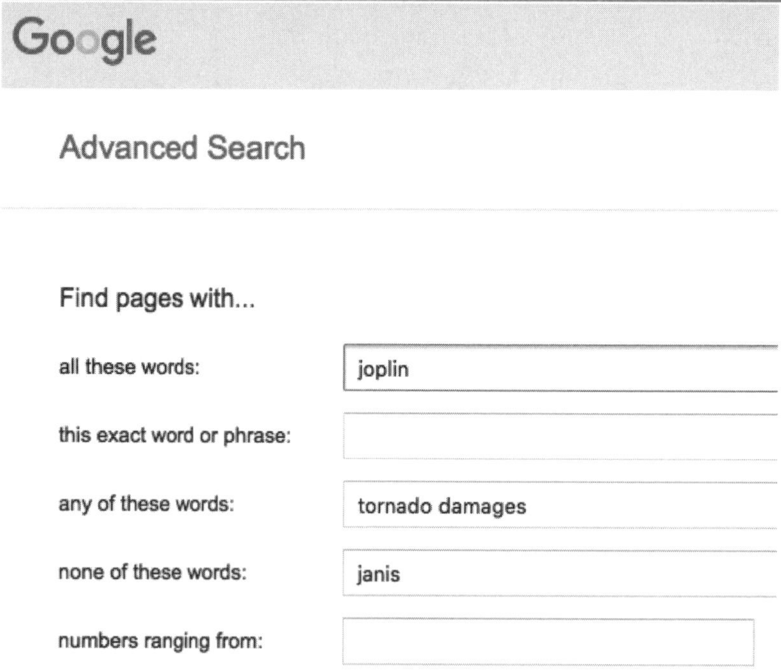

## Google

### Advanced Search

Find pages with...

| | |
|---|---|
| all these words: | joplin |
| this exact word or phrase: | |
| any of these words: | tornado damages |
| none of these words: | janis |
| numbers ranging from: | |

### FUN SEARCHING TIP—TRY USING THE VOICE SEARCH OPTION IN GOOGLE CHROME

- Click on the **Microphone** icon in the Google Search box.
- Plug in your mic, or use the computer's built-in microphone.
- You may need to allow Google search to access the microphone in your computer.
- Say your search term aloud.
- Watch the results come in!

## ADVANCED SEARCH FEATURES

When searching with Google, a few advanced search options will help you and your students get more targeted results. Here are a few tips for getting the most out of your Google searches.

- *Keywords:* In Advanced Search, adding additional terms or key words is vital to refining your search and making the most relevant sites come to the forefront of your results. You can add key words in the **all these words** field. This will set the order of your results. Instead of looking for Joplin, Missouri, we're now looking for damages in Joplin.

- *Phrases:* Another important element of searching with Google Advanced Search is linking two words together as a phrase. When you utilize the field **this exact wording or phrase**, your search limits the results to only your key words when they are listed together. For our example, the results with the phrase "Joplin tornado" are given the top priority in our search. This means anything dealing with the singer Janis Joplin or the composer Scott Joplin won't display in our results.

- *None of These Words:* Many times, a search will include related terms due to the large amount of material on the web. Another way to refine your search is to exclude pages that have **any of these unwanted words**.

Just using a few simple key-word filters in our search can change the results dramatically. Earlier, we had more than 26 million results by using Google Basic Search and the term "Joplin." Now, after using Google's Advanced Search, we have dropped to 464,000 results. This means we got rid of more than 84 percent of unwanted search results. As we go through the list of results, we will find that the top listings all deal directly with damages from the tornado due to our use of specific key words.

## Need More Tools?

As we've just learned, Advanced Search can help you filter your results when you manually type in key words and phrases. If you continue down the Advanced Search menu options, though, you'll find a heading that says **Then narrow your search by?** Here, you'll have access to filters by site, file type, usage rights, and more (see Figure 12.4). Let's explore a few of these in greater detail.

*File Type:* Another terrific use for Advanced Search is to search for a specific file type (see Figure 12.5). As you know, a standard search in Google provides you with a list of websites that you can use as resources for information. What if you really need a PowerPoint or an Excel spreadsheet, though? It would be almost impossible to search through the pages of results, hoping to find a file amidst the numerous sites—unless, of course, you use Google's Advanced Search to help you find what you're looking for.

Under the File Type heading, you can filter for a specific extension on a file. There are 10 different file types that can serve as filters for your content. Just type in your desired topic, and select the appropriate file type. This is a great way to find a teaching resource or a form on the district website. For your students, it's a fantastic resource for finding examples of various multimedia projects.

*Search Within a Site or Domain:* This filter gives you the choice to search for a specific resource on a particular site. You can perform your search on one website versus searching the entire Internet. This can be very helpful when searching on a large site with thousands of possible pages.

**Figure 12.4 More Tools in Advanced Search**

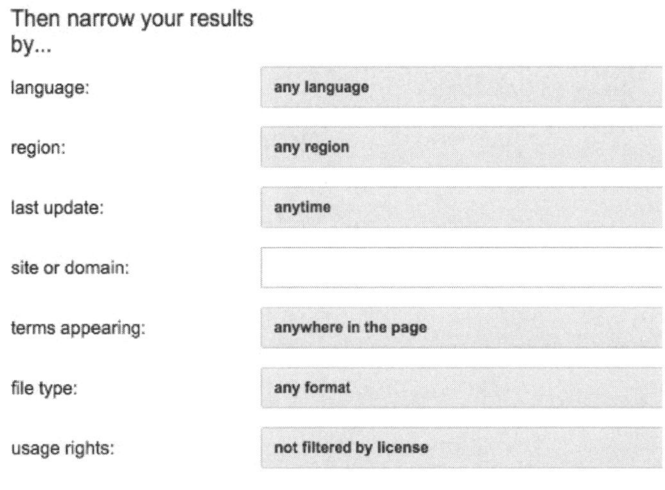

Then narrow your results by...

| | |
|---|---|
| language: | any language |
| region: | any region |
| last update: | anytime |
| site or domain: | |
| terms appearing: | anywhere in the page |
| file type: | any format |
| usage rights: | not filtered by license |

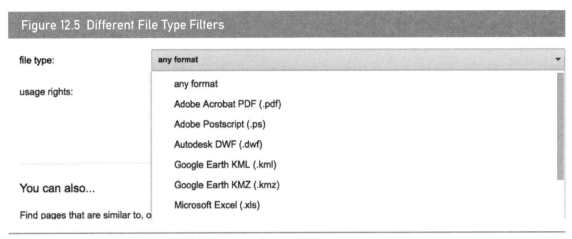

Figure 12.5 Different File Type Filters

file type:

any format

| any format |
| Adobe Acrobat PDF (.pdf) |
| Adobe Postscript (.ps) |
| Autodesk DWF (.dwf) |
| Google Earth KML (.kml) |
| Google Earth KMZ (.kmz) |
| Microsoft Excel (.xls) |

usage rights:

You can also...

Find pages that are similar to, o

*Usage Rights:* This filter is extremely useful if you're planning to search for images or other multimedia content. A basic Google search provides user with access to an amazing amount of material. The problem is that Google doesn't provide users with copyright access to any of the content coming back in search results. Google may show you thousands of images, but that doesn't mean you have permission to use them in your school projects! Usage rights breaks down multimedia content into a variety of areas—all of which eliminate content for which copyright permission has not been provided.

After using a few of these Advanced Search techniques, you may never perform a basic Google Search again. Advanced Search isn't a cure-all for your Google queries, but it can dramatically improve your ability to find the right resources on the web.

## INSTANT RESULTS

Google Instant is a new way to view your search results while you are typing your search term. In a nutshell, while you start typing a search term, Google Instant will begin to predict your possible searches and instantly show results.

### Why Google Instant?

In the world of search results, speed is essential. Google felt that using predictive text and results could save users time in conducting their routine searches. Less time typing and searching means more time learning.

Using Google Instant means you only need an initial idea to begin your search. As soon as you begin typing the letters, Google will share possible conclusions to your search. Because you don't need to finish typing your search term, you'll reach the content more quickly than ever. With Google Instant, you don't even need to hit the Search button!

Now, I know there are those of you out there who want no part of predictive results. If you don't want to use Google Instant, you can always turn it off by following these steps (see Figure 12.6):

Figure 12.6 Turning Off Google Instant

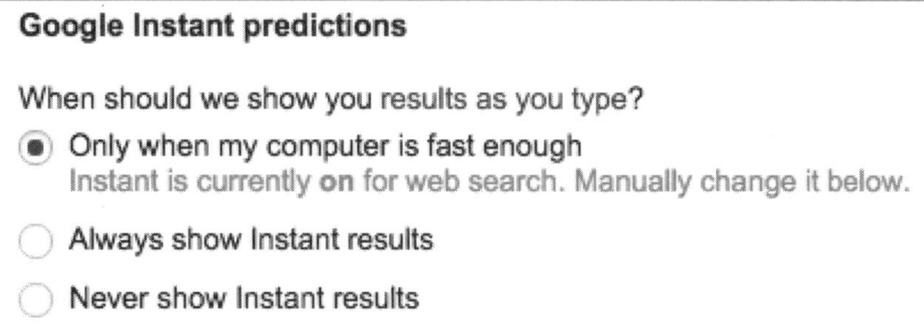

**Google Instant predictions**

When should we show you results as you type?

⦿ Only when my computer is fast enough
Instant is currently **on** for web search. Manually change it below.

◯ Always show Instant results

◯ Never show Instant results

1. Go into the **Search Settings** on Google.com.

2. About halfway down the page, you'll find the option, **Never show Instant results**. Click the button, and you've disabled Google Instant. You can always turn it on again later.

For those of you who like the sound of this searching tool, here is what's in it for you and your students:

- *Faster Searches:* By predicting your search and showing results before you finish typing, Google Instant can save 2 to 5 seconds per search. Imagine how much time the average student can save on one research project!

- *Smarter Predictions:* Even when you don't know exactly what you're looking for, predictions help guide your search. The top prediction is shown in grey text, directly in the search box, so you can stop typing as soon as you see what you need.

- *Instant Results:* Start typing, and results appear right before your eyes. Until now, you had to type a full search term, hit return, and hope for the right results. Now results appear instantly as you type, helping you see where you're headed, every step of the way (Google, 2016).

## KNOWLEDGE GRAPH

First introduced in 2012, the Knowledge Graph is Google's next attempt to consolidate information into easily accessed panels of content. Let's look at the example of the 2016 presidential election. Many people may be looking to find out information about a candidate such as Donald Trump. By conducting a basic search on Donald Trump, you'll find the same great access to links and other web content, but along the right side of your results, you'll find a summary of facts about Mr. Trump that provides a snapshot of information (see Figure 12.7).

The Knowledge Graph can also show how many pieces of data are related to one another. For example, many people who are searching for Donald Trump are also interested in learning about other figures from that time period, or they may want to have quick access to facts about other presidential candidates. To access this related content, you'll simply click on the **People Also Searched for** option at the bottom of the information panel. A panel of related content will display across the top of the screen, allowing you to quickly change your search to

Figure 12.7 Google Knowledge Graph

## Donald Trump

Businessperson

Donald John Trump is an American businessperson and media personality. He is the chairman and president of The Trump Organization and the founder of Trump Entertainment Resorts. Wikipedia

**Born:** June 14, 1946 (age 69), Queens, New York City, NY

**Net worth:** 4 billion USD (2015) Forbes

**Spouse:** Melania Trump (m. 2005), Marla Maples (m. 1993–1999), Ivana Trump (m. 1977–1992)

**Children:** Ivanka Trump, Tiffany Trump, Donald Trump, Jr., Eric Trump, Barron Trump

**Education:** Wharton School of the University of Pennsylvania (1968), More

On the issues: Economy and jobs

"Raising the prevailing wage paid to H-1Bs will force companies to give these coveted entry-level jobs to the existing domestic pool of unemployed native and immigrant workers in the U.S., instead of flying in cheaper workers from overseas," wrote Trump.

similar content to your original query. Google's Knowledge Graph uses data compiled for billions of searches to provide this carousel of related searches.

## GOOGLE IMAGE SEARCH

Google Image Search is both a blessing and a curse for education. It is a huge benefit to your classroom because Image Search can help you and your students find an enormous amount of visual content from the web (see Figure 12.8). You can find pictures to illustrate concepts in a report or presentation. It's amazing the power that an image can have in developing content knowledge. After all, it is no surprise that a picture is said to be worth 1,000 words.

But then there's the curse of Google Image Search. Because Google's search engine looks at everything on the web, it can be difficult to filter out inappropriate content. By default, Google is searching only for the term you or your student typed; it isn't trying to determine the appropriateness of the images themselves.

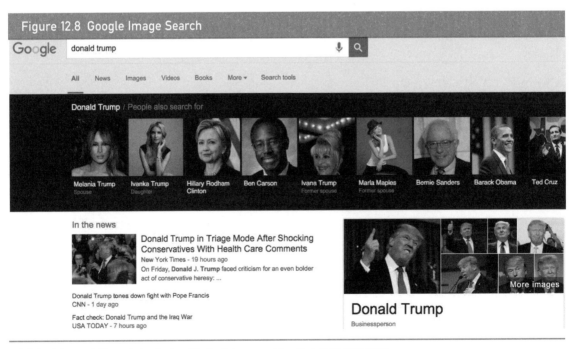

Figure 12.8 Google Image Search

Another big issue with Google Image Search is copyright. Just because Google helped you find a series of images doesn't mean you have permission to use them. Remember, all the images that Google locates in its searches are already on the web; someone put those images on a website, and Google found them. Before your students use the pictures in a project, in many cases you still need to get permission from the original owner.

In spite of the issues surrounding Google Image Search, it is a wonderful tool, and it can help your students see information in many new ways. Let's take a closer look at how to use the tool.

## Finding and Saving an Image

To find and save an image using Google Images, do the following (see Figure 12.9):

1. Go to google.com and click on the **Images** link in the top left corner of your screen.

2. Type your search term in the **Google Search box**.

3. Your results will come back as a giant grid of images. Hover your mouse over a specific image, and you'll receive additional information about the picture.

4. To save a particular image, double-click on the thumbnail version. The image will display in its own window.

5. Right click on the image, and choose **Save Image As** from the menu on the screen.

Figure 12.9 Saving an Image From Google Images

© 2016 Google Inc. used with permission. Google and the Google logo are registered trademarks of Google Inc.

## Additional Search Options in Google Images

Besides saving images, there are a variety of filters in the Google Images search function that can help you find and use the images you're looking for in the database (see Figure 12.10). Once you conduct a basic image search, you'll find an option Search Tools that provides you with several useful options.

*Sorting by Relevance:* Use the **Sort by relevance** option to organize your results by subject. Instead of looking through hundreds of unrelated images, you can see images arranged by a similar feature. Type "mountains" into the **Images search box**, and you'll find that several categories of mountains are available for viewing. When you click on the **Sort** option, the mountains will be arranged based upon their category.

*Size:* You can filter image results by their size (click **Any size** at any time to get back to unfiltered results):

Use these options if you want to see results for a specific range of sizes.

- Click **Medium** to find images with resolutions between 400 x 300 pixels and 1024 x 768 pixels.

- Click **Large** to find images with resolutions bigger than 1024 x 768 pixels.

- Click **Icon** to find square images with the following resolutions: 50 x 50, 64 x 64, 96 x 96, 128 x 128, and 256 x 256.

It will also show you images with widths and heights less than or equal to 50 pixels.

For most pictures, you'll want to look at the largest size possible. Why? Once you download an image, you can always resize it to be smaller if necessary. However, if you download a small version of an image, you may not be able to increase the size without pixelating it, which distorts the image.

*Color:* You can filter results by color (click **Any color** at any time to get back to unfiltered results):

- Choose **Full color** to see the greatest number of photos available. However, you can filter for **Black and white** if you only want to see those types of images.
- Click a colored square under the **Specific color** link to find images containing that particular color. For our earlier example of mountains, clicking on either **red** or **orange** will result in many of your images having a desert or red rock mountain landscape.

*Type:* The second group of links filters results by their type. Google Images can automatically detect whether an image is a face, a photograph, clip art, or a line drawing (click **Any type** at any time to get back to unfiltered results).

*Time:* Allows you to filter images based upon their upload date. This is great for finding recent images that relate to your content. You can choose a variety of time options including the past day, week, month, or year, or create your own custom date search.

*Usage Rights:* Using Usage Rights will help you and your students avoid selecting images for which you don't have copyright permission. Within Usage Rights you'll find several different options for selecting images, but the one that will provide you with the biggest library is Labeled for Reuse.

A hidden gem of image search is the ability to search for information on a topic using the images themselves. How often have you seen an image and you can't quite remember the information

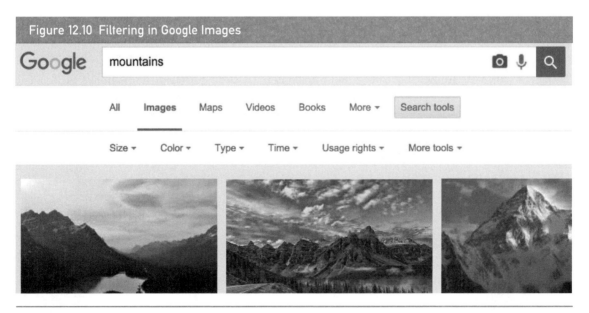

Figure 12.10  Filtering in Google Images

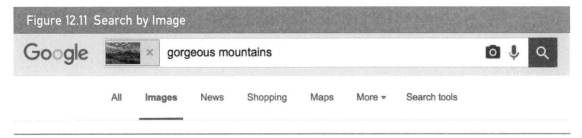
Figure 12.11 Search by Image

Google  gorgeous mountains

All  **Images**  News  Shopping  Maps  More ▾  Search tools

about the subject? Well, using Search by Image (the camera icon in the search box), you don't have to perform your search using text, rather you simply click and drag a photo into the search box (see Figure 12.11)! Immediately Google will search the web for information about the image. Many times the search will result with content about the history of the image, complete with the background of the subject in the picture.

## SAFESEARCH: PROTECTING STUDENTS FROM INAPPROPRIATE IMAGES

I mentioned earlier that a big concern of many teacher and parents is students being exposed to inappropriate pictures in Google Images. The Google Images search lets you search with a filter called SafeSearch, which should keep adult images out of your results (see Figure 12.12). The default is a moderate filter setting, but you can change that by doing the following:

1. Click on the **SafeSearch preferences** on the right side of the screen on your Google Images results page.

2. In the drop-down menu, select the level of filter you'd like to enable. Choose from: **Off**, meaning no filtering is taking place; **On**, meaning that Google will filter explicit results.

3. The settings will be immediately changed to your chosen selection.

4. You can **Lock** your SafeSearch preferences by going to your Google account settings.

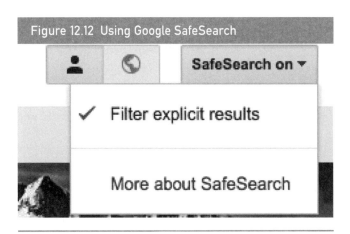
Figure 12.12 Using Google SafeSearch

SafeSearch on ▾

✓  Filter explicit results

More about SafeSearch

## GOOGLE BOOK SEARCH

So far, we've looked at many different ways Google can be used to search for information. One of the key educational sources of information for our students is that of books. For most of us, books were the only way we could conduct research when we were in school. Today, books are still valuable resources for information, but now there's a new way to find them.

Google is committed to creating digital copies of books and storing them within the Google databases. These books are free for you to access and read online. Finding them is as easy as searching for other content with Google. Here's how it works:

1. Go to google.com and click on the **More** link on the menu across the top of the screen.

2. In the drop-down menu, select the **Books** link.

3. The Google Books entry page will display. Here, you can search for books by typing in a key word, title, author, or line from a specific book.

4. Click on a book title, and you'll see basic info about the book, just like you'd see in a card catalog. You might also see a few snippets from books—sentences that use your search term in context.

5. If a publisher or author has given Google permission, you'll see a full page from the book and be able to browse within the book to see more pages. If the book is out of copyright, meaning the book is now in the public domain, you'll see a full page, and you can page forward or back to see the full book.

6. Clicking on **Search within this book** allows you to perform more searches within the book you've selected.

7. Last, you can add the book to a digital library within Google Books, so you can always go back to the book again later.

Google Books is an ambitious project, but its impact can and will be felt by schools for years to come. Who knows? There may be a day where the classroom is full of books, but the shelves are all empty.

## GOOGLE'S SEARCH TRICKS

Google has limitless amounts of information to search through. At times, it can seem overwhelming. To make the information more manageable, Google has provided some ready-reference categories of basic information that you can search with your students.

The advantage to using these time savers is that your students can find this information quickly, and much of the data are updated in real time. To try any of these searches, go to Google.com, and use the search box. Let's look more closely at a few of these search tips.

*Weather:* When you type "weather" and the name of a city or zip code in the Google Search box, Google will immediately load a 4-day forecast for that spot. You'll also get the current conditions for that location. This information would be great for studying the weather in a science class or as part of an elementary weather unit.

*Example search: weather 90210*

*Unit Conversion:* You can use the unit conversion search to make quick reference to a variety of measurements. You can convert distances, weights, volumes, and more to help your students understand the different units of measurement. Just type the desired conversion, and let Google take care of the rest.

*Example search: 2,000 feet in miles*

*Dictionary:* Google can help your students find definitions for unknown words. Just type "define" along with the word, and Google will search the web for a list of definitions. Along with the definitions is a reference to the site that provided the information.

*Example search: define education*

*Calculator:* One of the hidden gems in Google Search is a built-in calculator. Now, you might think that this calculator can only perform basic functions like addition, subtraction, multiplication, and division, but it can handle so much more. Google Calculator can perform operations such as tangents, sine, percentages, and so on. The hardest part of using Google Calculator is knowing how to type the equations. If you can type it, Google can solve it.

*Example calculation: 5\*9+(sqrt 10)^3=*

*Fill in the Blank:* How many times have you gone to Google to search for the answer to a specific question? Fill in the Blank is the answer to your search needs. Type your statement and put an asterisk in the blank part of your query. The search results will return with your answer bolded in the site descriptions.

*Example search: Cheese is made of \**

*Public Data:* This search provides you with information about recent trends in population and unemployment rates across the United States. Type your desired search, either population or unemployment, and then the state for which you'd like the data. Google will provide you with a graph summarizing recent trends for that data search (see Figure 12.13). This could be used in a geography or business class when looking for current information and trends.

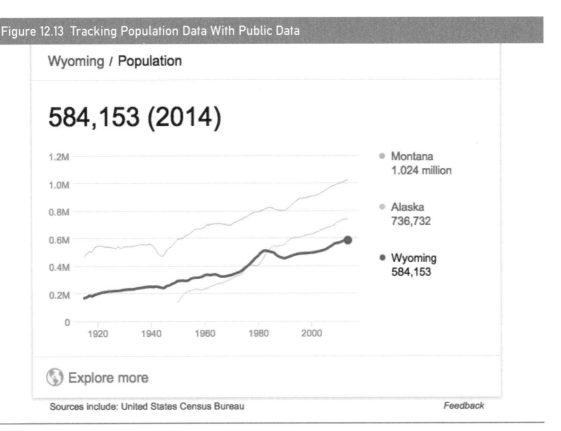

**Figure 12.13 Tracking Population Data With Public Data**

© 2016 Google Inc. used with permission. Google and the Google logo are registered trademarks of Google Inc.

*Example search: population Wyoming*

*Classroom Timer:* Google can provide you with a countdown timer you can use for activities with your students. The timer has basic controls that allow you to start, stop, and reset the clock. When the clock is up, an alarm will sound, indicating the end of the activity.

*Example search: 1-minute timer*

## Project Idea: A Google a Day

One of my favorite search activities for students is to have them play A Google a Day. You can access this search game using the *URL*—http://www.agoogleaday.com/. Additionally, there are a ton of content-specific games to search for at http://www.google.com/intl/enus/insidesearch/searcheducation/lessons.html#challenges. These particular games will be more teacher driven as they are summaries from the Google a Day website that relate to science, math, social studies, and more.

**ISTE S Standard 3 Objective a**

*Students plan and employ research strategies to locate information, resources or media for their intellectual or creative pursuits. (ISTE, 2016)*

A Google a Day provides students with specific search challenges and awards them points for how quickly and accurately they can find information. You can have students work on these challenges either individually, as a self-starter, or as an exit ticket. Likewise, forming student groups and developing challenges as teams is another fun option for students.

a **Google** a day

*There's no right way to solve it, but there's only one right answer.*

START PLAYING

## FROM A GOOGLE GURU

For the past 17 years, I've taught in a middle school setting. Middle schoolers, like most students, are perfectly happy to Google for basic resources but are easily overwhelmed by the wealth of resources they find and frustrated by time it can take to filter through the resources they encounter, often settling for the one that looks the most interesting or has the most accessible information. If Advanced Search isn't taught explicitly, ideally in the context of a research project or in a mini-lesson prior to a larger research task, we're missing an opportunity for impact and allowing students to waste precious research time.

Each year, I work with our sixth grade faculty to do a mini-lesson with their students on using Google Advanced Search prior to students beginning in-depth research for their speech unit, where students become grade-level experts on a specific topic in U.S. or Minnesota history.

In the class immediately before the lesson, students are given a homework assignment to search as they normally would for resources on their topic. They are asked to limit their searches to about 15 minutes and document their best three sources.

The next day, our students (sitting in pairs or groups of three, based on related topic selection) spend a couple of minutes discussing the results of their online research. As a class, we then discuss the quality of the searches to get a feel for overall satisfaction.

By this point, we've already done one mini-lesson on evaluating resources in sixth grade, but a refresher is needed. We discuss our trust levels in terms of various sources and when to be cautious. Next, we do a basic Google search for Abraham Lincoln. Students usually notice that it shows up as abraham lincoln in the search box. Lesson #1—case doesn't matter.

When students are asked what they notice in the search, they will mention things like this:

- Around 77,000 hits
- Images
- Quotes
- Books
- Links and info from Wikipedia
- News stories
- A link from the White House
- Multiple .com sites

At this point, I ask students which resources they think would be good and how they know. Prepare for kids to debate a bit. This is a good part of the process—questioning assumptions.

Now I demo three methods to get to Advanced Search:

1. https://www.google.com/advanced_search
2. http://google.com>**Search>Advanced Search**
3. Doing a Google search and clicking the **sprocket>Advanced search**

Next we do a search with the same search term but choose just one of the domains, such as .gov or .edu. Then we ask students what they notice.

Given that Abraham Lincoln is a pretty broad topic (but familiar enough to most students to know a little about him), I ask what the speech might choose to focus on. The two most common areas kids suggest are biography and assassination. (Note: Be prepared for some students to notice the three-letter word pattern as you're typing. Again, I teach middle school ☺.) We narrow all of the areas that seem appropriate—language, region, domain, terms appearing, and so on. Then we discuss the results, comparing to what we'd seen in the previous search.

Next, we discuss how Advanced Search can help for other types of topics:

- If we weren't looking at a historical topic, we could change the Last Update.
- If there are terms with synonyms, enter them into Any of These Words.
- If there are things we don't want to find—say we're searching for Ben Franklin, we don't want dime stores—we could use None of These Words.
- If we're specifically looking for images to use in a project, we could explore Usage Rights.

We also look at the search bar and how Advance Search appears there. I tell students that it's a matter of understanding how the search terms work. Once they're comfortable with the formatting, they can do it on their own.

Now I give kids time for guided exploration. Expect this to take a while. If your school has a tech integrationist, this would be a good time to call him or her in to partner or for backup. Lessons like this are ideal for team teaching.

Here are some variations:

- With older students, you may want to go directly to Advanced Search.
- With controversial or current events topics, explore the process with Incognito mode versus non-GAFE accounts, so students begin to explore how the search algorithms work and previous searches impact later results.
- For projects incorporating images, try using Advanced Search for image searches.
- Demonstrate how Google Search handles spelling errors.

## BIOGRAPHY

Tami Brass

St. Paul Academy and Summit School, St. Paul, MN, US

Teacher and Director of Instructional Technology

Twitter: @brasst

Website/blog: http://www.tech4teaching.org

### More Ideas for Going Google

- Now that you've learned some new search techniques, try making another search story. By using better searching tools, your students can really tell some interesting stories.
- You can use all of these search techniques on a mobile device. Even if students don't have smartphones, they can use the Google mobile app to receive search results on other devices.

## TIPS FOR THE GOOGLE CLASSROOM

- Try using Google Chrome as your default browser. One of my favorite features is the built-in search in the address bar. Instead of going to Google.com to create a search, simply type right in the address bar, and you'll get the search results you desire.

- Google provides tons of search-related training and resources at http://www.google.com/intl/enus/insidesearch/searcheducation/. Here you'll find recorded webinars, lesson plans, and tip and tricks for classroom uses for search.

## CHAPTER 13

# Google Custom Search

## FIVE Things to Know About Google Custom Search

1. Custom Search can be embedded in your classroom website.
2. You choose the sites you want used in the search.
3. Your custom search engine can be edited if unwanted results occur.
4. Custom search can be done in a variety of languages.
5. There are many different options you can configure for your search (images, voice, etc).

Before we leave the topic of searching, one last tool we need to address is Google Custom Search. What is it? With Custom Search, educators can create a filtered search on a specific group of pages. For example, rather than having my students conduct a search on Martin Luther King, Jr., on the entire web, I can create a search engine for some specific sites that provide quality information about Dr. King. This means my students aren't exposed to resources that aren't valid and may contain questionable materials. As the teacher, I control which sites are included in the search, so I can help determine which sites my students are exposed to.

> ### ISTE T Standard 3 Objective d
>
> *Teachers exhibit knowledge, skills, and work processes representative of an innovative professional in a global and digital society. Teachers model and facilitate effective use of current and emerging digital tools to locate, analyze, evaluate, and use information resources to support research and learning. (ISTE, 2008)*

## HOW TO SET UP A CUSTOM SEARCH

To set up a Custom Search, go to www.google.com/cse and click on **Sign in to Custom Search Engine**. You can then configure your search in three steps (see Figure 13.1):

1. Set up your search this way:

   a. Look under the **Sites to Search** header.

b. Add one *URL* to each line in the search box. As you add a URL a new address box will appear after you press **Enter** or **Return**.

c. Choose your desired language. The default is English.

d. Complete the section **Name Your Search**.

e. Agree to the terms, by clicking **Create**.

2. The second step in setting up your Customized Search Engine is to choose how you want to use it. You'll find two primary options: **Add It to Your Site** or **View It on the Web**.

3. Once you've created the Custom Search Engine, Google will provide you with the *HTML* code to add the search box to your website. You can grab this code using the **Get Code** button. If you don't have a website, Google will host your results for you.

4. Your second option is to **View It on the Web**. Google will provide you with the custom URL for your search results. Click on the button for **Public URL**, and you'll see your custom search window. Share the URL with students, and they're off and running.

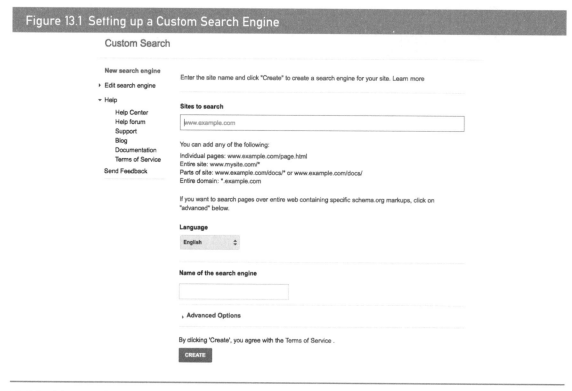

Figure 13.1 Setting up a Custom Search Engine

## SHARING YOUR CUSTOM SEARCH WITH STUDENTS

Sharing your Custom Search with students requires a final step (see Figure 13.2).

- While in the editing mode, you can choose your custom search from along the left side of the screen.

- You'll find it under the **My Search Engines** link.

- You can also find and manage your search engines from www.google.com/cse (see Figure 13.3). Just click the link for **Manage your existing search engines**.

- Choose your search engine from the list that displays on the screen.

- Copy the link in the URL window, and provide this to your students.

- All the search results will come from your Custom Search Engine and the sites you selected to include.

"Google Custom Search Engine is incredibly useful for teachers. Essentially, you create your own search engine by selecting the sites that Google will index. It searches only the sites I specify, bypassing a lot of the junk" (Nate Grondin, social studies teacher, as quoted in Google, 2011b).

Using Google Custom Search is a nice alternative to costly filtering and unsupervised searching. For younger grades, it's a great way for teachers to help students learn the power of searching while providing them with a productive and safe environment.

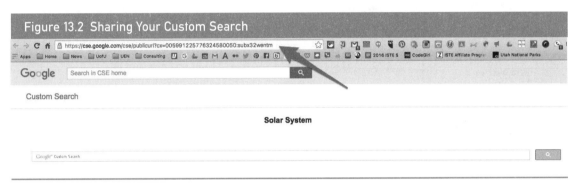

**Figure 13.2 Sharing Your Custom Search**

Solar System

© 2016 Google Inc. used with permission. Google and the Google logo are registered trademarks of Google Inc.

## FROM A GOOGLE GURU

We want our students to learn how to use the Google search engine, but we don't necessarily want them searching everything on the Web. The younger students might not have enough knowledge about the topic they are searching to determine if the information they find is correct and unbiased. Many sites on the Web are above the reading level of the elementary student, and combing through multiple pages of results to find a site that is readable is very time-consuming for the student. In addition, doing a Google search could lead students to sites that are not appropriate for them.

**Figure 13.3 Managing Your Custom Search**

© 2016 Google Inc. used with permission. Google and the Google logo are registered trademarks of Google Inc.

To avoid these problems, in past years, teachers have located web sites for students to use and created lists of these in Diigo, Delicious, Symbaloo, and other curations sites. The teachers had the students use the sites on these curated lists for their assignments.

However, a directory of sites takes a long time to go through, too. Even if there is a search tool on the site's page, it is still difficult for students to locate information.

A great solution for keeping students on sites that are appropriate and useful, but which also allows them to search all of the sites on the teacher's list at the same time, can be found by the teacher creating a Google Custom Search Engine.

A Google Custom Search Engine allows the teacher to add the list of sites to be used by students to a simple form, and a web page is created with what looks like a typical Google search box (see Figure 13.4). When students use this special search box, they are only searching the sites the teacher has designated.

Figure 13.4 Google Custom Search

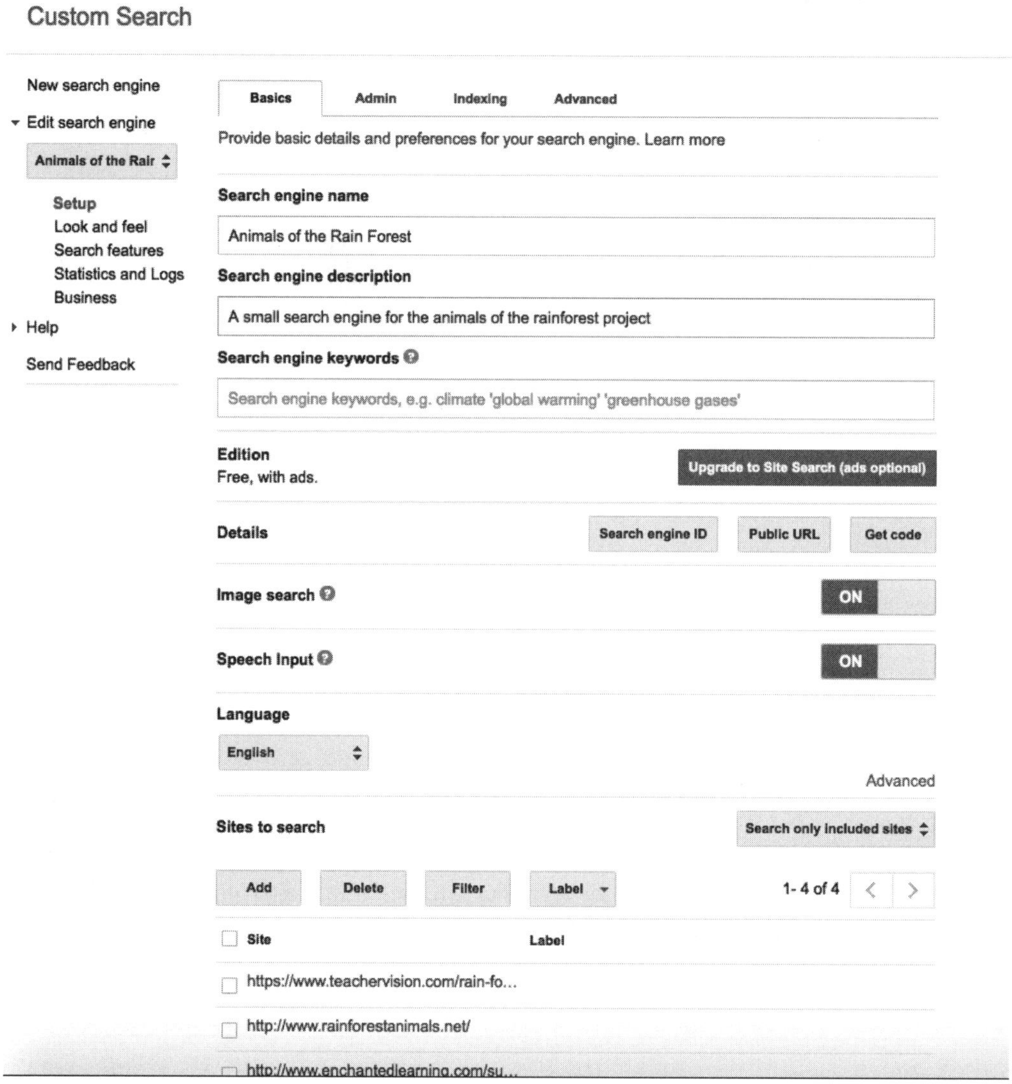

© 2016 Google Inc, used with permission. Google and the Google logo are registered trademarks of Google Inc.

The URLs of these Google Custom Search Engines are lengthy, so the use of a URL shortener is a good idea when presenting the addresses to students.

Here is the link to a small Google Custom Search Engine to support an animals of the rainforest project. It is set to include image results, too, which is another choice when setting up the engine:

Public URL: https://cse.google.com/cse/publicurl?cx=001208881090021362570:f2vwv51rsqq

Bitty shortened URL: http://bit.ly/rainforest_animals

Another very useful feature of the Google Custom Search Engine is the ability to share the administration of it with others. In schools, it would be great to have all the teachers in a grade level work on the same Custom Search Engine by each adding sites they find. This collaborative effort will lead to a much richer set of resources for the students!

## BIOGRAPHY

Kathy Schrock

Wilkes University, PA, US

Online Faculty, Independent Educational Technologist

Twitter: @kathyschrock

Blog: http://blog.kathyschrock.net

Website: http://kathyschrock.net

### More Ideas for Going Google

- You can have your students create a Custom Search Engine as part of a research project they develop. This is an interesting way for students to find useful sites and share them with other members of class. An activity like this will help students think critically and evaluate web resources.

## TIPS FOR THE GOOGLE CLASSROOM

- You can embed your Google Custom Search Engine on your classroom or school website. When you are in the **Manage Your Site** mode, look under the **Control Panel** menus (down the left side of the screen) for **Get Code**. This option will provide you with the HTML code you can use to embed the custom search on a website.

## CHAPTER 14

# Google Chrome

## FIVE Things to Know About Google Chrome

1. Google Chrome is the number one browser for surfing the web.

2. Using Sync, you can have all your bookmarks, passwords, and other tools regardless of device.

3. You can add different profiles to your Chrome browser, enabling quick switches from one account to another.

4. Chrome Extensions allow you to customize your browser with a variety of shortcuts and applications.

5. Chrome is the platform for Chromebook laptops—so it will always be up to date with the latest changes.

When Google Chrome first launched 6 years ago, it joined a crowded browser market. With Internet, Safari, and Firefox all leading the way, it was unclear whether or not users would adopt this new tool. As of 2016 more than half of the market share for downloaded browsers belongs to Google Chrome (see Figure 14.1; Martin, 2016).

In this chapter we're going to look at what makes Google Chrome so popular for many teachers and students. Additionally, we'll explore the Chromebook and how devices leverage the Chrome browser to improve student learning.

> **ISTE S Standard 1 Objective b**
>
> *Students personalize their learning environments to enhance knowledge or peruse their own curiosities.*
> (ISTE, 2016)

**Figure 14.1 Google Chrome Leads the Way in Surfing the Web**

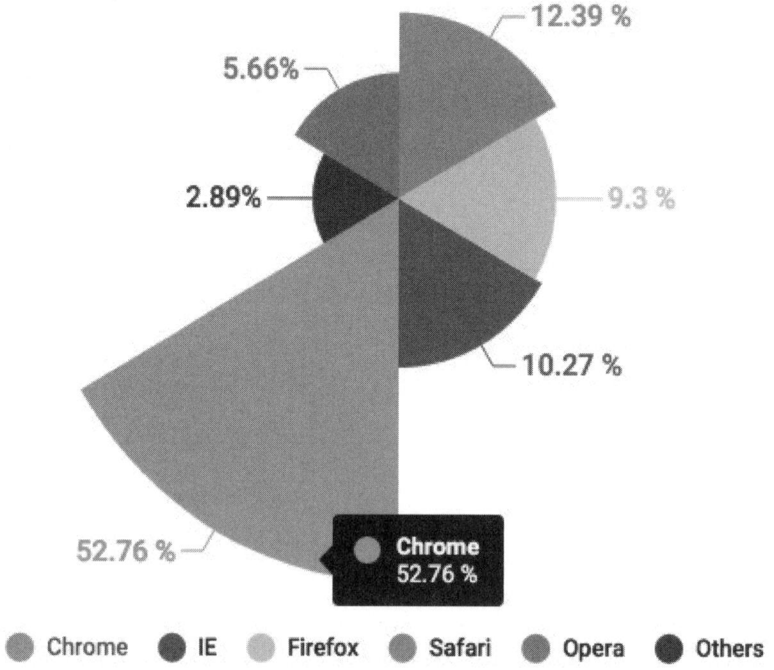

12.39 %

5.66%

2.89%

9.3 %

10.27 %

52.76 %

Chrome
52.76 %

● Chrome　● IE　● Firefox　● Safari　● Opera　● Others

## SYNC ALL YOUR CONTENT

The world has changed. We can no longer be tied down to a single machine as the source for all of our Internet content. The cloud has made us device independent as we seamlessly transfer among desktops, laptops, and mobile devices. The trouble is that many of our browsers are tied into specific machines. Well, Google Chrome looks to break free from constraints of platform or machine. Using the Sync Chrome option, users can easily manage customized tools, such as bookmarks, history, and passwords on a multitude of devices (see Figure 14.2). This means teachers can have the exact same browser whether they are on their computer at work or their phones at home. The content travels with you!

Typically, when you login into your Google account, you are simply logging in to the various tools that Google provides. This includes many of the tools in this book, like Google Calendar, Google Drive, Gmail, and more. If you sync devices you'll automatically have access to all your content, and you won't be limited in finding your web content.

To enable Google Sync, follow these steps:

- Access the settings on your Google Chrome browser.
- The settings icon is in the top right corner of your screen and appears as **three horizontal bars**.
- A menu will drop down, and you'll want to select **Settings**.

Figure 14.2 Setting Up the Screen for Google Chrome

# Set up Chrome

Sign in to get your bookmarks, history, passwords, and other settings on all your devices. Learn more

| Email |
| Password |
| **Sign in** |
| Need help? |

No thanks                    ☐ Choose what to sync

- A new tab will open in your browser—look for the **Sign In** heading. By signing in with your Google account, all the content that is saved in your account will be available on your current machine. This includes bookmarks, favorites, history, and passwords.

Tip—Google Sync will sync all your data if you allow it, so be cautious about logging into a shared or public computer and performing a sync. Just imagine the trouble you could cause yourself by syncing your passwords to the computer you used at the public library!

You can sync multiple accounts in your Google Chrome browser—this is a nice feature if you have more than one Google account (personal and GAFE). Switching back and forth between accounts is easy and quickly accomplished.

## SECURE YOUR BROWSER

One of the largest fears with saving content online is fear of hacking. Although Google boasts one of the most secure browser on the web with Chrome, there is always a chance that data can be breached. One of the best ways to avoid having your account hacked is to follow a few simple guidelines:

- Don't use the same password for every website account. I know that it's hard to remember new passwords all the time. The point is that a simple, repeated password is the easiest way for your data to become vulnerable.

- Sign out of shared or public computers. Often I teach classes where users login to their Google accounts and forget to uncheck the Remember Me or Save This User options found on many online tools. Signing out at the end of your session will save you a ton of headache later.

- Use 2-Step Verification. I find that this is one of the best security measures someone can take to protect their Google account. It makes it so that your account cannot be accessed from a new device without entering a code that gets sent to a different approved device. For example, if my account has an attempt to login from an untrusted computer, a prompt will appear asking the user to enter a unique code. Here's the thing—the code will only come to my cell phone. This means any attempt to hack into my Google account will be thwarted because the hacker won't have access to my phone, and thus he or she can't access my data.
  - Look in your **My Account** settings (click on your user icon in the top right corner of your account).
  - You'll find an option for **Sign In & Security**.
  - Choose **2-Step Verification** to enable this security measure.
  - Enter in the phone number for your mobile device and authenticate that device.

## Extending Your Ability

Like other browsers before it, Google Chrome has its limitations. Truthfully, it is impossible to include all the different features someone may want in an Internet browser. Some users want tools to enhance their productivity. Others want to add options to increase creativity. There is no single solution that will work for everyone.

Chrome looks to address this by allowing developers to create extension programs that can be added to your browser. Most of the extensions are free to install and easy to download using the Chrome Web Store. There are thousands of different extensions from which to select, so we'll look at a few popular choices used by teachers and students.

### Installing an Extension

- Visit the Chrome Web Store at the following address: https://chrome.google.com/webstore/category/apps.
- In the top left corner of your screen, select the option for **Extensions**.
- Next you'll want to choose your desired category of Extensions. There are more than a dozen choices available.
- Select the desired extension. A pop-up window will display, showing you the features and reviews of the extension.
- Click on **Add to Chrome** to install the extension in your browser.
- Installed extensions will display in your browser on the right of the omnibox (address bar).
- Click on the extension and follow the on-screen instructions. You're ready to go!

## Can't-Miss Extensions

Here are a few of my favorite extensions.

*Google Tone:* Released in 2015, Google Tone allows teachers to easily share websites with students. Once you're on the website you want to share, click on the Google Tone extension and you'll hear an odd little sound. This may not mean anything to you, but the other computers in the room with Google Tone installed will hear the sound and prompt the user to a link for your website. This is a must-have for any teacher with a Chromebook lab!

*Synergyse Training for Google Apps:* There's a lot to learn in the Google suite of tools. Even with all the great print resources out there (like this book), sometimes it helps to have a video or animation to help guide you through a feature. Synergyse provides users with a search box where they can type a question. When they select the different results, a custom animation will launch that guides users through the specific action, complete with audio and callouts to help with understanding.

*Hootsuite:* With many using social media sites to post and share content, we all want an easy way to share a link across different sites. With Hootsuite you can write one post and have it sent to multiple social media sites, including Twitter and Facebook.

*Goo.gl URL Shortener:* I love this extension! I have too many situations in which I need to take a long **URL** and shorten it into something I can share with others. This extension allows me to create the short URL in one click. With a second click I can also create a QR code to share as well.

*Awesome Screenshot:* If you ever need to make a screen capture of something in your Internet browser, this is an incredible tool. Not only can you take pictures of your screen, but you can add symbols (i.e., arrows) and text. This is a huge help when making your next handout of an online website or program.

*Print Friendly and PDF:* I love to use current events articles as part of my class—either as a self-starter or at the start of a class discussion. The problem is that printing an article from the Internet gives you annoying ads and tons of extra stuff that aren't part of the article. Print Friendly allows you to strip out all of this unwanted content and leaves just the text. You can save this clean version of the file as a PDF or share it as a new URL.

## Chromebooks: Your Device for the Cloud Classroom

Beginning in 2011, Chromebooks cemented the Chrome experience for many users as these computers provided an easy way to access all the cloud content so many of us use on a daily basis. In fact, it is reported that almost 30,000 Chromebooks come online in schools each and every day (Norris & Solloway, 2016). Why? What is the appeal of these simple machines? Not only are Chromebooks an easy platform to use for students, but many schools have jumped on the bandwagon as these devices provide a flexible, cost-effective, scalable set of computers that allow teachers to teach and students to learn.

### Advantages to Using Chromebooks

*Cost Savings:* Chromebooks cost a fraction when compared to many other one-to-one devices. Entry-level Chromebooks start out as low as $149—compare that with the iPad mini, which begins around $350 for the base model. That may not seem like much, but translated over several hundred devices, schools can save thousands.

*Management:* One of the best parts of a district adopting GAFE is the ease of control for deploying settings. Admins can quickly establish groups with different levels of permissions, depending on the tools required to complete various assignments. With one click, settings can change, and updates are immediate.

*Cloud Based:* Chromebooks exist as an Internet-based tool, so content is readily shared, easily accessed, and immediately saved. Both teachers and students love how quickly they can get into their projects, and because of the GAFE environment, many of their favorite tools all use the same login.

## FROM A GOOGLE GURU

Chrome extensions are an amazingly valuable tool for managing your files, resources, and your time. They can be found in the Chrome Store but are often overshadowed by apps. However, the smart Chrome user should really understand and leverage extensions. Extensions are utilities or tools that you can add to the Chrome browser that are usually available in every browser window, found to the right of the omnibox, or address bar. (I say usually because there are a few outliers.) Extensions can be simple, like a timer, or incredibly complex, like a file management system or bookmarking tool that turns about 10 minutes' worth of work into one.

If you are going to start exploring extensions, I usually suggest that you start with Extensity. This extension helps you manage all of your other extensions, and it is one that I keep open all the time. Another extension that I often tell people to start with is Google Drive Quick Create. This is a great time saver because one click on that extension saves the user about five steps usually needed to create a new document, spreadsheet, or set of slides. What is also great about that extension is that if you have multiple accounts, like your school and personal accounts, you can set it up so that it knows which drive to make the new document in.

Shortcuts for Google is another great extension that you can customize. It simply gives you access to all of your Google tools in any Chrome screen. This way you don't have to keep going back to a Google window and looking for the Apps icon. Many extensions are customizable, and this one has a lot of features. To customize an extension you need to right click (or control-click on a mac or alt-click on a Chromebook) on the extension and choose **Options**. For this extension there are tons of options that put certain tools right at your fingertips that you normally have to search for.

If you do any kind of searching on the web, One Tab is an extension to look at. I use this extension all the time for myself and with my students. To use it well you must understand tabbed browsing. That means you have a list of sites in a search window, like Google gives you, and you hold down the command key on the Mac or the control-key on a PC or Chromebooks then click on the link. It will open in a tab next to the list. You could have five tabs open or 50. As you review each tab, you may want to keep it open or close it. You may not even have enough time to review all the tabs you had open. With One Tab you can click on the **funnel icon**, and it takes all of the open tabs and puts them on a list on one page. You can share this list, edit it, or even make a web page out of it.

If you do any kind of work with struggling readers or writers, then you should check out the extension Read&Write for Google. It really is extraordinary what this adds to the Chrome experience. It gives you a toolbar in Google Drive, webpages, and PDFs that have some great tools such as word prediction, speech to text, highlighting features, vocabulary list creation, and voice notes. Imagine students reading a web page and highlighting words that they need to define. They can highlight the words and have them read to them, translated, defined with words or pictures, or sent to a Google Doc as a list with the definitions and images next to them. Imagine a student trying to write and using word prediction and speech to text right within his or her Google document or presentation. It is just incredible to see these tools open up a world of reading and writing for students who struggle.

There are so many more wonderful extensions out there. If there is a service or web tool that you or your students use often, there is probably an extension for it. My students and I have used extensions for Padlet, Symbaloo, Pinterest, EasyBib, Google Classroom, and many more. My goal for using extensions, and sharing them with teachers and students, is to make the Chrome experience work for us, so we can have more time to do exciting things in our classrooms. If you use extensions well, you will feel like you have superpowers.

## List of Links

### Chrome Store Extensions

https://chrome.google.com/webstore/category/extensions?hl=en

### Extensity

https://chrome.google.com/webstore/detail/extensity/jjmflmamggggndanpgfnpelongoepncg?utm_source=chrome-ntp-icon

### Google Drive Quick Create

https://chrome.google.com/webstore/detail/google-drive-quick-create/ckcbfnpodigdcbjjmhmolh-khlfbepnca?hl=en

### Shortcuts for Google™

https://chrome.google.com/webstore/detail/shortcuts-for-google/baohinapilmkigilbbb-cccncoljkdpnd?hl=en

*One Tab*

https://chrome.google.com/webstore/detail/onetab/chphlpgkkbolifaimnlloiipkdnihall?hl=en

*Read&Write for Google™*

https://chrome.google.com/webstore/detail/readwrite-for-google-chro/inoeonmfapjbbkm-dafoankkfajkcphgd

*Padlet*

https://chrome.google.com/webstore/detail/padlet-mini/kcljbbiddpoeaknnjaminoceoojdbikp

*Symbaloo*

https://chrome.google.com/webstore/detail/symbaloo-bookmarker-050/cnjfgbikbkcmick-dalamlmpmkhmbollm

*Pinterest*

https://chrome.google.com/webstore/detail/pin-it-button/gpdjojdkbbmdfjfahjcgigfpmkopogic?hl=en

*EasyBib*

https://chrome.google.com/webstore/detail/easybib-toolbar/hmffdimoneaieldiddcmajhbjijmnggi

*Share to Classroom*

https://chrome.google.com/webstore/detail/share-to-classroom/adokjfanaflbkibffcbhihgihpgijcei

## BIOGRAPHY

Samantha Morra

The Elisabeth Morrow School, Englewood, NJ, US

Middle School Technology Integrator

Twitter: @sammorra

https://twitter.com/sammorra

http://samanthamorra.com/

## TIPS FOR THE GOOGLE CLASSROOM

- Quickly switch between different Google accounts using the Profile tab located in the top left corner of your Chrome browser. This is a seamless way to go back and forth between your school GAFE account and your personal Google account.

- Unlimited Computers in One—settings in the Chromebook are completely customizable. You can create a different computer for each individual who uses the machine. This is great in schools. With iPads, students typically have to use one device throughout an entire project. Chromebooks can be readily exchanged, and students can still access their individual assignments.

## CHAPTER 15

# Google Alerts

## FIVE Things to Know About Google Alerts

1. Alert notifications come to your Gmail account.
2. You can set up Alerts at the bottom of search results under the News tab in Google.
3. There is no limit to the number of Alerts you can receive.
4. You can choose which type of materials you want searched (blogs, news, etc).
5. You can manage Alerts at alerts.google.com.

Teachers seem to love using Google as a search engine to help them, as well as their students, research a variety of subjects. As teachers conduct these Google searches, one of the biggest challenges they face is trying to find the latest research on topics for their classes. There is so much information, and no one has the time to sort through the endless amounts of material.

What if there was a way that Google could help you by sorting through the vast quantity of information on the Internet? Enter Google Alerts—it finds the best material from the web and sends you links to it on a regularly scheduled basis. It's a great way for you and your students to conduct research without needing to spend hours searching the Internet.

> ### ISTE T Standard 3 Objective c
>
> *Teachers exhibit knowledge, skills, and work processes representative of an innovative professional in a global and digital society. Teachers communicate relevant information and ideas effectively to students, parents, and peers using a variety of digital-age media and formats. (ISTE, 2008)*

## WHAT ARE GOOGLE ALERTS?

Google Alerts are compiled lists of articles and websites sent to you in the form of emails when Google finds new results—such as web pages, newspaper articles, or blogs—that match your search term. You can use Google Alerts to monitor anything on the web. For your next classroom research project, imagine having Google search for the latest information on the web. This is basically how it works:

1. Enter a query in Google Alerts that you're researching.

2. Google Alerts checks on a scheduled basis to see if there are new results for your query.

3. When there are new results, Google Alerts sends you an email with the new information.

## USING GOOGLE ALERTS

To use Google Alerts, do the following (see Figure 15.1):

1. Go to alerts.google.com.

2. Enter your query. It works just the same as a normal Google search. You can use multiple search terms or identify specific query modifiers for your search.

3. You can preview your search results to get a sense of the information that pertains to your query.

4. Select the type of search results you want. Choose from news, blogs, discussions, video, and more.

5. Choose how often you want to receive the alerts. You can select from the following options:

    a. *As It Happens:* This is the fastest return of results, but you will likely receive a large amount of material. For a popular topic, you'll receive a constant stream of emails.

    b. *Once a Day:* This is the default setting for Google Alerts. On a daily basis, you'll receive a compiled list of the relevant search results.

    c. *Once a Week:* Every week, you'll be emailed a list of the compiled search results.

6. Select the volume of your search results. You can choose to receive all the possible search results, or you can have Google send you only the best results.

7. Enter the email address to which you want your alerts delivered. I'd naturally suggest you choose your Gmail address, but it's not a requirement.

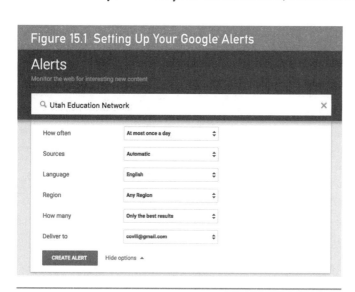

Figure 15.1 Setting Up Your Google Alerts

8. If you aren't signed in to your account, Google will send you a confirmation email to validate your new alert. If you are signed in to a Google account when you create an alert, you don't need to confirm it.

That's it! Your alert is now active. From this point forward, you'll receive an email whenever Google Alerts finds new results for your search.

You can manage your alert in each email message (see Figure 15.2). Also, each email you receive contains a link to delete the alert, so you can cancel any time you want.

## Google Alerts Tips

- Try to be as precise as possible. The more precise your search terms are, the more relevant your alerts will be.

- Use quotes around words if you are looking for them together.

- Examples:
  - "white house"
  - "Barack Obama"

- Use a minus sign (-) in front of words that you want to exclude.

- Examples:
  - paris -texas
  - apple -fruit

- Put a plus sign (+) immediately before a word to match that word precisely as you typed it, excluding synonyms and spelling variations.

- Examples:
  - +ford (to stop Google including results for Ford)
  - Michael +Jackson (to stop Google including results for Michael Jackson)

- Use the site: operator to limit your search to specific sites.

- Examples:
  - physics site:.edu
  - congress site:nytimes.com

- Use the site: operator with a dash to exclude specific sites.

- Example:
  - "joebloggs" -site:twitter.com (Google, 2011e)

For your next research project, have your students set up Google Alerts to help them find the most current information. While you're at it, using Google Alerts can help you find the materials you may need to supplement your lessons or research as well.

## FROM A GOOGLE GURU

### Google Alerts for Keeping Up With the Web

As a board member and current president-elect of the Utah Coalition for Educational Technology (UCET) Organization, I'm always trying to be aware of any news articles, blogs, or web postings about our organization that are being posted to the Internet. One method to do this is to do a daily or weekly Google search of terms like UCET, "Utah Educational Technology," and even my own name. Despite my best intentions, I often forget to do this and miss out on a lot of new items that are posted online about UCET.

Therefore, I've set up a Google Alert through my GAFE account. This way Google will do the searches for me and send an email either once a day, once a week, or as it happens for up-to-the-minute notifications. Additionally I can select from what sources I will receive alerts. Currently I keep it set to automatic, so nearly everything new to the web about UCET will be emailed to me, but it is possible to narrow down your alerts to come only from news, blogs, or the web. Finally, I can also set the language or region or choose the types of results from the web search I'd like to see: best results or all. With some Google Alert summaries, I find myself skimming through unrelated posts that just might happen to have the words "Utah," "Education," and "Technology" in them. This doesn't take much time, however, and is worthwhile in helping to eliminate any important and relevant posts I would otherwise miss.

Google Alerts has made it very easy for me to see what people are saying about UCET, address questions that might come up, and correct any misinformation that might get posted to the web about our yearly educational conference dates and events. The daily emails also serve as a reminder to me that I need to be sharing positive news and updates online more often.

## BIOGRAPHY

Michael Hakkarinen

President 2016–2017, Utah Coalition for Educational Technology, Salt Lake City, UT, US

Technology Trainer

Twitter: @EdTechHakk

---

**More Ideas for Going Google**

- Teach a lesson on safe practices on the web by having your students create a Google Alert on themselves. This is a good way to see what is being said about you on the Internet.

- Have students create a key-word alert that tracks their school or the district as a class project to find what information is being published to the web.

## TIPS FOR THE GOOGLE CLASSROOM

A great way to organize your Google Alerts is to create a filter in your Gmail inbox (see Figure 15.3). This means all the alerts for a specific topic will filter directly into a folder rather than cluttering up your inbox. If you're working on a lengthy research project, the Google Alerts emails can become a bit overwhelming if you don't have a plan for organizing them. Here's how to set it up if you're using Gmail:

1. Click on the **Settings** icon in the top right corner of the screen.

2. Choose **Mail settings** from the *drop-down menu.*

3. Select **Filters** from the menu within the **Settings** tab.

4. Click the **Create a new filter** link at the bottom of the window.

5. This menu gives you several choices for how to filter your messages. I find the easiest way to filter is by key word using the **Has the words** field.

6. Click the **Next** button.

7. Now you want to determine the effect of the filter. Generally, I find I want to accomplish two things with the filter:

   a. **Skip the Inbox** with alerts, so they don't go to the inbox.

   b. Move the alerts inside their own folder by **Applying a new label**.

8. Once you've checked the appropriate boxes, click the **Create Filter** button. You're done!

**Figure 15.3 Creating a Filter in Gmail**

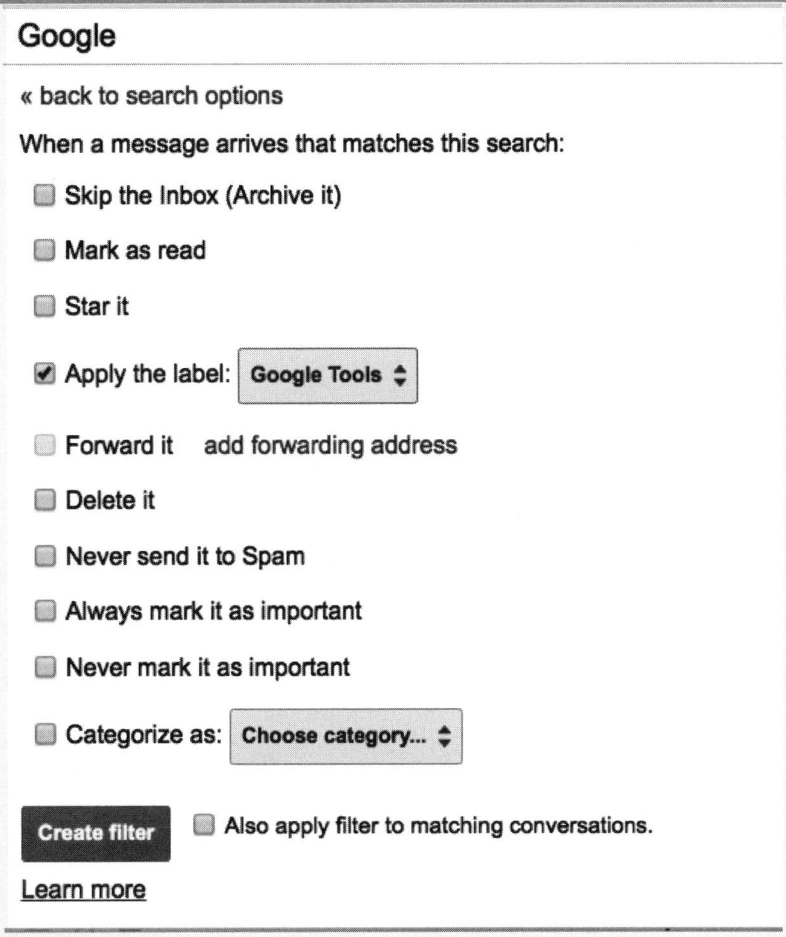

### Google

« back to search options

When a message arrives that matches this search:

☐ Skip the Inbox (Archive it)

☐ Mark as read

☐ Star it

☑ Apply the label:   Google Tools ⇕

☐ Forward it    add forwarding address

☐ Delete it

☐ Never send it to Spam

☐ Always mark it as important

☐ Never mark it as important

☐ Categorize as:   Choose category... ⇕

**Create filter**    ☐ Also apply filter to matching conversations.

Learn more

## CHAPTER 16

# Google Translate

## FIVE Things to Know About Google Translate

1. Google Translate can translate into up to 50 different languages.

2. You can translate entire documents using Google Translate.

3. Google Translate can pronounce words in the new language and provide definitions of the words.

4. Using the mobile app for Translate, you can translate street signs on the fly.

5. Google Translate can translate websites into a variety of languages.

Google's databases contain dozens of different languages from which to search. With so many languages at its disposal, it begs the question: Why can't Google simply translate text from one language to another? Ask no more; let's look at Google Translate.

Google translate accepts voice input for 15 languages and allows translation of a word or phrase into one of more than 50 languages. Translations can be spoken out loud in 23 different languages.

> **ISTE T Standard 2 Objective C**
>
> *Communicate relevant information and ideas effectively to students, parents, and peers using a variety of digital age media and formats.*
> (ISTE, 2008)

To translate words and phrases, simply select your translation languages and start typing. The translation result should appear instantly as you type, without your having to click a single button. Or, you can always click the **Translate** button to trigger a translation.

When you translate a single word, you may see a simple dictionary at the bottom of the page indicating parts of speech and possible word variations. Be sure to check for multiple definitions as the first definition may not be the most common.

If you aren't sure what language you're attempting to translate, the Detect Language option can figure this out for you. The accuracy of the automatic language detection increases with the amount of text entered (see Figure 16.1), so as you keep typing in Google Translate, it gets better at recognizing words and phrases.

Figure 16.1 Google Translate Interface

## TRANSLATE WEB PAGES

One of the best features in Google Translate is the ability to translate an entire web page.

- To complete the translation, simply enter the web page's address (e.g., www.uen.org) into the input box, and click Translate.
- Instantly, your web page will transition from English to your language of choice. What a tremendous option to help our ESL students in their new classrooms!

If you hover your mouse over the translated text, the original text for the highlighted segment is displayed in an info bubble just above the translated text. To see all of the original text of the page, click the **View: Original** radio button in the top frame of the translated page.

## TRANSLATE DOCUMENTS FROM YOUR COMPUTER

Google Translate also provides an easy way to translate entire documents without the need for copying and pasting large blocks of text. Simply click the **translate a document** link and submit your file as a PDF, TXT, DOC, PPT, XLS, or RTF. In just a few moments, your document will display in Google Docs in the new language.

### ISTE S Standard 7 Objective a

*Students use digital tools to connect with learners from a variety of backgrounds and cultures, engaging with them in ways that broaden mutual understanding and learning. (ISTE, 2016)*

Please note that the translation may not always be in the most conversational language. Google Translate has been known to present a fairly literal translation, which gets the meaning across, even if it uses words or phrases that some native speakers would not typically use in conversation.

## Project Idea: Using Google Translate in Your Classroom

Imagine having a built-in translator available 24/7 for use with your students. Here are some possible ideas for its use:

- *Dictionary for Foreign Language Students:* Rather than buying an expensive dictionary, have your foreign language students use Google Translate to help them with basic vocabulary. The students can work in both languages to ensure they are using words and phrases correctly. As a quick assessment tool, Google Translate can help kids know if they are learning the right words.

- *Pen Pals With Foreign Students:* Using Google Translate, you can have email communication with students from different countries. Gmail can automatically translate the messages from the students. Students in the foreign country will have your students' messages in their native tongue. The messages your students receive can be read in English. What a great way to bring the world's students together!

- *Translate School Documents for Parents:* Be sure to have copies of the important classroom documents available in the languages your students' parents speak. Using the Translate Document feature, you can have your files available for everyone. Even better, you can show parents how they can use Google Translate at home so they can get copies of every document they need to read. This is a great way to include ESL students and their parents in your classes. It builds a sense of community and lets every voice be heard.

- *Take Google Translate on the Road:* Using the Google Translate mobile app, you can now take a translator with you anywhere you go. For 15 different languages, Google Translate can use your camera app to capture street signs in a foreign language and immediately translate the sign into a variety of different languages. Imagine taking a group of students on a trip abroad and having each student with their own personal translator!

## FROM A GOOGLE GURU

I am a high school Spanish teacher in Memphis, Tennessee, and I encourage my students to use Google Translate as a trusted resource to find a word or a phrase that they need. As a major part of my class, students blog as a way of tracking their writing progress, so as they're writing in Blogspot and need a moment to check a certain word, I encourage them to use Google Translate as a spot check. This is one of several ongoing resources that we use in our weekly blogging.

One particular assignment my students have is to write about what they've read, watched, or listened to in Spanish during the week. As they're blogging in Spanish, they may need to make sure they are using the correct word in context, so Google Translate helps with that. In our district, one of the three modes of communication we work with in our world language classes is the interpretive skill of reading and listening. Doing spot checks with Google Translate is a quick and easy way to make sure they are staying on track with understanding the message.

Students who use Google Translate have up-to-date access to a variety of dialects, so they get the best translation and choice for what they want to say. One thing I tell my students about Google Translate is how it will give you an accurate representation of what they input, so I prefer they use it to check their comprehension of one or two words that they may not remember. Overall, the students have been able to use this tool in an ethical way as they practice their skills in writing Spanish.

Here are some samples of student work. The main point is for students to write in their own words, so although they're not grammatically perfect, they are the students' own ideas and writing.

Here is a weekly blogging assignment from S. Donlon, Spanish 4 Honors, who writes about her weekly activities in Spanish:

http://spanish4sd.blogspot.com/2016/01/activity-log-14–18.html

Here is a weekly blogging assignment from J. Holmesn, Spanish 4 Honors, who writes about his weekly activities in Spanish:

http://jhspanish4h4blog.weebly.com/activity-log/4–8-enero-2016

This sample is from A. Collins, Spanish 2 Honors, who writes about the *quinceañera,* a 15th birthday celebration similar to Americans' Sweet 16: http://alannaccollins26.blogspot.com/2015/04/celebraciones.html

Here is a sample of a blogpost from K. Cathey, Spanish 2 Honors, who writes about her food choices and what she likes to eat:

http://keniciac.blogspot.com/2015/03/unit-3-writing-revision.html

## BIOGRAPHY

Paul Jennemann

Spanish Teacher, White Station High School

Shelby County Schools, Memphis, TN, US

Twitter: @profepj3

I blog with Path2Proficiency.com and at profepj3.weebly.com.

## TIPS FOR THE GOOGLE CLASSROOM

- Google Translator provides a very literal translation of most foreign phrases. Be careful not to assume that any translation is going to be in perfect conversational text. Although it may not be a perfect translation, Google Translate does allow for a good exchange of ideas from one language to another.

- The Google search engine can also be translated into other languages. Rather than having your ESL students use Google in English, you can change the settings to display the Google interface in a variety of different languages. This can be changed in the Settings option in Google search.

## CHAPTER 17

# Google Keep

## FIVE Things to Know About Google Keep

1. Google Keep is an online posting board that can be accessed using the cloud on any Internet-connected device.

2. Reminders allow notes to have a set due date.

3. Notes can include multimedia content including images and voice recordings.

4. Notes can be shared with others.

5. You can organize your notes using labels.

Google Keep maximizes the cloud to provide teachers and students with an online "everything" board. Google Keep gives you a space to make your to-do lists. Need to jot down a quick note? Google Keep is for you. What about adding a photo reminder of a homework assignment? Check! Google Keep will even keep your personal dictation as you record thoughts for later.

> **ISTE T Standard 3 Objective b**
>
> *Collaborate with students, peers, parents, and community members using digital tools and resources to support student success and innovation.*
> (ISTE, 2008)

## GETTING STARTED

To create your Google Keep board, visit http://keep.google.com:

- Login with your Google account, and your board is ready to go.
- To add a new note, click on the box near the top of your Google Keep screen.

Figure 17.1 Creating a Note in Google Keep

Take a note...

- You'll find three different default options for your new note:
- Simply type in the box (see Figure 17.1), and you'll be able to add a basic note—see what follows for your options in adding content to your note.
- Click on the **bulleted list icon**, and you'll create a list.
- Select the **mountain range icon**, and you'll add an image note.

## Adding Content in a Note

With Google Keep you can create several different types on content for your board (see Figure 17.2). Whether text based or using media, Google Keep is an easy way to share and save your content.

*Notes*: the default content in Google Keep is to create a note. Notes don't have a character limit, so you should have plenty of room to jot down your thoughts.

Figure 17.2 Adding Content in Google Keep

*Reminders*: Reminders give teachers the option to add a time frame to a note. This provides a lot more structure than the basic sticky note. By using the check boxes, you can quickly visualize what you've accomplished and what is left to go before your due date.

*Share*: One of the best features of Google Keep is the ability to share your content with others. This is a great option for teachers looking to share a to-do list with their students. Simply add the email address of a student, and you're good to go.

*Labels*: To help you organize your content, you add a variety of colored labels to different notes. This allows you to sort and filter your content based upon the labels you've applied.

*Images*: This is a great option for your board is to upload images. This gives your Google Keep board a Pinterest feel and makes it easier to visualize content.

## Project Idea—Create a Board With Voice Comments

There are several different tools you can use to create bookmarks and save images. Most of the allow you to upload text, images, and some video. One thing that is missing from these tools is the ability to record audio. Using the Google Keep app on your mobile device, you can easily record messages as notes. This is a great tool for younger students or ESL students who struggle with reading comprehension.

Note: This project must be completed on a mobile device.

To create a voice message, follow these steps:

- Launch the Google Keep app.
- Click on the microphone icon at the bottom of the screen.
- A recording screen will launch, and you'll immediately be able to record your voice for a memo.
- The memo will be transcribed as text in addition to the ability to play the message.

## FROM A GOOGLE GURU

As a professed Google addict, Google Keep came as a surprise to me. I thought I was actively using the majority of tools Google offered in both my personal and professional life at school. Discovering Google Keep was truly a game changer for me this school year. In the past I've struggled with keeping an ongoing to-do list in one place. I might jot things down on sticky notes (or random scraps of paper), make notes on my phone, or star emails, and yes, I've even tried a variety of apps on my phone. The problem was my lack of consistency and ability to pull it all together. Which tasks were for student assistants? Which were for my library assistants? What was that deadline? Where did I put that note?

Enter Google Keep. It does everything I need and more. Accessible on my phone? Check. Synchs to my computer? Check. Easy to share with others? Check. Easy to use? Double-check. The fact that Google Keep looks like virtual sticky notes is just a bonus for me, the self-proclaimed queen of sticky notes.

Google Keep is where I empty my brain of all of the various things that need to be done. I use different notes labeled for different categories. I have ongoing notes for both school and personal tasks. My school notes are shared with coworkers like my library assistants, tech coach partner, and/ or even student assistants depending on the category or task. I love that the notes are viewable anywhere, and when you finish a task, you can check it off, which also strikes through the task. (Yes, it's just as satisfying as writing a list and crossing through each task as you finish it!) I have notes that I share with myself across Google accounts and between my school Google account and my personal Gmail account. This keeps me on track with completing tasks and deadlines (most of the time)!

The phone app is probably my favorite part of Google Keep because my phone is always in hand. As I travel from class to class, it's convenient to add tasks I need to complete for teachers into Google Keep by typing them, adding a photo, or even recording a voice message. I can even copy the note to Google Docs if needed. When I return to my office, the notes and tasks are all there on the keep.google.com tab that is always open in my chrome browser.

I feel like I've just begun to scratch the surface with Google Keep and want to explore it more with students. I've already recommended it to students as a tool for keeping organized with group tasks as well as a great tool for self-organization, but I think there is much more.

## BIOGRAPHY

Sherry N. Gick

Rossville Consolidated Schools, IN, US

Library and Instructional Technology Specialist

@SherryGick

thelibraryfanatic.com

### More Ideas With Google Keep

- Create lists of materials students can use in a Makerspace. Share the list with students, and provide the final projects without giving them instructions on how to create the project. Everyone gets the same list of materials and project goal, but they can all take their own paths in getting there.

- Upload images to create a private Pinterest board of content. This is a great way for you share student work in a private space. Or feel free to share your board with others and make it more social!

## TIPS FOR THE GOOGLE CLASSROOM

- Use the Labels menu to create new boards. This is a great option to create a board for different subject areas in elementary classes, or secondary teachers can make a different board for each of their preps.

- Create your own to-do lists. These lists are great because you can check off different items on your list. Completed items will be crossed out, making it easy to see what you've got left.

- Use color as a way to categorize content. Simply click on the **color palate** when creating a note, and you can choose from several different colors. This is a great way to help students quickly identify what type of content is being shared.

# Conclusion

Over the course of this book, we've explored how Google can help the classroom teacher and his or her students achieve 21st century learning skills. With a basic Google account, there is so much you and your students can accomplish. They can collaborate, create, share, produce, find, develop, and communicate with each other and with the world. It's incredible to consider the power contained within the tools we've discussed in the previous chapters.

Still, there is one key Google feature we have yet to address, and it could be the most important yet in developing a technology implementation strategy in your classroom. GAFE allows your entire school or district to adopt a suite of Google tools for use with all students and faculty.

## WHAT'S INCLUDED IN GOOGLE APPS FOR EDUCATION?

We've explored a dozen Google tools you can use in your classroom, but there are only a few that were important enough to include in GAFE. This exclusive library of tools includes Gmail, Google Calendar, Google Drive, YouTube, Google Sites, and Google Classroom. Your school or district can include additional tools in your version of Google Apps, as there are several more apps, or applications, to choose from.

## WHY ADOPT GOOGLE APPS?

With Google Apps, you have access to tools that provide your school with a fully supported email system. Your school can have its own video repository, safe and private, for only your students and faculty. Google Apps provides you with a secure library for all your documents, spreadsheets, and presentations. Best of all, Google Apps is completely free for your school or district!

Imagine all the costs your school would save. Without paying for each of these systems, you can use those funds in other ways. In a time when budgets are tight, this is a huge benefit to your school's bottom line. In addition, here is a quick list of reasons why many schools have chosen to use Google Apps.

> 1. Students will love you for it—Schools tell us that when they ask their students what email they'd prefer, they overwhelmingly say Gmail.
>
> *"Our students approached us about a year ago, saying that we needed to improve our email and collaboration services. We actually had our student government tell us, 'We want you to implement Google Apps.'"*—Wendy Woodward, Director of Technology Support Services at Northwestern University

2. Save money—Outsourcing the maintenance of servers to Google frees up resources that would have been spent on additional licenses and upgrades.

*"This helped our IT staff understand that their focus should be on strategic enterprise solutions to help us reach our educational objectives, not just overseeing commodities like email. Had we not gone with the Google solution, we'd be looking at proposing a significant increase in student fees."*—Eric Hawley, Associate Vice President for Technology at Utah State University

3. Innovate in real time—What better way to prepare your students for the newest technology in the workplace than by giving it to them as a part of their education?

*"The response from the university community has been extremely positive because we are now partnering with cutting-edge technologists who understand that we're trying to provide the latest, most innovative technologies available today."*—Roy B. Roberti, Director of Information Technology Planning, Hofstra University

4. Collaborate globally—Google Docs doesn't just give students and teachers access to the same documents. It actually allows students to work on the same document at the same time from anywhere in the world.

*"Constructing lesson plans and unit plans is no longer a solitary activity. It's a collaborative process that's happening not only with teachers on a building level team but with teachers at a grade level from a variety of schools. Our teaching is made better as a result of this collective intelligence."*—John Krouskoff, Director of Technology, Clarkstown Central School District (Google, 2011c)

Google Apps is the primary way in which many schools and districts are implementing an organized approach to technology integration. That being said, it's not the only way to have a Google-assisted classroom. Even if your school or district doesn't choose to adopt Google Apps, you can still incorporate Google Tools in your classroom. Several of the activities in this book don't even require a Google account for students to be successful. As you work with different Google tools, you'll find ways to incorporate technology in your teaching.

Throughout this book, we've explored the impact that Google can have in your daily activities. Using a combination of Google tools can impact several areas in your classroom. From using Google Calendar to help you organize your lessons and share information about the class schedule with parents and students to creating innovative multimedia projects with Google Earth, there are so many different ways that Google can complement your teaching practice.

## THE CONSTANT OF CHANGE

Google has always been known for innovation in their tools. That is wonderful for users as the products they love keep getting better with each additional feature. The problem comes in trying to use a book like this as a final answer to every question about the tools. Just think, in the four short years since the first edition of this book was published, Google has discontinued tools such as Google Reader or iGoogle and created new programs like Google Classroom and Google Photos. Rather than giving you a complete list of all the menus and features for each Google tool, I hope this book has been an example of what is possible when implementing the programs as part of your curriculum.

Even as the tools change, the ideas remain constant. Google Drive will allow your students to collaborate with one another on a variety of documents. Google Earth will provide innovative options for exploring the world and creating your own unique tours of different locations. Google Sites will help you share your classroom events, materials, and information with parents and students. Despite the changing menus and displays, you can feel confident that Google will continue to provide you and your students with the tools you'll need to achieve 21st century skills.

## GOING GOOGLE IN THE 21ST CENTURY CLASSROOM

Using 21st century skills as the foundation for your curriculum will move you toward technology tools that can positively influence your students' achievement. By using Google tools with your students, you'll find that they can more effectively communicate with the world, they will be able to create projects that illustrate their innovative ideas, and students will become problem solvers— able to think critically about issues and concepts.

At the beginning of this book, I shared the simple message on a bumper sticker—"I've Gone Google." Whereas "going Google" has been interpreted as using Google tools as part of one's everyday workflow, going Google in the 21st century classroom means more than using an Internet search engine. Going Google in the classroom is a commitment to technology integration and 21st century learning skills. It is a desire to use tools to promote collaboration and communication, to develop creativity and innovation, and to strengthen the critical thinking and problem-solving abilities of our students.

I hope that this book has provided you with a model of how Google tools can help you in your classroom. Don't be afraid to use Google for much more than a search engine—to truly "go Google." You may be glad you did!

# Glossary

**Circles:**   Identifies a group of contacts in Google+. Typically, a circle is created as a way to separate contacts that have a similar relationship to the account owner (e.g., business contacts, friends, etc.).

**Cloud computing:**   Denotes a change in the way documents, images, and data are stored. Rather than storing information on your personal computer's hard drive, the data are uploaded to a secure web server where you can access the content. For example, your calendar wouldn't live on your Dell computer; it would live on Google's server, and you would access it with Google Calendar.

**Drop-down menu:**   A menu type found in several Google tools. Drop-down menus provide users with additional options to help them find content. A drop-down menu is identified by an upside-down triangle.

**Embed code:**   Internet or HTML-based text can be copied from various web applications and pasted into a website or other tool.

**Gadget:**   A small module of information for Google Sites. Gadgets are created by third-party developers and are available for you to add to your Google Site.

**GB:**   Stands for gigabyte. It is a unit to measure the amount of space for computer storage; 1 GB equals 1,000 MB, or megabytes.

**Hangout:**   A live video chat room from Google that can have multiple participants. You will need a webcam and microphone to make video chat work.

**HTML:**   Stands for HyperText Markup Language. This is a programming code used to develop websites.

**ISTE:**   Stands for International Society for Technology in Education. You'll find reference to their standards for teachers and students throughout the book. These standards are the accepted norm for technology integration in K–12 schools.

**MB:**   Stands for megabyte. It is a unit to measure the amount of space for computer storage; 1 MB equals 1,000 KB, or kilobytes.

**Pixel:**   A unit of measurement for determining the size of digital content. Your computer screen's resolution is measured in pixels.

**Placemark:**   An icon indicating a location on a map. Placemarks are used in Google Earth, Picasa, and Google Maps.

**PLN:**   Stands for personal learning network. People use social media sites like Twitter, Facebook, Google+, and blogs to share information with colleagues as part of their PLNs.

**Real-time data:**   Indicates that the information provided on a website is updated within seconds to minutes. This information is dynamic and provides accurate content for the user.

**RSS:** Stands for Really Simple Syndication. RSS feeds are found on most blogs as a way to help users subscribe to content that is updated frequently. Google's Blogger has an RSS feed built into its service, so you can share your blog with others.

**Templates:** Premade document files or website files you can use for your own classroom. You'll find templates in Google Sites and Google Docs.

**URL:** Stands for Universal Resource Locator. The URL is the online address for a particular website. It is located across the top of the Internet browser in the address bar.

**Wiki:** A webpage that allows collaboration among multiple people. Wikis are editable, and the changes are saved directly to the web. Wikis can be open to the public (e.g., Wikipedia), or they can be private, where a login or password is required to make changes.

# References and Further Reading

21st Century Schools. (2010). *What is 21st century education?* Retrieved December 30, 2011, from http://www.21stcenturyschools.com/What_is_21st_Century_Education.htm

Anderson, N. (2006). *Teens: Email is for old people* [Web log message]. Retrieved December 30, 2011, from http://arstechnica.com/old/content/2006/10/7877.ars

Brown, E. (2015, October 28). U.S. performance slips on national U.S. test. *Washington Post.* Retrieved April 22, 2016, from https://www.washingtonpost.com/local/education/us-student-performance-slips-on-national-test/2015/10/27/03c80170–7cb9–11e5-b575-d8dcfedb4ea1_story.html

Boren, Z. (2014, October 7). There are officially more mobile devices than people in the world. *Independent.* Retrieved March 13, 2016, from http://www.independent.co.uk/life-style/gadgets-and-tech/news/there-are-officially-more-mobile-devices-than-people-in-the-world-9780518.html

Boss, S. (2008, November 13). Teaching with visuals: Students respond to images. *Edutopia.* Retrieved January 4, 2012, from http://www.edutopia.org/visuals-math-curriculum

Boss, S. (n.d.a). Google lit trips: Bringing travel tales to life. *Edutopia.* Retrieved January 4, 2012, from http://www.edutopia.org/google-lit-trips-virtual-literature

Boss, S. (n.d.b). New York children take a Google Lit Trip. *Edutopia.* Retrieved January 4, 2012, from https://www.edutopia.org/economic-stimulus-education-technology-new-york

Bulley, B. (2011, January 23). Heidi Rogers: Technology & community. *CDAPress.* Retrieved January 4, 2012, from http://www.cdapress.com/lifestyles/article_2af7f86a-c3fb-5c7c-87c2–6e24d3ab7d0a.html

Carr, N. (2008, July). Is Google making us stupid? *The Atlantic.* Retrieved January 4, 2012, from http://www.theatlantic.com/magazine/archive/2008/07/is-google-making-us-stupid/6868/

Carvin, A. (2006, May 22). What exactly is a blog, anyway? *PBS.* Retrieved January 4, 2012, from http://www.pbs.org/teachers/learning.now/2006/05/what_exactly_is_a_blog_anyway.html

Common Sense Media. (2015). The Common Sense census: Media use by teens and tweens. Retrieved February 2, 2016, from https://www.commonsensemedia.org/sites/default/files/uploads/research/census_executivesummary.pdf

ConsumerSearch. (2011, July). *Google review.* Retrieved January 4, 2012, from http://www.consumersearch.com/search-engine-reviews/google

Dodge, B. (2007). *Webquest.org.* Retrieved January 4, 2012, from http://www.webquest.org/

Dretzin, R. (Executive Producer). (2010). Digital nation [Television series episode]. *Frontline.* Arlington, VA: Public Broadcasting Service.

EPortfolio Step-by-Step Process. (n.d.). Portfolios with GoogleApps. Retrieved December 10, 2015, from https://sites.google.com/site/eportfolioapps/overview/process

Google. (2011a). *Google for educators: Google Docs.* Retrieved January 4, 2012, from http://www.google.com/educators/p_docs.html

Google. (2011b). *Google for educators: The Google custom search engine.* Retrieved January 4, 2012, from http://www.google.com/educators/p_cse.html

Google. (2011c). *Ten reasons to choose Google Apps.* Retrieved January 4, 2012, from http://www.google.com/apps/intl/en/edu/sell.html

Google. (2011d). *Top ten advantages of Google's cloud.* Retrieved January 4, 2012, from http://www.google .com/apps/intl/en/business/cloud.html

Google. (2011e). *What are Google Alerts?* Retrieved January 4, 2012, from http://www.google.com/support/ alerts/bin/static.py?page=guide.cs&guide=28413&topic=28416&answer=175927

Google. (2016). *What is Google Instant?* Retrieved January 15, 2016, from https://support.google.com/ websearch/answer/186645?hl=en

Google. (n.d.a). *Google in education.* Retrieved January 4, 2012, from http://www.google.com/edu/purpose .html

Google. (n.d.b). *Inside search: Meet the new way to search: Google instant shows results as you type.* Retrieved January 4, 2012, from http://www.google.com/landing/instant/

Google. (n.d.c). *Module 1: Google apps education edition.* Retrieved January 4, 2012, from http://edutraining .googleapps.com/Training-Home/module-1/chapter-1/3–1

Google Search Statistics. (n.d.). *Internet Live Stats.* Retrieved July 1, 2016, from http://www.internetlivestats .com/google-search-statistics/

Graves, M., Juel, C., & Graves, B. (2006). *Teaching reading in the 21st century* (4th ed.). Boston: Allyn & Bacon.

Hunt, J. (2010, February 8). *More creativity in the classroom* [Web log message]. Retrieved January 4, 2012, from http://www.huffingtonpost.com/jim-hunt/more-creativity-in-the-cl_b_453244.html

ISTE. (2008). *ISTE Standards for teachers 2008.* Retrieved January 4, 2016, from http://www.iste.org/ standards/standards/standards-for-teachers

ISTE. (2016). *ISTE Standards for students 2016.* Retrieved June 27, 2016, from http://www.iste.org/ standards/standards/standards-for-students

Jackson, L. (2011, July 18). Blogging? It's elementary, my dear Watson! *Education World.* Retrieved January 4, 2012, from http://www.educationworld.com/a_tech/tech/tech217.shtml

Jackson, T. (2007, October 31). *How our spam filter works* [Web log message]. Retrieved January 4, 2012, from http://gmailblog.blogspot.com/2007/10/how-our-spam-filter-works.html

Martin, J. (2016, June 23). *Best web browser 2016 Chrome vs Firefox vs Edge vs Safari vs IE and more.* PC Advisor. Retrieved June 23, 2016, from http://www.pcadvisor.co.uk/feature/software/best-web-browser-2016–3635255/

Melanson, M. (2010, July 30). *Google Earth shows real-time weather.* Retrieved January 7, 2012, from http:// readwrite.com/2010/07/30/google_earth_shows_real-time_weather/

Meloni, J. (2009, August 18). Getting started with Google Docs in the classroom. *Chronicle of Higher Education.* Retrieved January 7, 2012, from http://chronicle.com/blogPost/Getting-Started-with-Google/22641/

Nightingale, J. (2011, January 11). Get creative in school with digital media. *The Guardian.* Retrieved January 7, 2012, from http://www.guardian.co.uk/classroom-innovation/creative-schools-digital-media

Norris, C., & Solloway, E. (2016). Chromebooks: Things we love, things we love not so much. *The Journal.* Retrieved February 12, 2016, from https://thejournal.com/articles/2016/02/16/chromebooks.aspx

Pace, K. (2016, February 25). Google for educators: The best features for busy teachers. *Edutopia.* Retrieved April 23, 2016, from http://www.edutopia.org/google-for-educators

Partnership for 21st Century Skills. (2004). Framework for 21st Century Learning. Retrieved January 7, 2012, from http://www.p21.org/overview/skills-framework

Partnership for 21st Century Learning. (2015). Retrieved July 1, 2016, from http://www.p21.org

Paulson, F. L., Paulson, P. R., & Meyer, C. A. (1991). What makes a portfolio a portfolio? *Educational Leadership, 58*(5): 60–63.

Pearlman, B. (n.d.). Students thrive on cooperation and problem solving. *Edutopia.* Retrieved January 7, 2012, from http://www.edutopia.org/new-skills-new-century

Prensky, M. (2010). Digital nation [Television series episode]. In Dretzin, R. (Executive Producer), *Frontline.* New York: PBS.

Rogers, M., Runyon, D., Starrett, D., & Von Holzen, R. (2006). *Teaching the 21st century learner.* Retrieved January 7, 2012, from https://docs.google.com/viewer?url=http://depd.wisc.edu/series/06_4168.pdf

Shelton, J. (2011, March 15). *Taking "boring" out of the classroom* [Web log message]. Retrieved January 7, 2012, from http://www.ed.gov/blog/2011/03/taking-"boring"-out-of-the-classroom/

Simple K12. (2010, November 11). *8 Google tricks for your classroom* [Web log message]. Retrieved January 7, 2012, from http://blog.simplek12.com/education/8-google-tricks-for-your-classroom/

Soard, L. (2014, August 4). How big data can help schools improve performance. *Insight.* Retrieved April 23, 2016, from http://www.insight.com/content/insight-web/en_US/learn/content/19086242-how-big-data-can-help-schools-improve-performance.html

Standen, A. (n.d.). The good earth: See the world with Google's mapping program. *Edutopia.* Retrieved January 7, 2012, from https://www.edutopia.org/good-earth

Teacher Created Materials. (2002). Why WebQuests. *Internet4Classrooms.* Retrieved January 7, 2012, from http://www.internet4classrooms.com/why_webquest.htm

Tumbleson, A. (2011, January 2). Students use Google Earth to explore the history of West. *West Yellowstone News.* Retrieved January 7, 2012, from http://www.westyellow stonenews.com/news/article_478521de-167c-11e0-afa2-001cc4c03286.html

Tyson, T. (2009). *Keynote address.* Presented at Utah Coalition for Education Technology conference, Salt Lake City. Retrieved January 5, 2012, from http://www.ucet.org/inUCETnew/archives/2009/conference/index.html

U.S. Department of Education. (2015). *National Education Technology Plan 2015.* Retrieved January 4, 2016, from http://tech.ed.gov/netp/

# Index

A SAGE Publishing Company

**CORWIN HAS ONE MISSION:** to enhance education through intentional professional learning.

We build long-term relationships with our authors, educators, clients, and associations who partner with us to develop and continuously improve the best evidence-based practices that establish and support lifelong learning.

# Solutions you want. Experts you trust. Results you need.

AUTHOR CONSULTING

## Author Consulting

On-site professional learning with sustainable results! Let us help you design a professional learning plan to meet the unique needs of your school or district. www.corwin.com/pd

INSTITUTES

## Institutes

Corwin Institutes provide collaborative learning experiences that equip your team with tools and action plans ready for immediate implementation. www.corwin.com/institutes

ECOURSES

## eCourses

Practical, flexible online professional learning designed to let you go at your own pace. www.corwin.com/ecourses

READ2EARN

## Read2Earn

Did you know you can earn graduate credit for reading this book? Find out how: www.corwin.com/read2earn

Contact an account manager at (800) 831-6640 or visit **www.corwin.com** for more information.